BRITAIN by BRITRAIL

"Provides highlights of attractions, suggested day tours, distance and travel times, information about connections (including sea and air), selected departure schedules, and details about different grades of passes."

—The Associated Press

"Makes it easy to plan an itinerary with frequent stopovers in all the major cities of Britain, along with many day and overnight side trips to less traveled and historic villages nestled in the mountains and countryside."

—*Small Press* magazine

D1559824

BRITAIN by BRITRAIL
HOW TO TOUR BRITAIN BY TRAIN

Fifteenth Edition

written by
George Wright Ferguson

edited by
LaVerne Ferguson and Christian Martin

A Voyager Book

OLD SAYBROOK, CONNECTICUT

**TO THE MEMORY OF
JACK WATSON
FRIEND, CORRESPONDENT,
AND RAIL NOMAD EXTRAORDINAIRE**

Photographs on pages 16, 20, 38, and 62 courtesy British Rail.

Library of Congress Catalog Card Number: 87–640215
ISBN: 1-56440-502-8

Manufactured in the United States of America
Fifteenth Edition/First Printing

FOREWORD

This 1995–96 Edition of *Britain by BritRail* extends a hearty welcome aboard to all who have joined the ranks of its readers since its first year of publication (1980) and to those who have made use of the author's first rail-travel guidebook, *Europe by Eurail*. Adapting to British Rail's unique rail network throughout England, Scotland, and Wales, *Britain by BritRail* follows the format of its predecessor, *Europe by Eurail*, by adhering to the time-proven base city–day excursion format. Because of its adaptability, London has been selected as the base city for day excursions within England and Wales. The capital of Scotland, Edinburgh, with Glasgow as an alternative, serves as a base of operations for day excursions northward into the Highlands.

Readers are assured that everything written was learned through the personal research and experiences of the authors. Our pledge to check, revise, and improve each edition continues.

Ferry crossings from Britain to Ireland and to the continent of Europe form a very important part of travel within the British Rail system. Consequently, several chapters describing the various ferry crossings are a permanent part of *Britain by BritRail*'s format. With the opening of the English Channel tunnel (also known as the "Chunnel") on May 6, 1994, Britain is linked with the Continent in another way. At press time, international rail freight is utilizing the Chunnel, and Le Shuttle trains provide automobile, coach, and lorry service between Folkestone, England, and Calais, France. The Eurostar passenger train service, however, is not expected to be in full service until 1995. We plan to include helpful information regarding the Eurostar passenger service after the schedules and fares are solidified.

Britain by BritRail is dedicated to the rail systems of England, Scotland, and Wales. *Britain by BritRail* presents to its readers a compact yet comprehensive volume on British Rail travel. Armed with a BritRail Pass or a BritRail Drive Pass and a copy of *Britian by BritRail*, readers are ready to plan and then enjoy their British Rail itineraries.

Train schedules, fares, and prices appearing in this edition are updated to press time. They are, however, for planning purposes only. We cannot be held responsible for their accuracy. All photographs are by the authors except as credited.

THE FERGUSON TEAM

George Wright Ferguson was born in Philadelphia twenty minutes after his mother was taken from a Washington-New York express train. He grew up alongside the Baldwin Locomotive Works on the "Pennsy" main line, and trains have continued to play an important role in his life.

A graduate of Penn State, George served in Europe during World War II as a test pilot and engineering officer with the Eighth Air Force. His first European train ride was aboard a vintage 1918 "40-and-8" freight car between Munich and Antwerp, a trip that lasted four days and four nights!

After a stint as editor, and later publisher, of a farm-equipment magazine, George was recalled to active military duty, with assignments in Korea, Japan, and Vietnam and at the Pentagon in Washington, D.C. George retired from the Air Force in 1967 with more than 5,000 flying hours in his log book. As a senior Air Force logistician, he was commended by Defense Secretary Robert McNamara for his study of the Air Force's worldwide-movement capabilities.

George's international experiences continued with research assignments in Thailand, Iran, South America, and Germany for the Battelle Memorial Institute, headquartered in Columbus, Ohio. There he met the other member of his "team," LaVerne.

LaVerne Ferguson first discovered her love for travel in a third-grade geography class. Determined to see "the world," she has collected brochures and information about various countries for many years. LaVerne majored in social studies and English at Ohio State University, then became an executive secretary and later a technical writer. She also has completed courses in library research and business communications.

In addition to researching and writing rail guidebooks and articles, the Fergusons also own Rail Pass Express, Inc., a rail-only sales agency in Columbus, Ohio. Their trained staff members are experts in all aspects of European rail travel. George and LaVerne welcome comments and suggestions. You can write to them at Rail Pass Express, Inc., 2737 Sawbury Boulevard, Columbus, OH 43235–4583; or call toll-free (800) 722–7151.

CONTENTS

1 IN THE BEGINNING

As Edna St. Vincent Millay put it, "My heart is warm with the friends I make,/And better friends I'll not be knowing;/Yet there isn't a train I wouldn't take/No matter where it's going."

Britain by BritRail! You are about to embark on a unique and rewarding traveling experience. Like thousands of other discerning visitors, you are about to learn that the British Rail system offers a truly delightful way of vacationing throughout the length and breadth of Europe's only English-speaking nation—Britain.

In size, Britain is a rather compact nation. It's about two-thirds the size of California or approximately one-third larger than the New England area of Maine, Vermont, New Hampshire, Massachusetts, Rhode Island, and Connecticut—the North American area to which Britain has contributed much of her heritage since Colonial days.

London is a tourist magnet, but despite what other writers say, London is not Britain. Britain has some of the most beautiful countryside in the world. Its mountains are no match for the Alps; its seas are not azure blue like the Mediterranean. But what it might lack in spectacular scenery is offset by a magical quality of green so peaceful and picturesque that, in a mere glance, the visitor becomes aware that what he sees is history. A visit to Britain that does not include at least a few days in the countryside is unthinkable.

The difference in traveling along Britain's congested highways and on British Rail's InterCity trains must be experienced to be believed. By rail, it is a smooth, relaxing journey uninterrupted by traffic lights and traffic jams. Rent-a-car visitors are usually too involved with starboard steering and keeping a close watch on the car in front to appreciate much more about Britain than the fact that the road signs are in English.

In Britain, you'll find more than 15,000 trains traveling to more than 2,400 destinations daily. The service is so frequent that if you miss a train, chances are you won't have to wait more than one-half hour to an hour for another. The British frequently seize such an opportunity to nip into a nearby pub for a quick pint and a game of darts. So follow the adage, "When in Rome, do as the Romans do." It applies equally well in Britain, which inherited some of Rome's customs, too!

Aboard a British Rail train, the driver (that's what the British call their train engineers) takes care of all the driving while you sip on a beverage, enjoy an uninterrupted view of the countryside, and stretch out in a comfortable seat. You can even respond to "nature's call" at your own option rather than sweating out making it to the closest petrol (gas) station—many are closed on weekends and holidays!

There are few places in Britain that cannot be reached by train. By employing the base cities of London, Edinburgh, or Glasgow, the splendor of Windsor Castle, the academic aura of Oxford and Cambridge, or the Old Course at St. Andrews are all but an easy, comfortable train ride away. It is true that a number of branch and feeder lines have been shut down in the past decade or so. The main lines, however, still connect all of the major cities and population centers throughout England, Scotland, and Wales—the three countries served by British Rail. Northern Ireland, by the way, is a part of Great Britain, but its railways are operated by a separate company that does not accept the BritRail Pass. It does, however, accept the BritIreland Pass, covering England, Scotland, Wales, Northern Ireland, and the Republic of Ireland.

Millions of Americans have either forgotten or have never had the opportunity to learn what travel by train can be like. In the post–World War II days, when America was rebuilding its industries and highways, it failed to do the same for its railroads, which had provided the majority of the transportation needs throughout the conflict. The demise of the great passenger trains followed rapidly. Within a single decade, the Santa Fe's Super Chief, the New York Central's 20th Century Limited, and the Southern's Crescent disappeared. Not so in the lands across the Atlantic. You may rest assured that in Britain, as well as in the rest of Europe, the passenger train is alive and well today.

Britain by BritRail is a train travel guidebook written for the purpose of bringing train and train-related information to its readers in a direct, pragmatic manner. *Britain by BritRail* does not rate or recommend hotels. A quaint coaching inn or a hotel's convenient location to rail services may gain comment. The book's primary purpose insofar as accommodations are concerned, however, is to point out the most convenient tourist information center or hotel booking (reservations) facility.

Restaurants are treated in the same manner. We appreciate good food, along with the service that complements it. But with few exceptions, the choice of what to eat and where to find it remains the option of the reader perusing the wealth of excellent publications catering to this most worthy pursuit.

Britain by BritRail, like its sister publication, *Europe by Eurail*, is devoted to the visitor who goes to Britain expecting that its train services will provide the necessary transportation for a holiday that is different. We have gone ahead of you, probed what can be done, and solved the problems of doing it long before you will arrive. Every city and day excursion has been personally experienced, and we are pledged to constantly recheck, revise, and expand subsequent editions. This is being accomplished by personal visits and through our British and European network of correspondents in the areas described.

10

Britain by BritRail

Britain by BritRail presents a concept for comfortable, unhurried travel by train in Britain. By utilizing the economy of a BritRail Pass, along with the innovative, *fully* described base city–day excursion method, you can really see Britain at its best—by train.

Britain by BritRail is the perfect traveling companion for visitors using the BritRail Pass. This book helps to introduce and establish the reader in the base cities of London, Edinburgh, or Glasgow. Once you are ensconced in affordable, comfortable accommodations and your sightseeing and shopping are attended to in the base cities, *Britain by BritRail* then introduces its recommended day excursions to interesting places based on train schedules that will assure your return each night to the same hotel room. With a BritRail Pass and a current copy of *Britain by BritRail,* you become your own tour guide and avoid the constant packing and unpacking that accompanies most bus tours attempting to cover the same territory. By BritRail, if it's Tuesday, it's London, unless you have made the decision to pack and move on to another base city. You are calling the shots, not the tour bus driver.

Britons and their Continental cousins have employed British Rail's services for "holiday-making" on the British Isles for decades. Train travel is too fast for any possible chance of boredom setting in, yet it is leisurely enough to enjoy fully the constantly changing scene of hills and hamlets, farms and forests, countrysides and cities—everything that forms Britain's fascinating landscape.

Should you pause to ponder why, for example, an English gentleman would leave his motorcar at home when he's "off on holidays," you will find the answer very quickly when your train parallels a major highway or flashes across a bridge through the center of a British city. The superhighways right down to the ancient, narrow streets are packed with vehicles—all proceeding at a much slower pace than you and your train.

In the chapters describing the base cities and day excursions, *Britain by BritRail* meets the traveler upon arrival at the base-city airport or train station and then methodically *leads* him—in a relative order of priorities—to those essential facilities such as currency exchange, hotel accommodations, and tourist information sources. *Britain by BritRail* does not dwell on all the sightseeing opportunities offered by the base city. It provides an overall picture and then gives *explicit* directions on how to get to the city's tourist information office to obtain the most current information available to visitors. Readers requiring advance information regarding the base cities of London, Edinburgh, or Glasgow should direct their inquiries to the closest British Tourist Authority office listed in the appendix of this edition.

Britain by BritRail does concentrate on the day-excursion opportunities made possible from the base cities' geographic locations and rail facilities. A resumé of the day excursions follows the book's introduction of each base city so that the visitor may begin sorting out those excursions personally preferred.

Whether you admit it or not, everyone has a problem budgeting vacation time. It's human nature to try to see as much as possible in as little time as possible. This "sightseers' syndrome" could be dangerous to your vacation. Avoid it by planning an itinerary that allows ample "free time." Also, vary the day excursions by going on a short one following a particularly long outing away from the base city. Press too hard by trying to see and do too much on your vacation and you will return home as a living example of the old adage, "A person who looks like he needs a vacation usually has just returned from one."

To avoid reader frustration when searching for a single item of information or a telephone number, *Britain by BritRail* groups much of this data in its appendix for ready reference. Along with addresses of information sources, useful telephone numbers are all compiled in the appendix. Station plans and maps of transportation lines can be located easily near the end of the book.

Train schedules between London and the base cities of Edinburgh and Glasgow in Scotland are listed on pages 79 and 81 of chapter 10, which describes London. This particular information should prove to be helpful when you are initially planning your BritRail trip. Train schedules for the day-excursion trips out of the base cities are provided in the text describing each day excursion. Trains departing from the base cities are normally on morning schedules; trains returning from the day excursions usually run in the late afternoon and early evening. Each day-excursion section begins with the distance and average train time for the trip, because we realize that there may be some days when you prefer a short trip rather than a great adventure. If the twenty-four-hour times shown in the train schedules boggle your mind, we suggest that you consult the "time converter" clock on page 306 of this edition.

Please remember that the timetables and schedules appearing in this edition are provided for planning purposes only. Every care has been taken to make the timetables and schedules correct. The information is checked with authoritative sources up to press time. *Britain by BritRail* and/or its publisher cannot, however, be held responsible for the consequences of either changes or inadvertent inaccuracies. Current rail schedules are posted in all British Rail stations, and timetables from the base cities to every day-excursion point are available for the asking in the base-city stations. Please consult them.

Travel Economy

"Know before you go," the slogan of the U.S. Customs Service pertaining to what you may return with, also applies to the financial aspects of vacation planning. The rise and fall of the dollar's purchasing power in Europe over the past few years has left a lot of us wondering whether or not we could afford a vacation on the other side of the Atlantic. Although the inflation rate in the United States has been reduced to what bankers term "acceptable," it is still difficult to determine what effect Europe's inflation will have on your dollars once you're there.

Advance planning and purchasing vacation needs in advance (particularly transportation) in American dollars are probably the most effective ways to combat inflation and price fluctuations. Basically, the program calls for buying as much of your vacation needs as you can before you go and planning to limit your out-of-pocket costs paid in foreign currency to a minimum. In this way, you are well protected against fluctuating currency values.

The idea of doing things that were previously thought impossible—like putting $48 worth of gas in a Ford Escort—emphasizes train travel in Europe as the best means of effectively stabilizing your travel dollars. Prepayment plans, such as the BritRail Pass, are ideal. Not only do you purchase the pass with American dollars prior to departure, but the BritRail Pass also provides the most inexpensive way to travel in Britain—the quickest, too!

American travel agents still have a penchant for wanting to sell a "fly-drive" program to any client who wants to vacation in Britain. But, in general, car rentals have one basic fault—"the price you see" is never "the price you pay," which is *always* higher. As a rule of thumb, add to the quoted price another 20 percent for personal accident insurance, collision insurance, and taxes. After that, consider fuel costs. And don't forget about the 17.5 percent value-added tax (VAT). Then, ask your agent to provide you with an economical BritRail Pass. If he doesn't sell them, you can order one by calling BritRail's sales agent, Rail Pass Express, Inc., at (800) 722–7151.

Accommodations almost always account for the greatest share of a traveler's budget. Low-cost air fares and transportation bargains like the BritRail Pass can get the traveler *to* and *around* the British Isles, but the real bite out of the buck comes when the visitor opens his wallet to pay for a night's lodging. Attractively priced accommodations packages are being offered by some American tour operators. But too few suit the needs of those preferring individual itineraries, as is the case for travelers on a BritRail vacation. With advance planning and advance payment, however, savings can be realized by those who are willing to put forth the extra time and effort.

Well ahead of your intended departure date—preferably two months in advance, but no less than six weeks—write to one of the British Tourist Authority (BTA) offices listed on page 287 of this edition and request information regarding lodging (including the "bed-and-breakfast" places) in the areas you intend to visit during your BritRail journey. You may make reservations, or "bookings," as the British call them, in various ways. Hotel accommodations may be arranged by mail with central booking offices in London and Edinburgh but generally not elsewhere. The best assurance that you will have a room waiting upon arrival is to make an advance deposit directly to the hotel, then take care of the balance with the hotel's cashier when checking out. By the way, always ask the hotel to confirm the room rate when you check in. This will avoid delays and possible financial embarrassment when leaving.

One final bit of advice on reducing the cost of accommodations in Britain—use your BritRail Pass. Too many of us overlook the fact that the BritRail Pass can actually provide exceptional savings in housing costs by permitting you to stay outside the base city's center, where hotel rooms, pensions, bed-and-breakfast housing, and the like are far less expensive than their downtown counterparts.

London particularly lends itself to such a suburban arrangement because there are many areas outside the city's center that are readily accessible by rail. Anytime downtown accommodations become difficult to find or too demanding on the budget, tell the housing people you have a BritRail Pass and can easily stay in the suburbs.

Staying in London's northern or western suburbs has other advantages, too. From many of the suburban stations, you can board a fast InterCity train for a day excursion without ever going into a London terminus. You can return to the suburbs in the evening, too, without becoming involved in London's rush hours.

Watford Junction, sixteen miles from London's Euston Station, is one of the stations in London's suburbs that offers excellent InterCity connections to such day-excursion points as Birmingham, Chester, and Coventry. Most InterCity departures from Euston Station on weekday mornings pick up at Watford Junction sixteen minutes later. On weekday evenings, most InterCity trains set down at Watford twenty minutes ahead of their arrival times in Euston station.

Other rail points in London suburbs are Luton, for direct rail connections to Nottingham and Sheffield; Stevenage, along the main line to Edinburgh via York; and Slough or Reading, for connections to Bath as well as the Welsh cities of Cardiff and Swansea.

There are times when accommodations in the base cities are extremely limited. Edinburgh, during its annual festival every August to September, is an excellent example. Lodgings in the suburbs, à la BritRail Pass, can be more economical and just as convenient as those in the base cities.

If you have your heart set on lodgings in London when inquiring as to their availability, you will be asked the inevitable question, "Where do you want to be near to?" Naturally, when you're traveling by rail, your response will be, "Near the rail station." You are in for a surprise—at last count, London had fourteen rail stations. Because these terminals rim the vast, sprawling city, a better site-selection statement would be to ask for a hotel nearby one of the major lines of the Underground (subway). There are thirteen of these "tube" stations from which you can reach the British Rail stations. Of the ten Underground lines operating beneath London, the Circle Line serves the most rail stations. Confirmation of London's rail-station count may be made by turning to the map illustration appearing on page 294 of this edition. Opposite, on page 295, is a graphic presentation of the Inter-terminal British Rail Lines with the London Underground. The complete London Underground system is depicted on pages 296 and 297.

InterCity 225, a series of high-speed electric trains operated by British Rail, provides rail service at speeds up to 140 miles per hour. Not only do passengers reach their destinations quicker on the 225, they also enjoy a more comfortable ride in state-of-the-art coaches. Special features include push-button–operated exterior doors, carpeted floors and walls, and diffused ceiling lighting. Full-height smoked-glass partitions divide the interior of the cars, making the atmosphere more private and restful. One car on each train is specifically designed for disabled travelers.

2   PLANNING A BRITRAIL TRIP

Webster's Dictionary defines a plan as "a program of action." Plans vary in detail and complexity, according to the nature of the user. For example, one person may require a detailed, hour-by-hour, appointment-by-appointment schedule for a day's activities; another may merely plan to get up in the morning and see what happens after that. This example categorizes the two general types of rail travelers we have observed down through the years—one adventurous, the other conservative.

Time is the first consideration when planning any kind of journey. "Do I have enough time to go shopping today, or should I plan to go tomorrow?" That is a basic question we frequently ask ourselves. "Do I have enough time to visit Britain this year, or should I plan to go next year?" Basically, the latter question is the same as the former, the only variance being the time frame— one day or one year. Yet the second question has more impact than the first because the decision involves considerably more elapsed time than that for a routine shopping trip.

How long should your BritRail tour be? There are many factors bearing on such a determination, the most important being the individual. How much annual vacation time do you have? How do you use it—all at one time or in two or more segments? The folks issuing BritRail Passes are ready to accommodate just about anyone's personal needs, with passes ranging from eight days to one month of travel and flexible passes ranging from four days of travel to fifteen days in one month (two months for youth). The passes permit travel on all scheduled British Rail trains, including the InterCity 225 train shown on the opposite page.

Travel magazines and the travel sections of the Sunday newspapers are usually loaded with one-week trips to almost anywhere—mainland Europe and the British Isles included. Based on our own experience, we believe that going to Europe for any period of less than two weeks is a waste of time and money.

In support of the foregoing statement, we invite you to take a look at the logistics involved in a European trip. It takes an entire day to reach Britain by air from North America and an entire day to return. Although the flying time aboard a jet airplane ranges from seven to eight hours, airport to airport, it will be day two before you arrive in Britain. (Most eastbound transatlantic flights depart at night during day one and arrive the following morning—day two.) During the flight, you will be exposed to a cocktail hour, a dinner hour, a break for an after-dinner drink, followed by a full-length, feature motion picture. In the morning, as the sun rises in the east over Britain, you'll be awakened an hour or so before landing to be served breakfast.

Add up the time consumed by all the scheduled events while en route, and you'll quickly conclude that your night spent in the sky over the Atlantic Ocean consisted of many things—except sleep. Even if you did manage to sleep during the entire trip instead of eating, drinking, and watching movies, your body and all its functions will be arriving in Britain a few hours after midnight by North American time. You will crave adjustment to a phenomenon known as "jet lag," which will be trying its best to interrupt your plans for a carefree vacation.

When you discount the two full days utilized for air travel, plus a minimum of one day to get your sleep-eat cycle functioning properly again, the number of days left in a one-week visit hardly seems worth making the trip. Most of the economical excursion fares for transatlantic air travel evolve around day fourteen, meaning that your minimum time spent in Britain after departing from North America must be fourteen days in order to qualify for the reduced fares. Consequently, in consideration of both time and money, we recommend your stay in Britain be a minimum of two full weeks.

Having determined the length of time you will have for your BritRail trip, the next step is to develop a clear idea of where you want to go in Britain, what you want to see, and what you want to do. This process of developing objectives should be completed well before your departure date. We disagree with those who believe that anticipation of travel is more rewarding than its realization. But we do agree that the planning phase can also form a fun part of your trip. Properly done, this "homework" will pay substantial dividends when travel actually begins.

To get things started, write to the British Tourist Authority and BritRail Travel International, Inc., for information. You'll find the appropriate addresses listed on page 286. *Be specific.* In your request, indicate *when* you will be going, *where* you wish to go within Britain, and *what* in particular you would like to see. If you have any special interests or hobbies, be sure to mention them in your request. Spelling out your information needs will produce better responses.

Don't overlook your local library as a valuable information source. For example, you will find an excellent condensation of British history in the Encyclopeadia Britannica. Back issues of *National Geographic* magazine are excellent sources for first-person explorations of the British Isles. Seek out friends and neighbors who have been to Britain. No doubt you'll find their experiences flavored with their own likes and dislikes. Nevertheless, any and all information you can gather prior to your trip will eventually find its place in your memory bank. Surprisingly enough, you'll find yourself recalling many of these fragments of information during your own journey.

You are now ready for the decisive phase of your trip planning—constructing an itinerary. The moment of truth is at hand! Your only limitations during this portion of the planning phase are the lack of more than twenty-four hours in a day and the fact that the week does not contain more than seven days.

First, draw a blank calendar-style form covering a period from at least one week prior to your departure to a few days following your return. Make extra copies of the form—you'll need them. (Perfection is a long time coming in this project!) Now begin to block your itinerary into the calendar form, being mindful that the itinerary can be changed, but the number of days in a week remains fixed at all times. Possibly by the third time through the exercise, you'll begin to "see the light at the end of the tunnel." It's human to try to cram too many activities into a twenty-four-hour day, but it's better to discover your planning errors before starting your trip rather than during the middle of it.

With your itinerary in a calendar format, now you can determine your housing requirements, seat and sleeper reservations, and the other facets of your forthcoming trip. The days blocked out in advance of your departure can show your "countdown" items, such as stopping the newspaper, having mail held at the post office, and so on. Make several copies of your completed itinerary and leave some behind for the folks with whom you want to stay in touch. Above all, take copies of your itinerary with you—you'll refer to them frequently. If there have been any break-ins in your neighborhood, you should take steps to assure that it doesn't happen to you while you are gone. Alert the neighbors to keep a watchful eye for suspicious people and their activities. Many professional thieves have been known to park in a driveway in broad daylight with a moving van. The police should be advised regarding your absence. Also check with the insurance agency that writes your homeowner policy. "Am I covered?"—as they ask in television commercials—is what you ask. You may need additional coverage during your absence. One final caution. Don't have your forthcoming vacation plans announced in the newspapers. Thieves read, too. Save it for your return.

One item that you can't leave home without is a passport. If you do not have one or if yours has expired, write immediately to one of the U.S. passport offices listed on page 309 for information and applications. Allow a minimum of one month to obtain your passport. There are ways to expedite the process, but be safe by planning ahead and making this the first order of business when you've decided to make your trip abroad. U.S. citizens are admitted to Britain with only a passport. A visa is not required. Carry an extra certified copy of your birth certificate and two extra passport photos with you. If your passport is lost or stolen, go to the nearest U.S. Consulate.

What to Take?

Obviously, the practical answer to this question is "as little as possible." A tourist tends to pack everything he conceivably might use during a vacation, lug it everywhere, use it very little, and return home with longer arms. In these

Train travel is conducive to establishing new acquaintances or starting new friendships. When travelers (vacationers or business persons) are sitting next to you, they naturally will be inclined to strike up a conversation—if you are so inclined, too.

20

days of wash-and-wear fabrics (and deodorants), this is no longer necessary. A good rule of thumb is to take one medium-size suitcase and a shoulder bag. Hold to this rule and you will have a more comfortable trip. Regardless of how comfortable the weather at your destination is expected to be, pack a sweater. Brief cold spells in Britain are not uncommon. Stow a small pocket flashlight in your shoulder bag together with a collapsible umbrella in the "unlikely event" that you may need them.

If you must take expensive jewelry with you, take as well a copy of its insurance appraisal as proof of purchase to customs officials upon your return. Same for watches produced by foreign manufacturers. You may have bought that solid-gold Rolex in a St. Louis pawnshop for a song, but the customs inspector may have you singing a different tune if you can't come up with the paperwork!

If you wear prescription eye glasses or contact lenses, take a copy of the prescription with you. The same applies for prescription medications. Even if you only use over-the-counter drug products, we suggest taking an adequate supply of the item. Many such products are not available in Europe or are sold under a different label or packaging.

Samsonite, one of the major manufacturers of quality luggage, has published an interesting booklet on the subject of suitcases and travel. With the catchy title *Lightening the Travel Load—Travel Tips and Tricks*, it is crammed with helpful tips, everything from analyzing your luggage needs and the basic points of safeguarding it through packing for a trip. Helpful hints on carry-on luggage, how to tip, how to clear customs, and how to stay healthy while on your trip are also included. For a free copy, write to Samsonite Traveler Advisory Service, P.O. Box 39603, Denver, CO 80239. Be certain to include a self-addressed business envelope with postage affixed to cover up to two ounces first-class.

We also recommend the *Thomas Cook European Timetable* as part of your BritRail trip planning. It contains complete timetables covering every major rail route in Britain honoring the BritRail Pass. We suggest you purchase a copy before departing on your BritRail trip.

In the United States and Canada, copies of the *Thomas Cook European Timetable* can be purchased from major bookstores or from the distributor, Forsyth Travel Library, P.O. Box 2975 Dept. ER, Shawnee Mission, Kansas 66201. Telephone toll free (800) 367–7984. In Britain, the timetable may be purchased at any Thomas Cook Travel office. If you find the timetable too bulky to take with you, keep in mind that rail schedules are available at all major rail stations.

How to Get There

Transatlantic air traffic is so frequent and varied today that no description of it—short of an entire book—could do it justice. Excursion fares are still available in a multitudinous variety. Charter flights are available, too, and they are still mostly money savers. But some excursion rates are less expensive than charters. It is not uncommon on a regularly scheduled airliner winging its way to Europe to find that every passenger in your row of seats paid a different fare for the same flight on the same schedule with the same service!

We refer readers to their travel agents for airline information. But there has been an erosion of such information in travel agencies, brought about in general by the proliferation of air fares. The agencies face the almost impossible task of keeping tabs on the rapidly changing airline industry. Let's put it this way. If you've dealt with a reputable travel agency over the years, contact them the moment you've decided to BritRail through Britain, and ask them to come up with some air-excursion-fare options. At your leisure, call the various airlines' "800" telephone numbers and ask them for suggestions and fare information. We have listed the 800 numbers of a few airlines on page 310. Don't be disturbed if you receive a variety of responses. Sift them out until you find what you're looking for. Even if your travel agent didn't suggest the air fare you prefer and found through your own research, employ the agent's services in getting the tickets. You will pay the same price whether you obtain the tickets directly from the airline or from your travel agent. So give him the opportunity of collecting the commission and at the same time realizing that you are a pretty savvy client, and he will probably give you more personal service on your next trip.

Long-distance calls can be made in the United States without charge when calling businesses that have "800" service numbers. Obtaining the proper "800" number to call is easy: Dial (800) 555–1212 and tell the special operator the name of the airline information office with which you wish to speak.

Regarding charter flights, inquire about them but investigate them thoroughly before making any final decisions. Here again, get your travel agent involved, even if it's only to obtain the tickets. Even some of the most reputable air-charter carriers still operate on a "Go–No Go" basis. This means that if enough passengers sign up for the flight, it will go as scheduled; if there are not enough passengers booked, the flight will be scrubbed.

BritRail Passes

The BritRail Pass is a ticket for any train operated by the British Railways in England, Scotland, and Wales. There are two types of passes to choose from: BritRail Pass and BritRail Flexipass. You don't have to purchase a rail pass to travel by train in Britain. Having one, however, is very convenient. For example, with a BritRail Pass, you do not have to purchase a ticket every time you want to make a trip somewhere by train in Britain. Just board any British Rail train that is going your way and travel whenever, wherever, and as often as you like throughout the period in which your BritRail Pass is valid.

BritRail Passes may be purchased for first class or for economy class, with special reduced rates for youths and senior citizens. First-class seats are wider; consequently, the first-class coaches are more spacious because they accommodate fewer passengers. British Rail's economy class, however, is also comfortable. With the exception of a few local lines on which some "vintage" equipment is still in operation, the economy-class seats are fully upholstered, and space is plentiful. One thing is common to both classes—the view. Either in first or economy class, you can lounge in comfort while watching the countryside glide by.

A Senior Citizen BritRail Pass may be issued to anyone age sixty or older. The holder travels in either first class or economy class at a reduced rate. Youth Economy BritRail Passes are available for those ages sixteen through twenty-five; youth passes, however, are not available for first-class travel. BritRail also issues child passes for those ages five through fifteen for travel in first class or economy class at 50 percent of the adult fare. See the appendix, "British and European Rail Passes" section, page 301 for BritRail Pass prices and ordering information.

When traveling in Britain on certain peak days, holidays, or summer Saturdays, seat reservations are recommended. You may make them at any British Rail station or at the British Rail counters in Heathrow and Gatwick airports. It is more economical to make your reservations in Britain than in the U.S. Reservations are usually obtainable up to the day of travel.

Any visitors going to Britain should consider purchasing a BritRail Pass if they plan to travel primarily by train in England, Scotland, and Wales. To help you decide whether or not to purchase a BritRail Pass, we have included a selection of British Rail one-way fares on page 307. The fares are listed in U.S. dollars. To obtain the rate for converting dollars into pounds, consult the financial section of your newspaper or the international department of your bank. Compare the individual fare costs with the BritRail Pass costs shown on page 301 for your itinerary.

Keep in mind, when comparing the straight rail fares to the cost of the pass, that convenience in travel has a value, too. Standing in line ("queuing") to purchase train tickets is an inconvenience that can be avoided. With a BritRail Pass, you need do this only once—when you validate your pass. The rest of the time, you need only to board the train and you are on your merry way.

Even short-time visitors to the British Isles may find it advantageous to purchase a BritRail Pass in lieu of point-to-point tickets if they plan to make more than one or two medium-length rail journeys. For example, the cost of point-to-point tickets for a circuitous journey—like a quick dash out of London for a look around Edinburgh, Aberdeen, and Glasgow—exceeds the cost of an eight-day economy adult BritRail Pass; the economy of the pass becomes

Ferguson team, George and LaVerne, journey to Britain frequently to update the text and the photographs appearing in *Britain by BritRail*. Their quest takes them to sites as ancient as Scotland's Stirling Castle (above) and as current as the Euro Tunnel terminal (below), near Folkestone in Kent County, England.

immediately apparent. Consider, too, that the London-Edinburgh-Aberdeen-Glasgow-London round trip could be made comfortably in as little as three days, leaving five more days of unlimited rail travel available to the pass holder. Even though you might not be able to change your plans to extend your stay, you would still save money, in this case, by purchasing the BritRail Pass.

Some travelers may prefer the flexibility of a BritRail Flexipass. It differs from the conventional BritRail Pass, in that it allows you to travel for any four, eight, or fifteen days within a one-month period. With this pass, you can stay in a favorite location for several days before continuing your travel. Like the regular BritRail Pass, the BritRail Flexipass is available for first-class or economy travel, with special rates available for those ages sixty and over. The Youth BritRail Flexipass is available for any four or eight days of travel in a one-month period or any fifteen days within two months.

Other BritRail products include the England/Wales Pass, the Freedom of Scotland Travelpass, and the Continental Capitals Circuit (rail/sea transportation between London, Paris, Brussels, and Amsterdam). Those who want to combine the thrill of driving of the left-hand side of the road with rail travel can opt for the BritRail Drive pass.

Casual, short-term, or business visitors to Britain may all benefit from a BritRail Pass tucked in their pocket before leaving home. BritRail has come up with a combination package it calls the "London Extra," which has been designed with this type of visitor in mind. The London Extra consists of a special "Network Southeast" Rail Pass (First Class or Economy Class) for three, four, or seven days combined with a three-, four-, or seven-day London Visitor Travel Card—the pass that permits you to travel unlimited on London's red double-decker buses and the Underground (subway). The Rail Pass and Visitor Travel Card are each valid for consecutive periods, but they need not be validated on the same day. You can save one or the other for later.

The London Visitor Travel Card is also available separately for increments of three, four, or seven days. BritRail Pass *must* be purchased in North America prior to departure. Expand your horizons—don't leave home without one! Consult the appendix, page 301, for a complete list of BritRail products and ordering information.

Trip-Planning Tips

Don't carry more cash than you can afford to lose; carry traveler's checks. Whenever possible, cash your traveler's checks at the branch-bank facilities located in or near railway stations and airports. The currency-exchange services operated by Thomas Cook are also acceptable. The banks and the official currency-exchange services are government supervised and are required to pay the official exchange rates. Hotel and store cashiers, in contrast, seldom give you the full exchange value and often add a service charge.

Take a credit card with you. It usually proves to be an important adjunct to your en route finances. American Express is a popular card to carry. The privilege of cashing personal checks at the American Express offices is invaluable. Card members may cash checks for up to $1,000 ($200 in local currency and $800 in traveler's checks). MasterCard and Visa have gained popularity in Europe and can be used in a number of places, mostly stores and restaurants. Diner's Club and Carte Blanche are also accepted by most establishments.

Concerning credit cards, be aware that there's a "plastic war" being waged against American Express by MasterCard and Visa. *International Travel News* reports some readers have had to pay a supplemental charge to cash American Express traveler's checks at some British banks. Until the dust settles, it might be discretionary to inquire before presenting any card company's traveler's checks for cashing or credit cards for payment of services or purchases.

Picking pockets is an art that is practiced throughout Europe. Gentlemen's breast pockets are the main targets. Foil the thief by sewing a medium-size button both above and below the pocket opening. Loop a piece of shoestring or other strong string around the buttons when carrying valuables. Avoid carrying anything more valuable than a handkerchief in hip pockets. Ladies' pocketbooks should be of the shoulder type and carried that way at all times. Don't let the thought of someone picking your pocket alarm you. Just be aware of it and protect yourself against it. Actually, it is mild compared to what could happen to you on Main Street in your own home town in broad daylight.

Don't leave your cash, cameras, and other valuables in the hotel room or locked up in a suitcase. Take them with you or leave them in the hotel safe.

If you normally bathe with a washcloth, take your own; most European hotels don't have them.

3   EN ROUTE—THE FUN OF GOING

With all the luxuries of flight that modern aircraft offer, there is still something about flying that makes it a bit more demanding on your system than a similar amount of time spent at home or in the office. A transatlantic trip with a minimum of incidents and inconveniences is what we're after. Here are some suggestions that we have found helpful on our flights; perhaps they may help on yours.

Cash, Cards, and Credentials
You'll need some cash on your flight to pay for tips, snacks, refreshments, and taxi fares at your arrival point. U.S. currency will do very well, but don't carry it all in one big roll—distribute it around in pockets, a briefcase, or a money clip. A money belt is an ideal way to carry the larger notes. Taxis plying the airport-hotel routes have no problem converting dollars to local currency. Check with the driver, however, before entering his cab.

List the number of each credit card you plan to take. Leave a copy at home and pack one in your suitcase or carry-on bag. List passport numbers, too. When anything is lost or stolen, the police are interested primarily in its serial number. A certified copy of your birth certificate and a few extra passport photos will save you days of delay if you lose your passport.

Luggage
One suitcase, one shoulder bag. Check the suitcase and carry the shoulder bag. Be sure the carry-on bag has a small supply of toilet articles, stockings, and underwear—just in case the suitcase disappears.

In-Flight Comfort
If you plan to catch some shut-eye en route, ask for a seat alongside a bulkhead. Bulkheads don't mind being leaned on, but passengers do. Passengers in the forward section of the airplane generally experience less vibration. Wear loose clothing. Unfasten your shoes, but don't take them off. Your feet will swell following several hours of immobility. The best remedy is to walk the length of the aisle in the airplane every hour or so. Try deep knee bends.

Flying dehydrates your body. Drink lots of water and watch what you mix with it—alcohol dehydrates, too. Special meals for special diets are no problem with the airlines, but requests should be made at the same time as reservations.

Cameras, Film
If you plan to take a foreign-made camera with you that you purchased in the United States, save yourself a lot of headaches by taking the sales slip with

you. Otherwise, go to a U.S. Customs Office before leaving the country and have your equipment registered. Carry a copy of the sales slip or the registration form with your passport and a spare copy tucked away in the camera case or shoulder bag.

Despite what airport officials tell you, their electronic luggage-checking devices can fog your film. The best way to avoid it is to report for check-in early and ask that your cameras and film be inspected by hand. Special lead-lined bags are available at most camera stores. Color film in Britain includes processing and is usually more expensive than that which you can buy at home. Solution? Take all the film you'll need with you.

Tax-Free Purchases

Every international airport has a "tax-free" shopping service. The routine is generally the same. You select your purchases, pay for them and add them to your carry-on luggage, find safe storage for it during the flight, and then haul it off the airplane. Yet there are variations. For example, at JFK in New York, you select the items from a sample or catalog. The items are then delivered "for your convenience" to your departure gate for pick-up. The hazards of this system are many. If the delivery person gets things mixed-up and fails to make the right gate at the right time, you'll be off into the wild blue yonder sans purchases. Or if you are late passing the pick-up point, sometimes an unknown "benefactor" tries to help by taking your purchases on board the plane ahead of you. Finding this so-called "benefactor" can prove to be difficult. Solution? Buy your "booty" aboard the airplane while en route. Most international airlines carry aboard a good stock of "tax free" items, which you may purchase from the cabin crew. It's always best to check at the airline counter, however, to be certain that this "in flight" service will be available on your particular flight. "Tax-free," by the way, is a misused term. Most items, with exception of alcohol and tobacco, normally can be purchased cheaper in the arrival city.

Keep in mind that everything you purchase, "tax free" or otherwise, is subject to customs duty when returning home. Consequently, know your quotas and attempt to stay within them to avoid paying duty and the ensuing delays involved. Good luck with customs. Honesty is always the best policy!

Prior to Landing

Fill out all the customs forms your flight attendant gives to you and keep them with your passport and airline ticket. Keep this packet handy, but secure, until the credentials are required by the customs officials at the arriving airport.

28

Jet Lag and What to Do about It

Earlier, we mentioned jet lag. It can seriously affect your transatlantic trip unless you know how to deal with it. The following explanation of what jet lag is and some means to combat it should prove helpful to any traveler undergoing four or more hours of time change.

The human body has numerous rhythms; sleep is one of them. Even without sunlight, as in a cave, the body will still maintain a twenty-four-hour awake/asleep cycle. The heart rate falls to a very low ebb in the early hours of the morning, when you are usually asleep. Body temperature, which affects the mental processes, also drops during this time. Consequently, if an air traveler is transported rapidly to a time zone five or six hours ahead of that of the departure point, even though it may be eight or nine o'clock in the morning at the arrival point in local time, the traveler's body functions are at a low ebb. As a result, the traveler feels subpar, and this feeling can persist for as long as two or three days unless something is done to correct it.

To cope effectively with jet lag, start varying your normal sleep-eat-work pattern a week or so before your departure. If you are normally up by 7:00 A.M. and in bed around 11:00 P.M. or so, get up earlier and go to bed later for a few days. Then reverse the procedure by sleeping in a bit in the morning and going to bed ahead of your normal time. Vary your meal times, possibly putting off breakfast until lunch time. What all this erratic life-style will do is condition your body to begin accepting changes in routines. In turn, when the big transatlantic change comes, it won't be as much of a shock on your system.

To lessen the effects of jet lag en route, avoid excessive drinking and eating. After your arrival, exercise the first day by taking a vigorous walk, followed by a long nap. You should have set your watch to local time at your destination as you departed on your flight. By doing this, you subconsciously accelerate your adjustment to the new time zone. For example, how many times have you looked at your watch and then realized you were hungry? Get plenty of rest on the day of your arrival, and begin doing everything you normally do back home according to the new local time.

Some seasoned transatlantic travelers take even stronger precautions to avoid jet lag. They follow the rule of "no coffee, tea, food, wine, beer, or liquor" on the day of the flight to Europe, but they do advocate lots of fruit juices, vegetable juices, and water (no carbonated drinks). This method follows the theory that your body clock will then go on hold, waiting for you to restart it with breakfast the day you arrive in Europe. Resist the temptations of the airlines up to the point of breakfast and try to get some sleep. Respect jet lag by taking these precautions and you'll enjoy your vacation.

Plane to train. Facilities at London's Gatwick Airport (top) make it easy to transfer from the airport to British Rail's Gatwick Express (below) for the 27-mile trip into Victoria Station. The rail station is a part of Gatwick's south terminal, with interterminal rail service to the airport's north terminal. Nonstop rail service runs every 15 minutes during the day, hourly at night. Journey time is 30 minutes. $15 U.S. standard class; $22 U.S. first class.

4 ARRIVING IN BRITAIN

That big moment is about to happen. Years of dreaming, months of planning, and weeks of anticipation are about to become a reality. The NO SMOKING and FASTEN SEAT BELTS signs have been illuminated, and the cabin attendants advise that the aircraft will be landing in a few minutes. If this is your initial visit to Britain, you'll be straining to get your first glimpse of the land from your window; if you have been to Britain many times before, you'll be straining to get a glimpse of the land right along with the other passengers. There is always an unexplainable thrill about arriving in a foreign country. Enjoy this emotion; it's part of the reason for your journey—to experience the adventure of travel, to probe beyond the normal confines of your environment, to meet other people, to enjoy a bit more of the world than you did before the FASTEN SEAT BELTS sign came on.

The Airports

Within Britain, there are seven airports managed by the British Airports Authority—Heathrow, Gatwick, and Stansted in the London area; Glasgow, Edinburgh, Prestwick, and Aberdeen in Scotland. Your destination depends on the routing you selected and the air carrier taking you there. If your destination is London, you could arrive at either Heathrow, Gatwick, or Stansted. Check with the air carrier to be certain.

Should you need specific information regarding your arrival or departure airport in Britain, such as travel to and from the airport, airport services, or information services, ask your travel agent to check in the European edition of the Official Airlines Guides "Travel Planner." Another way would be to ask your agent to send a fax to Gatwick Airport, (0293) 50413; Heathrow Airport, (01) 745 4290; Scottish Airports, (041) 887 1699; or Stansted Airport, (0279) 81655. A fax message will ensure that the latest and most specific information will be obtained.

Transportation between London and the Heathrow and Gatwick airports is described on page 69. Similar information for Glasgow Airport in Scotland may be found on page 222.

Clearing Customs

The customs-information cards given to you by the cabin attendants before landing will expedite your clearance through arrival formalities. Actually, you will go through two processes—customs and immigration—although they appear to be integrated. Immigration officials will want to examine your passport.

This is usually conducted at a barrier gate en route to the baggage-claim area in the airport. After collecting the checked baggage, you should proceed to the customs-inspection area, where you will find two color-coded lanes—green for "Nothing to Declare" and red for "To Declare." Everyone has some apprehension about passing through customs. For the most part, the apprehension is based on the question, "Am I doing it properly?" Doing it properly in Britain consists of going straight through the "Nothing to Declare" channel (unless you are asked to stop by an officer) and moving through into the airport's general-assembly area.

If the customs officials want to examine your luggage, they will indicate so as you approach them. Don't go through the "To Declare" lane unless you have brought amounts of tobacco or liquor with you that exceed the duty-free limits or have purchased a gift that you will be leaving with someone in Britain with a value exceeding £36.

The type and amount of duty-free goods that you may bring into Britain vary with your point of departure—a European Common Market country or otherwise. For transatlantic passengers, the limit is 200 cigarettes and a liter bottle of liquor or two bottles of sparking wine and two bottles of still wine. You will have plenty of advance advice on duty-free imports posted in your departing airport and you can check with the cabin attendants on the airplane as well. Know before you go, and the clearing procedures in Britain will present no problem.

The phrase "know before you go" also applies to your return to North America. The U.S. Treasury Department publishes an informative booklet containing customs hints for returning residents. Write to the Department of the Treasury, Washington, DC 20229 for the *Know Before You Go* booklet. For U.S. Customs information while in London, telephone 499–1212 at the American Embassy.

When clearing through foreign customs, keep in mind that the average customs inspector is more interested in the luggage of a returning national than in yours. Always carry your customs declaration along with your passport and in full view as you unlock your luggage in case it has to be inspected.

British Currency

British currency is based on the pound sterling. The pound is divided into one-hundred pence, just as the U.S. dollar is divided into one hundred cents. When exchanging money in Britain, you will receive paper notes in denominations of £5, £10, or £20. Coins of 50p (seven sided), 20p, 10p, 5p, 2p, and 1p will be exchanged for amounts less than one pound. The £1 coin replaced the £1 note.

British paper notes, like the majority of world currencies, vary in size according to their value, and a variety of them can wreak havoc to the orderliness of a North American's wallet. Certain notes, the £10 and £20 in particular, will require folding before they will fit into a wallet designed to hold dollars. Use discretion when engaged in this folding process, especially in public.

British Telephones

Old-timers who first toured the British Isles under the auspices of General Dwight D. Eisenhower and their local draft boards will find that the British telephones with the dreaded "A" and "B" buttons are long gone. Many people thought that when the British removed all their road signs to confuse possible invaders during World War II, they added "A" and "B" buttons to the telephones to confuse—possibly even eliminate—telephone communications by invaders and visitors alike. We've even heard it whispered by off-duty State Department personnel that Britain was denied participation in the Marshall Plan because of the huge amounts of money the Americans had "hung up" in the British pay phones somewhere between the "A" and "B" buttons.

All that is legend. The modern, public, coin-box telephones now in operation throughout Britain are simple—with a bit of explanation, that is. Basic differences still exist between British phones and ours, particularly in the signals they make. A ringing signal is two short rings, followed by a pause. The busy signal sounds the same—only busier. An all-circuits-busy signal is a rapid series of high-low tones, but when you have reached a telephone number not in use, a high-pitched continuous tone reminiscent of a World War II air-raid siren is heard.

Coin operated phones are identified by a red stripe across the phone booth door. They operate much like ours, except when you hear a series of rapid pips, which is a signal that more coins must be deposited or your call will be terminated. Phonecard payphones are identified by a green stripe across the door. They require the use of a prepaid Phonecard, which you can purchase in £2 (20 units), £4 (100 units), and £20 (200 units) denominations. The cards are sold at post offices and wherever the distinctive green British Telecom (BT) Phonecard sign is displayed. Instructions for the use of Phonecards are posted inside each booth, or you can ask an information office for the pamphlet, "How to Call Home from the UK."

British Traditions

Some visitors entering Britain for the first time may find some of the British traditions, customs, and way of life a little difficult to understand. Perhaps what follows may assist in the transition.

If a Scot from Edinburgh, a Welshman from Cardiff, and an Englishman from London were traveling together in North America, they would describe themselves as being "British." But among themselves, they would be Scot, Welsh, and English. These three nationalities, joined by the Ulstermen of Northern Ireland, make up what we refer to as the United Kingdom. Since the BritRail Pass is not accepted for rail travel in Northern Ireland (as previously mentioned), references in this book are to *Britain* rather than the *United Kingdom*, and the term *British* refers to the peoples of England, Scotland, and Wales.

The British character will wear well on you after a few days. If you are taken by the strangeness of their manners, remember that the British are a well-disciplined people. If anything is at fault, more than likely it is the visitor, not the host. You might spill your tea the first time a waitress calls you "Dearie," but you'll learn very quickly that these figures of speech are actually a kind of politeness. You'll also learn very quickly that the British queue is the quintessence of "first-come, first-served."

On the surface, Britons may appear to lack a sense of humor. Once their facade is penetrated, however, you will find them capable of the highest mark of humor—they can laugh at themselves. This becomes most evident in their observations regarding their weather. "The way to ensure summer in England," snapped Horace Walpole, "is to have it framed and glazed in a comfortable room." Byron's observation was perhaps more terse: "The English winter—ending in July to recommence in August." Britain does have a tendency to be damp at times. You won't regret taking a small folding umbrella.

The Language Barrier

By now, you'll notice that there is one! It has often been said that the two great countries of America and Britain are divided only by a common language. Terminology, more so than pronunciation, appears to be the problem whenever an American and a Briton cannot communicate effectively. Several of our readers report that *British Self-taught, with Comments in American* by Norman W. Schur (New York, the Macmillan Company, 1973) can be most helpful during an initial visit to Britain.

Reading the daily newspapers and listening to the British Broadcasting Corporation (BBC) or watching the telly (television) are quick remedial methods for learning the language. These media communicate through a (more or less) middle-of-the-road lexicon. Regional and local dialects can be extremely difficult to comprehend on occasion. It has been said that if an Oxford graduate and a Cambridge graduate were locked together in the same room, neither would be able to converse with the other—even after being properly introduced.

One of the first things a visitor from "the Colonies" will notice is the manner in which directions are given. Americans geographically locate a point within a city by referring to the number of blocks distant from the point of inquiry, for example, "two blocks down the street." Britain's early road builders, however, never thought too much about a grid system and permitted their streets to wander along the easiest gradient. Consequently, directions given by a constable or a man on the street will usually be in terms of linear directions, that is, "straight-away for one-hundred yards," "a quarter-mile," "a mile or two," and so on. Visual objects are employed as well: "straight-away to the pub," "keep walking till you come to the third traffic light," and the like. Cabbies (taxi drivers) are particularly good sources for directional information and advice. Every cabby carries a street map in his taxi and will be glad to assist you.

Nuances in the American/British vocabulary can sometimes lead to trouble. In a public place, such as a train station, those in search of toilet facilities will do well to employ the term *lavatory* in their quest. The *WC* (water closet) seems to be losing its effectiveness in Britain, although it still brings direct results when used in Continental Europe. But if you want to be up on slang expressions, you might ask for the *loo*—that's where the "in crowd" goes to "spend a penny." Requesting directions for the *bathroom*, particularly in a train station, might lead you to the public showers. So take our advice and stay with lavatory.

Terminology in a train station should not present much of a problem. The baggage room is *left luggage*, and *lost property* translates easily into lost and found. Elevators are labeled *lifts*, but *subway* means a pedestrian, underground street crossing. The Underground, or *tube,* is the British version of our subway.

A *carriage* is a (rail) coach, and a *coach* is a long-distance bus. Should you hear the term *goods wagon* or *goods train,* that translates to a freight car or a freight train in American terminology. Aboard a train, the conductor usually is referred to as the *guard;* the engineer becomes the train *driver.*

The British measure their body weight in stones—a stone being a unit of fourteen pounds. A person weighing fourteen stone six pounds would gross out at 202 pounds avoirdupois. A popular measurement of elapsed time is *a fortnight,* meaning fourteen days or two weeks. Britain's conversion to a decimal currency system has not changed the slang for the pound sterling—it's still a "quid." You may hear a price quoted in *guineas,* a holdover from the old days meaning one pound and one shilling.

British Pubs

The pub is uniquely British and can be found only on the British Isles, because the ingredient that makes a true "public house" is not its construction, architecture, furniture, or the spirits it dispenses—it's its clientele. The "local," as most British pubs are lovingly referred to, is an organic part of the community. It ranks in importance along with the local postal office and the town hall—perhaps even higher. It is supported by "locals," who generally prefer to

35

Local Hangout, The Gallows Pub in Edinburgh takes its name from the fact that it is located on the site of Gallows Hill, where executions by hanging were held in days not too dim in the city's past. British public houses frequently have taken their names from the activities previously conducted in the area, like Smugglers—or from folklore— George & Dragon. The Wicked Lady near St. Albans, however, has us puzzled.

36

stand when they imbibe, for pub etiquette must be observed at all times. Pub etiquette also dictates that you pay for the "round" when served and if you accept a drink, you are expected to buy a round in return.

The term *public house,* means just that. Everyone is welcome—even Americans and Australians. To accommodate the differences in drinking etiquettes of these visitors, most pubs have a second bar area, which is identified as a lounge or a saloon. There are more seats and usually the drinks cost a bit more.

When are the pubs open? Licensing hours now generally permit English pubs to remain open from 1100 to 2300 Monday through Saturday and Sundays from 1200 to 1500 and 1900 to 2230 in England and Wales; 1230 to 1430 and 1830 to 2300 in Scotland. You must be over eighteen to buy or consume alcoholic beverages in a pub. Children fourteen years and older may be admitted legally to a pub and may consume nonalcoholic drinks. Children of all ages are usually admitted to licensed restaurants; they are also admitted to "beer gardens" and family rooms, which many pubs have.

Closing time in a pub is quite an event and frequently can create confusion among the uninformed and the uninitiated. At the appointed hour, the owner or head barkeep announces, "Time, gentlemen!" in a loud, authoritative voice. At that instant, a bar towel is draped over the beer pumps, and everyone quickly attends to drinking up and hastily departing the premises. Without prior knowledge of this procedure, visitors have frequently mistaken closing time for a fire drill and have begun evacuating the building via the closest window!

A pub is usually rated by the congeniality of its owner, and unless "on holidays," he or she is usually found on the premises during operating hours. An entrepreneurial lot, many owners offer "pub grub" in their establishments. Visitors find it a good alternative to Wendy's or McDonald's for a snack or a lunch because a Frosty can never really compete with a good pint of ale or porter.

A pub's personality greets you at the door. You can tell in an instant whether or not it's your kind of place. If its ambience reaches out to you, enter. No doubt a local or two will note your entrance with a friendly nod as the barmaid beams at you and asks, "What'll you have, governor?" When advised, she'll then indicate with a slight directional nod of her head that it will be served in the lounge area. Pay when served. Tip the barmaid, but never tip the owner in the event he brings the drinks to the table to bid you welcome. He's the host; you are the guest. Later, you might join the locals at the bar; but remember, remain standing and pay for a round when it's your turn to buy. Who knows, the locals might suggest that you drop around again.

Food on the move includes a variety of service and menus. InterCity trains (above) feature three types of menus: Gold Star, Main Line, and Grill. Buffet service (below) offers a wide range of snacks and drinks. Food-service cars (carriages) are identified by an exterior red band above the windows.

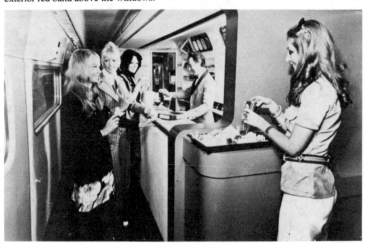

5 BRITISH RAIL SERVICES

Over the last decade, the services on the British Rail passenger network have come a long way—with yet a long way to go. There is still a discernible difference between the operating speeds and the passenger comforts of the railroads of Continental Europe and those of the British, the latter being inferior; yet the gap is narrowing.

The front runner of British Rail's stable is its High Speed Train (HST), the InterCity 125. Nicknamed the "Journey Shrinker," the world's fastest diesel train is shrinking journeys on many of the main routes out of London. From King's Cross Station, for example, the Flying Scotsman, an InterCity 125, covers the 393 miles between London and Edinburgh in four hours flat—an average of ninety-eight miles per hour, and that includes a station stop at York and Newcastle in England before crossing the Scottish border. Hourly service by 125s links the two capitals. InterCity 125 service also extends from London to Plymouth and Penzance. Leading the 125 fleet to England's west is the Golden Hind, appropriately named after Sir Francis Drake's famous sailing vessel.

InterCity 125 trains offer comfort as well as speed. They have a whole range of luxury features, including air conditioning, soundproofing, automatic interior doors, and a wide choice of meals, snacks, and drinks. The trains are powered by two 2,250-horsepower diesel-electric engines—one at each end of the train. The 125 coaches are identified by letter (A, B, C, etc.), and the stations they serve have their platform positions marked accordingly.

The mainline between London and Edinburgh, which is particularly popular with overseas visitors, was electrified. The use of electric locomotives cut the time for the 393-mile journey to only four hours. The light at the end of BritRail's tunnel grows brighter and brighter. By InterCity 125 service from London, you can now reach Cardiff, in Wales, in one hour and forty-seven minutes; York, in one hour, fifty-seven minutes. Running times are being slashed on all major British Rail lines. A train trip from London to Glasgow used to take six hours; now you're there in only five hours and five minutes!

Aside from the InterCity 125s and the equally fast and comfortable all-electric passenger trains operated by British Rail on its major routes (the London-Glasgow line is completely electrified), there is a paucity of modern commuter-type trains on many of its intermediate lines. For example, although train service south of London is completely electrified, for the most part it is served by four-car units, some of which have already passed their thirty-eighth "birthdays." These trains have seen yeoman duty through the years and show more than a fair amount of wear and tear.

Along with Beatlemania, graffiti arrived in Britain accompanied by modern packaging, which produces litter in abundance. The older trains, however, were designed in the days when cleaning labor was plentiful and cheap. Washing as many as eighty windows on a single coach wasn't a problem then, but it is now. Moreover, air conditioning is nonexistent in the older trains, although that's no great problem because summers in the British Isles are generally milder than those in North America. But heating can be a problem. Not many years ago, train passengers set out on their journeys wrapped in heavy overcoats and shod with thick-soled shoes. Full heat in the coach brought complaints of stuffiness. Today's grumbles from thinly clad travelers are very much the opposite.

The "old units" are gradually being replaced by new suburban-type trains, and some of the vintage units are being refurbished with more comfortable seats, better lighting, heating, and soundproofing. Nevertheless, it will be a while before the "generation gap" in British Rail's rolling stock is overcome.

Possibly on a day excursion off the main lines, you may ride in a locomotive-hauled coach with an exit door for each compartment. We've counted as many as nine doors to a side on some coaches. These cars are relics from the days when station porters opened and closed the doors for passengers. Consequently, you won't find any door handles inside the compartment. To get out, lower the window and open the door from the outside.

Sleeping, restaurant, buffet and Pullman cars are operated by British Rail, along with the standard passenger carriages (coaches). British Pullman cars differ from the Pullmans of North America in that they do not convert at night to provide sleeping accommodations. Instead, British Rail Pullmans are the elite of the line, the best in daytime comfort, and exclusively first-class. Even travelers holding first-class BritRail passes are required to pay a supplemental fare for occupancy, and seat reservations are obligatory. This luxury service operates on the London-to-Manchester/Liverpool route. Basically, it is designed to offer the businessman morning and afternoon services between England's capital and its leading commercial center. It is worth the experience, but we suggest that you dress appropriately for the occasion if you want to engage in tycoon-to-tycoon conversations with other passengers. In London, the Pullman trains depart from Euston Station. When accommodations are available, last-minute reservations and supplementary payment can be arranged with the conductor.

First-class sleeping cars have single-berth compartments; economy-class sleepers have two-berth compartments. Sleeping-car charges in Britain are economical—$57 per person for first class and $48 per person for economy class. The sleeping cars are equipped with fresh bedding, washing facilities with soap and towels, a shaver outlet, and bottled drinking water. Sleeping-car passengers are served with morning tea or coffee and biscuits free of charge, and they generally can remain in the sleeping cars at destination until 7:30 A.M. The charge is standard for all destinations regardless of the distance.

With such attractive prices, an overnight trip aboard a sleeper may outweigh the alternative of seeking a night's lodging in a city and an early morning departure in order to make your destination on time. Consider the sleeping cars for excursions to Plymouth, Penzance, and Inverness.

Sleeper services operate between London and the main centers in Scotland, the north of England, south Wales, and the west of England. "Nightcap" service is available, too, in case you're interested.

Most InterCity trains haul restaurant cars. If not, there usually is a buffet car from which you can obtain snacks and beverages. Aboard the InterCity fleet, restaurant cars offer a wide range of freshly prepared traditional dishes. Gold Star restaurant service is available on many 125s and on selected "business" trains—the Manchester/Liverpool Pullman, for example. Passengers holding first-class tickets who wish to take meals can reserve seats in the restaurant car or in adjacent coaches. Breakfast aboard British Rail trains has always been a great attraction. It's hearty and generally very good.

Some buffet cars offer "grill" meals, which you may enjoy either there, or back at your seat. Seating in the buffet cars is not assignable, thereby providing a reasonable opportunity to be seated while you select from the bill of fare. One innovation found aboard many British Rail food-service cars is beer and lager on draft. This, according to many railroad buffs, is an outstanding stride forward in the annals of railroad engineering!

Admittedly, dining aboard a speeding train is an unusual gastronomic experience, but it can be on the expensive side. Although British Rail's food catering aboard is far more economical than similar services on the trains of the Continent, those seeking less expensive food may want to utilize the food facilities found at most rail stations in Britain. They range in service from complete restaurants servicing a variety of hot and cold dishes to a snack bar–type operation. Some have off-license provisions allowing you to purchase alcoholic beverages for consumption elsewhere, but all bars operating in the stations, unlike those on the trains, must observe the local licensing hours for drinks.

The most economical food you may enjoy on a train in Britain is, of course, that which you bring aboard yourself. Many of the station restaurants will prepare box lunches for you to take on your trip. Ask for the "buffet-pack" service. Your hotel or bed-and-breakfast probably can provide the same service. We suggest that you make your initial inquiry a day ahead of your first planned day excursion.

First Class, Economy Class?

On most British Rail trains you have a choice of first- or economy-class travel. BritRail Passes and Flexipasses are sold for both classes. First-class seats are wider and more spacious. If that is the sort of accommodations you want, then it is worth paying the extra price. Economy class (also referred to as standard class) is, however, an excellent standard. All the facilities aboard the trains, such as restaurant and buffet services, are available for both first- and economy-class travelers.

The average British citizen usually travels by economy-class carriage (coach). In fact, it is so much the custom that if you want to purchase a first-class ticket, you must specifically state "first-class"; otherwise, you will automatically receive an economy-class ticket. This does not mean that you will find the economy-class carriages crowded, while the first-class sections remain vacant. First class offers extra comfort and is less crowded. First-class accommodations for weekend and holiday travel are particularly desirable. Seats may be reserved in both classes, which is a wise move if your journey is a "must" and the distance is great. "Riding the cases" (sitting on your suitcase for lack of a seat) is not a comfortable way to travel.

Seat reservations may be made in any major train terminal throughout Britain. In addition, Gatwick, Heathrow, and Stansted airports have British Rail ticket booths where you may make reservations immediately after your arrival. It is possible to obtain advance reservations prior to arriving in Britain, but it is far more economical to make them when you get there.

Travelers holding first-class BritRail Passes may travel in either first- or economy-class carriages—which is a nice option for bachelors when the good looking "bird" you've been yearning to chat with boards the economy-class section. It's a disaster, however, if she moves to the first-class section while you're holding an economy-class ticket!

You will find some single-class trains operating on branch lines. This means that the first-class accommodations are not available aboard that particular train. It is a nice, polite British way of avoiding the somewhat unrefined term *second class only*.

Similar to those on the Continent, first-class British Rail cars are marked distinctively by a yellow band running the length of each car above its doors and windows. On other-than-mainline service, where both first- and economy-class accommodations may be provided in the same car, a yellow band will be shown for only the first-class portion of the car. Restaurant cars, buffets, and cars containing other forms of food-catering facilities are identified by a red band above their doors and windows.

Except for those of the InterCity 125s and 225s, it is difficult to determine exactly where the first-class coaches will halt during an en route station stop. The non-English-speaking nations of Europe generally provide a diagram of each train's composition and where it will stop in the station. Not so in Britain. According to the equipment in use, the first-class section of a British train can be at the head, the rear, or the middle of the train. Through experience, we have devised a system that is relatively effective in determining where the yellow-striped cars will stop.

Position yourself midway on the platform and scan for the yellow band as the train enters the station. Should it pass you, take off to the head of the train; if it doesn't, head in the other direction. Should the yellow-striped car stop directly in front you, fate has been kind to you this day, but you can bet it won't happen again soon.

There is an increase in the nonsmoking accommodations aboard British trains. The overall percentage of nonsmoking seats currently is about 75 percent, reflecting the noticeable change in the public attitude toward smoking. There is a stiff fine for violating the rule. So if you are a smoker, keep your eyes alert for the red nonsmoking signs and smoke only in the areas so designated.

Train Schedules

British timetables are generally divided into sections according to the pattern of services provided. A typical two-part division is "Mondays to Saturdays" and "Sundays." You may run across a mix, however, including "Mondays to Fridays," "Mondays to Saturdays," or "Saturdays and Sundays." All days stated are inclusive. In other words, "Mondays to Saturdays" includes all six days. (The schedules appearing in *Britain by BritRail* are stated as "Mondays *through* Saturdays.")

Always be certain that you look at the correct part of the schedule for the particular day of the week on which you wish to travel. Another caution: Services may be modified on days preceding and immediately following bank holidays. Best bet for a "must" trip, a late night return, or an early morning departure is to check your plans with the British Rail personnel in the station travel centers. Extensive engineering work is often conducted on the British Rail system on weekends, which frequently affects passengers' schedules. Telephones may also be employed for inquiries. Useful telephone numbers are given on the *Britain by BritRail* schedules for this purpose.

You should experience little difficulty in verifying the departure time of your selected train or locating the platform from which it departs once you've made it to the station—providing that in London you've gone to the proper station. Airport-style digital displays are the usual source for such information in most British stations. You will find them in the main station halls and also on the train platforms in many stations. Even the old-fashioned train bulletin boards, however, can still provide the needed information. Augmenting displayed train-departure information are the usual vocal announcements in the station halls and on the platforms. For the most part, they differ from those made by Amtrak because you can understand them. Perhaps it's the accent that makes it possible.

Ask the Guard

Every British Rail train travels with a conductor aboard. As previously explained, his official title is guard. This gentleman carries with him—in either his handbook or his head—a potpourri of valuable information. For example, if you are required to change trains in order to arrive at your final destination, ask the guard. The London day excursion to Lincoln is one in which you should change trains at Newark Northgate, approximately one and one-half hours after departing London. Will the train departing there for Lincoln Central be standing across the platform from the train you arrive on from London, or will a platform change be necessary? The guard has this information, and it's yours for the asking.

Perhaps en route you learn that the train you are traveling on will be passing a famous British landmark, say a castle. On which side of the train will it pass? If you are a castle buff, maybe you would like to come back on another day to visit the castle. Is there a local train station near the castle? Is there a local bus to take you there if the castle is beyond walking distance? Is there a pub or inn in the vicinity? Surprisingly, you'll probably get responses to all of the above plus a condensed history lesson on the castle and its surroundings— all from the guard.

The guard becomes invaluable when you decide to change your itinerary or vary the time to return to your hotel. With a quick reference to his handbook, he will be able to tell you the time of the next train or the last one you may take that evening. He is also an excellent source of the correct time, for his watch is always set to the second and checked with British Rail's master clock daily. In many ways, the guard becomes your unofficial tour guide—or guardian angel, as the case may be.

BritRail/Drive

Britain is compact, which makes it convenient to take the train and see the sights. There are but a few nooks and crannies within Britain that cannot be reached by train. Some vacationers to Britain, however, find an occasional need to go sightseeing by car. As a consequence, BritRail has devised a system with Hertz to fill this need.

BritRail/Drive combines a three- or six-day BritRail Flexipass with the rental of a Hertz car with unlimited mileage for three or seven days out of a one-month period. There are five different types of car models to choose from—two types with automatic transmissions, an absolute must for any driver experiencing the transition to "starboard" steering for the first time.

If you purchase the BritRail/Drive package, you will receive car-rental vouchers (one for each day's rental) along with your rail pass. Reserve your first car at least seven days prior to your departure date by calling Hertz, toll free, at (800) 654–3001 and tell them that you have purchased a BritRail/Drive package. You should make these reservations as early as possible, particularly if you want a car with an automatic transmission. For the remainder of your car-rental reservations, Hertz has rental offices and Freephones at rail stations throughout England, Scotland, and Wales.

Since your car-rental vouchers may be used only during the validity period of your BritRail Flexipass, the most economical way of using them is to arrange for a car to meet your train at a day-excursion point, do your exploring, and return the car to the same station before returning to your base city by train. By the way, prebooked requests for a car to meet your train will be honored seven days a week.

Each car-rental voucher includes a twenty-four-consecutive-hour rental with unlimited mileage, no drop-off charge, and government tax (VAT) of 17.5 percent. The renter is responsible for collision damage, personal accident insurance, and gas. Payment of these charges may be made by credit card or a deposit at the start of each rental period. Aside from the gasoline, the other charges average about $11 U.S. per day.

If you are traveling alone, a single supplement will be charged in addition to the per-person price. The amount of the supplement varies according to the duration of the BritRail Flexipass and the car category. BritRail/Drive rates are based on two adults per car. The minimum age for rental is twenty-one.

Complete fare information and a *Go BritRail* catalog detailing BritRail's many economically priced programs may be obtained free of charge by calling toll free (800) 722–7151.

Weekend/holiday travel need not be avoided on British Rail services as long as you accept the fact that trains will be crowded. Seat reservations in advance will help. Aids to passenger control, such as this queue marker, do much to expedite boarding for holiday destinations.

6   TRAIN TRAVEL TIPS

"What affects men sharply about a foreign nation," wrote G. K. Chesterton, "is not so much finding or not finding familiar things, it is rather not finding them in the familiar place."

For many of us coming to Britain for the first time, we find a confusion of terminology and learn too late that what we sought was really available throughout our visit. Our problem was merely not knowing the proper place to look or the proper name to ask for. Perhaps some things might be set in better order for the pleasure of your BritRail adventures with the following train-travel tips.

Handicapped Travel

One important tip to mention first is that British Rail is leading the world in providing facilities in its stations and aboard its trains for the disabled and the handicapped. Through such efforts, rail travel is becoming more and more a chosen method of transportation and recreation for disabled persons. Many aids for the handicapped have been incorporated into British Rail's code for station design. Trains are being designed with wider doors for wheelchair access; some even have a removable seat to make room for a wheelchair. Ramp access to toilets, buffets, and other facilities is being provided. Folding wheelchairs are also available at main stations so that occupants may be transferred to a regular seat once aboard the train. British Rail is most eager to provide as comfortable a journey as possible for the disabled passenger. To do this, prior advice of the intended travel plans would be most helpful to both the traveler and the authorities.

For those readers who want to learn more about this innovative approach to travel for the disabled and the handicapped, we suggest writing to the Royal Association for Disability and Rehabilitation, 25 Mortimer Street, London, W1N 8AB, England, for details. The association has published *A Guide to British Rail for the Physically Handicapped.*

If you plan to travel in Britain with a handicapped person, write or call BritRail Travel International, 1500 Broadway, New York, NY 10036–4015 (telephone 212–575–2667) as soon as you establish your itinerary and begin making arrangements. The same applies to the airline you'll be using for your transatlantic flight. Provide them with all the details of your itinerary, the nature of the disability, and any other information that will help them to help you.

Specifically, special diets, medications, and toilet and medical-attention requirements should be made known. With these details attended to, you can look forward to a pleasant journey.

Baggage Carts

Many otherwise able train visitors to Britain impose a severe disadvantage upon themselves by arriving with more luggage than three men and a small boy could possibly carry. Train porters are an endangered species, and their demise is being expedited by the luggage trolley—Britain's version of our baggage cart—an elusive device that, whatever your position on the train platform, haunts the extreme opposite end. Our number-one tip (repeated from chapter 2) to all train travelers is to "go lightly." At most, take one medium-sized suitcase augmented by a modest shoulder bag. There still will be times when you will wish you could completely unburden yourself by discarding your suitcase. If you have purchased a model with built-in wheels, however, it usually will follow at your heels like a well-trained dog as you apply mini mum pulling power. Unlike a dog, the wheeled suitcase cannot climb stairs, so be prepared to lift it on and off the train.

Rather than relying upon the trolleys in the train stations, you might consider investing in your own baggage cart to take with you. You will see more and more train travelers proceeding through rail stations in Europe with such equipment. There are many types of carts on today's market. Airports and travel specialty shops are the best places to look for them. Like most items, the better ones cost a little more, but they're usually worth it. For our money, there is only one baggage cart worth buying—the Cart-A-Bag. It's collapsible and holds up to 150 pounds of luggage. It folds small and packs into its own vinyl case. When not on the road, we even use it around the office to cart books and things to the post office. TWA's Flight Shop sells them, and most of the better luggage shops do, too. Cheaper carts are available, but not for long. Within days of their purchase, you'll find parts of their wheels scattered about in some airport or train station and the rest of the device in a dustbin (that's British for trash can).

Another tip regarding the loading of your luggage onto a baggage cart, or one of British Rail's station trolleys, is to keep the load as narrow as possible. You must pass through ticket barriers going to and coming from the trains. The barriers are rather narrow. A Samsonite suitcase loaded sideways on your baggage cart or one of the station's trolleys will just clear, but a full-figured lady with a wardrobe case is in trouble every time. The trolleys provided by the station should not be taken aboard the train, although we've seen it tried. Again, if you are taking your own cart with you, fold it before boarding. If you don't, you may spend an embarrassing ten minutes or so on the station platform extracting a hapless fellow traveler from it as your train eases out of the station without you.

Using the Lifts

The greatest problem in using the train station's luggage trolleys (or your own baggage cart) is traversing the station hall to the platform area, because practically every station has stairs. You can overcome this problem by using the station's lift (elevator). This polite announcement is found posted in most British Rail stations: "Lifts are available for passengers who have difficulty in using the stairs. Please contact station staff if assistance is required." In searching for a lift, don't keep looking for a modern, automatic-door elevator brightly lit with soft music playing. What you will find instead is the old-fashioned, double-door, manually operated freight elevator, large enough to hold a Mack truck and usually illuminated with a single, bare light bulb—but it works. As the sign says, station staff will assist you. If you use the lifts frequently, however, you will develop the knack of handling them all by yourself. One word of caution: The lift will not operate until *both* barriers (usually a door and a gate) have been closed securely. Furthermore, the lift will be left inoperative if you fail to close the doors after you have used it. Be considerate of other passengers and the station staff by making certain that the lift is left operable for the next user.

As a matter of interest, if your rail journey takes you to Continental Europe, the use of rail-station lifts by passengers is usually forbidden.

Porter Services

Porter service is on the wane but still available in many train stations throughout Britain, particularly in the larger ones. The best way to locate a porter is to inquire at the "Left Luggage" (baggage storage) area or at the station's incoming taxi stand. If your luggage has been checked in at the station, there will be a handling charge, but the tip remains a personal item between you and the porter. We suggest 75 pence per parcel (with a £1.20 minimum) as a reasonable gratuity. Most porters will take your bags to the train and place them aboard in the luggage racks over your seats. Porters are rather scarce on arrival platforms. If you must have assistance, approach the stationmaster's office or the train conductor prior to departure with the request that a porter be asked to meet your train upon arrival at your destination.

If you are transferring between base cities or changing hotels from one city to another, you can request the hall porter at the hotel you are leaving to arrange for the arriving hotel's hall porter to meet your train upon arrival. A small tip should arrange everything.

The BritRail Difference

Readers who have traveled on the trains of Continental Europe will note a few basic differences between Eurail and British Rail operations. Car (carriage, if you please) markings include the standard pictographs for smoking or nonsmoking. First-class conveyances are appropriately identified with the yellow band, but unlike their Continental cousins, British Rail cars do not display the destination panel on their sides. (Eurail cars are marked with the name of the city from which they originated, the final destination, and the major in-between stops.) Nevertheless, British Rail trains do "split." Dual-destination trains in Britain will be identified in the departing station by dividing boards— first at the ticket barrier, where a bulletin board will state the train's composition. (For example: "First 4 Cars—Dover. Remaining Cars—Ramsgate.") At the head of the first four cars, you will find a platform sign advising RAMSGATE AHEAD. TURN BACK FOR DOVER. The best solution we have found in a situation like this is to *ask the train conductor (guard) before boarding and again on board the train when you present your BritRail Pass or ticket.*

Another thing missing on the BritRail scene are the vendors, trackside as well as aboard the train. The construction of the "four-car unit" makes access impossible to the other units making up the train. So the vendor and his "goodies cart" moving through the train while en route is automatically ruled out.

Most of all, we missed the trackside vendors who can provide all the essentials of life—food and beverage alike—through an open train window during a two-minute station stop. BritRail's counter to the trackside vendor are the snack-bar kiosks located on the train platforms. But leaving the train to make a purchase at one of the kiosks is a bit risky—particularly if spouse, kids, and *your* suitcase depart without you!

A Few More Trip Tips

A few more train-travel tips to make your trip more enjoyable: "Mind the doors!" British Rail cars of the vintage class appear to provide a door for each passenger. There is a great din of door slamming prior to departure and an equal amount of confusion each time the train makes a station stop. If you are waiting at an en route station for a train, stand well back from the platform edge. Passengers impatient to alight from the train are prone to open the doors before the train comes to a complete stop. In so doing, they're actually extending a bludgeon that could kill you, maim you for life, bruise you, or just scare the daylights out of you—the last being preferred over any of the others. British Rail has posters, positioned in all of its stations where these multi-door cars are in service, asking folks to "please don't open the carriage door until the train has stopped" and "please don't stand close to the platform edge." Most of the posters are illustrated by a picture showing a person being struck by a door. Be certain that you are neither the hapless victim nor the careless culprit by observing the rules. The final caption on the poster sums it up succinctly: "A moment's impatience, a lifetime of remorse."

Train Etiquette

Show your BritRail Pass, or ticket, upon request, and in the case of the pass, have your passport handy should the conductor like to see it. Don't place your feet on the seats of the train unless you have removed your shoes or have provided a protective covering for the seat. Place your luggage in the overhead racks provided for that purpose—not on the seats so that other passengers won't be able to crowd you. Observe the smoking/nonsmoking areas and rules. There are rather stiff fines that can be imposed for those smokers who violate the nonsmoking areas.

Observe seat reservations. Seating that has been reserved is marked. Even though it is apparent that a seat is unoccupied, if there are other passengers seated opposite, ask if the seat is open. It will avoid embarrassment later if the person holding the reservation happens to return.

Regarding dining-car reservations, on long-distance trains it is best to arrange for them soon after boarding. Inquire from the guard (conductor, remember?). If he cannot make them for you, a member of the dining-car crew will do so. Generally, they pass through the train prior to the first serving for that purpose. Usually, there are two servings, so be prepared to select the one to your liking. You can also inquire regarding the menu at the same time. The second serving is scheduled so that the dining-car crew has time to tidy up before the train reaches its destination. Therefore, the first serving is preferred by many because it does not seem to be rushed.

If you plan an overnight journey on a sleeper, ask the attendant to explain the manner in which the equipment in your compartment operates. For example, the newer sleeping cars have electric shades. A push of the button and they open; another push of the same button and they close. If you did not know the button's function, you just might try pushing the button while the train is standing in a station and you are not dressed for the occasion! It's proper to tip the attendant for his services; the proper time to do so is when he serves breakfast.

SeaCat catamarans ply between England and France at a cruising speed of 35 knots. 240 in length and with a beam of 85 feet, the SeaCats carry 450 passengers and 80 vehicles. Known as a wave-piercing catamaran, the SeaCat hull passes through the waves rather than riding over them. (Courtesy of Hoverspeed.)

7   SPECIAL ITINERARIES

In addition to the day excursions offered by this edition of *Britain by BritRail*, there are some special itineraries that are made possible through the unique features of British Rail services and its associated transportation facilities. Two of them, the Continental Quickie and the BritRail by Night excursions, are our own concoctions. Britainshrinkers have been offered by British Rail since 1973.

Continental Quickie

If you have never been to Continental Europe before, here's an opportunity to set foot on French soil, explore the seaport city of Boulogne, and yet return to London in time for a dinner appointment. Hoverspeed's service makes this day excursion possible by skimming across the English Channel in one of the company's super SeaCats between Folkestone and Boulogne in less than thirty-five minutes port to port! Train connections are made out of London's Victoria or Charing Cross Station to Folkestone Central Station. Read more about the amazing SeaCat on page 58 of this edition.

Boulogne is the largest fishing port in France. It was from Boulogne that Caesar set out to conquer England. Boulogne is really two towns—the Basse Ville that lies along the waterfront is very modern, while the Haute Ville poised on the hillside is much older and has a fine medieval wall surrounding it. You may want to include a side trip to Calais on this excursion. Rail and bus services between the two cities are frequent and convenient. If interested, make inquiry with the Boulogne tourist information center at the hoverport when you arrive.

If you are planning a day trip to France during the valid period of your BritRail Pass, you will need to purchase a Port-to-Port round-trip ticket. Your BritRail Pass will get you to the port and return you to London once you are back on British soil. If you plan to spend several days on the Continent, however, you should consider the BritFrance Railpass, which allows you to travel on both the British and the French rail networks. You can choose from any five days of travel to be completed within one month ($259 adult economy class, $359 adult first class, $220 youth) or any ten days travel within one month ($399 adult economy class, $539 adult first, $340 youth). The BritFrance Pass also includes one way travel across the English Channel on Hoverspeed services, which must be completed during the time the pass is valid. It does not, however, include use of the Chunnel.

By mid-1995, the new Eurostar passenger trains that go *under* the English Channel will make a London-to-Paris day excursion possible within only three hours, city center to city center.

Britainshrinkers

This sounds like it could be the title of a James Bond thriller—and well it may be. BritRail's *Go BritRail* brochure describing this program states: "You'll travel on a special network of BritRail trains and comfortable motor coaches. Because our trains are fast, we can show you much more on each tour . . . all in a relaxed, leisurely way. At your destination, a motor coach awaits to whisk you off to the 'must see' sights in the area."

Britainshrinkers is a program of fully escorted tours leaving London after breakfast and returning in time for dinner. Lunch in a genuine pub is included, as are the entrance fees to places of interest that you will visit. The tours are easy to take—just arrive at the London rail station indicated on your ticket. A guide in a red uniform will take your ticket at the Britainshrinkers check-in point, which is easily identified by its sign.

The Britainshrinkers also offer two-day tours called overnighters. These enable you to visit places more distant from London. They include first-class hotel accommodations for one night, along with dinner and breakfast. Two-day tours venture into scenic Scotland. Or you can opt for the three-day tour, which combines Cambridge and York with Scotland.

The Britainshrinkers and overnighter programs differ from *Britain by BritRail*'s day excursions and out-and-back excursions only in that the Britainshrinkers are fully escorted. The BritRail Pass or Flexipass is accepted as supplemental payment for the rail portion of the Britainshrinker tours—you could save up to 40 percent of the cost of each Britainshrinker tour you take if you have a BritRail Pass or Flexipass. As British Rail officials point out, the Britainshrinkers program was devised to serve the needs of visitors to London who were unable to take more than a day or two to visit the British countryside.

Other fully escorted train-plus-motorcoach tours include the five-day Silver Arrow and the six-day Tartan Arrow; or you can take each trip individually or combine the two. Prices include overnights in three- and four-star hotels with private bath, hot breakfasts, and table d'hote dinners each day; entrance fees; welcome drinks; and a special luggage service (you won't have to carry your own suitcases). Substantial discounts are available to BritRail-Pass holders.

For a complete BritRail catalog and details on purchasing Britainshrinkers programs, BritFrance Railpasses, and/or BritRail Passes, write to Rail Pass Express, Inc., 2737 Sawbury Boulevard, Columbus, Ohio 43235. Telephone toll-free (800) 722–7151 or fax your request to (614) 764–0711.

BritRail by Night

Here's something that you can do with your eyes closed. As a rule, we do not advocate using sleeper cars when traveling by train in Europe. In the case of the excellent sleeper services offered by British Rail—and their moderate cost—however, we are making an exception.

British Rail operates its sleeper services between London and the main centers in Scotland, the north of England, south Wales, and the west of England. First-class sleepers accommodate one person; connecting bedrooms are available. Economy-class sleepers offer double accommodations—the two berths are stacked one over the other like bunk beds. Both services provide wall-to-wall carpeting, hot and cold running water, soap and towel, a comfortable mattress, and that all-important call button that will bring you a nightcap or your wake-up coffee.

The cost of sleeper accommodations based on single occupancy is $57 for first class; $48 for economy class. Usually, you can take occupancy thirty minutes before departure time and stay aboard until 7:30 A.M., even if the train arrives at your destination several hours earlier.

The major sleeping-car routes to points described in this edition are: Paddington Station to Penzance and Plymouth and to Cardiff in Wales; Euston Station to Glasgow, Inverness, Edinburgh, and Aberdeen. Sleeper service also is available from either Edinburgh or Glasgow to Inverness.

Overnight sleeper service opens a new door to the adventurous rail traveler. The sleeper charge compares favorably to economical hotel rates, so you can make the sleeper your "hotel on the move." By reserving sleeper accommodations for successive nights, an itinerary could be planned for a night on the train; a day at the destination; a night on the train returning to London; sightseeing, shopping, or a short day excursion out of London; and a night to another destination.

Expanding on the above, an adventurous traveler could depart London's Paddington Station about midnight, arriving early morning in Penzance to begin an all-day sightseeing trek extending to Land's End. Back in Penzance, the adventurer could board the sleeper that evening for London, spending an entire day there before boarding another sleeper in King's Cross Station for Aberdeen, Britain's "oil city." After spending the day in Aberdeen, our traveler could reverse his travel and journey to either Edinburgh or Glasgow, where he could then board a sleeper bound for London—or board the Aberdeen sleeper direct to London. Another option is Inverness. After arriving in Edinburgh overnight from London, there's ample time in the day to entrain to Inverness, search for "Nessie" on Loch Ness, then return to Edinburgh on a late train out of Inverness in time to board the Edinburgh-to-London sleeper for the last of four nights' sleeper travel.

British Rail, in their subtle humor, came up with a cute poster promoting sleeper travel. A middle-aged British couple is seen getting off a sleeper, their faces wreathed in smiles. The caption on the poster reads, "Last night, for Ted and Alice, the earth moved." Need we say more?

The Eurostar passenger train departs from London's Waterloo International Eurostar Terminal and arrives at Paris' Gare du Nord in non-stop comfort. The jaunt, which used to take seven hours, now only takes three hours. Direct service is also available from London to Brussels in just over three hours.

Le Shuttle trains transport cars and trucks across the English Channel. The trip from the Folkestone, England, terminal to the Calais, France, terminal will take under an hour. Travelers drive their cars into the enclosed rail cars, where passengers ride in air-conditioned comfort.

8 THE CHANNEL TUNNEL AND CROSSING THE ENGLISH CHANNEL

The newest and fastest method of crossing the English Channel is to go *under* it via the tunnel ("Chunnel") connecting Folkestone, England, with Calais, France. At press time, however, the Eurostar passenger services are not yet available to the public. Full services are expected to be available by mid-1995 at airline-competitive prices. For updated Chunnel information and tickets (when they become available), please call (614) 889–9100.

Another convenient way of crossing the English Channel between Britain and the Continent is by the services of the British government subsidiaries of Sealink and Hoverspeed. Sealink is the conventional ferry service; Hoverspeed utilizes the hovercraft and SeaCat. For either service, you will be required to leave the train to board the water-borne conveyance. Unlike the European rail-ferry services from Denmark to Germany and Sweden, the rail coaches are not transferred aboard the ferries or hovercraft. Private shipping lines such as the Sally Line also provide channel service. All of the schedules and destinations are summarized later in this chapter.

The Chunnel and Eurostar Services

In 1888, Louis Fuguier proclaimed that "linking England and France will meet one of the present day needs of civilization." On May 6, 1994, England's Queen Elizabeth II and France's President François Mitterand inaugurated a new era in European train travel by witnessing the linking of England and France via a tunnel that runs underground and under the English Channel. More than 17 million tons of earth were moved to build the two rail tunnels (one for northbound and one for southbound traffic) and one service tunnel. The project cost more than $13 billion and took seven years to complete.

At press time, limited "discovery" passenger service is expected to begin November 14, 1994, with full service scheduled to begin in June. Operated by British Rail, the French (SNCF) and Belgium (SNCB) railways, the Eurotunnel will provide different types of service between England and the Continent. Eurostar will provide passenger service, and Le Shuttle will provide automobile, coach, and lorry service between Folkstone and Calais. International rail freight rounds out the list.

Eurostar service will be offered from London's new Waterloo International Eurostar Station to Paris' Gare du Nord or Brussels Midi stations. Travel times from London to Paris or Brussels will be reduced from more than seven hours to three hours, thus making a European Capitals tour nothing more than a day excursion. Eurailpass will not be accepted for service through the Chunnel. The sleek Eurostar trains (*Trans Mache Super Trains*) each carry 794 passengers (210 in first class and 584 in second class) and reach speeds of 200 miles per hour in France and 100 miles per hour in England with speeds through the Chunnel of 80 miles per hour. The trains are accessible to handicapped passengers. In the next few years international service will continue to expand providing day and evening trains to various destinations.

Sealink

Sealink services on the English Channel are one class only; both first- and second-class accommodations, however, are available on the boat trains between London and Dover. The BritRail Pass is accepted for the rail portion of the journey from London to the port. Separate tickets, however, must be purchased for the sea portion. These tickets are available at the ticket offices of London rail stations or at the Sealink Travel Centre at the head of platform 2 in the Victoria Station. Seat reservations are advisable throughout the year for the boat trains departing from this station. The term *boat train* applies to those trains departing from Victoria Station for direct connection at Dover's Western Docks with Sealink ferries crossing to the French port of Calais.

These boat trains go directly to the pier. Boat trains going to the port of Folkestone for SeaCat services do not stop at Folkestone's Central Station. Regular train service is available to Dover, terminating at Dover Priory (Dover's main station), and to Folkestone, where trains call at Folkestone Central but not at Folkestone Harbor. Due to the myriad of sailings to the Continent, we suggest that you check with the Sealink Travel Centre at the head of platform 2 in the Victoria Station for additional information, reservations, and current schedules.

Hoverspeed's SeaCat

Aboard a SeaCat, you get the sensation of traveling in a wide-body jet airplane. You can settle into an aircraft-style seat; or you can stroll around the cabin, which is four times wider than the largest jumbo jet; or you can watch the captain and the crew through windows just behind the bridge as they guide the ship across the busy English Channel at a cruising speed of 35 knots. Passengers are advised of the SeaCat's safety and emergency procedures by a video demonstration quite similar to the way that such briefings are now conducted on transatlantic aircraft. But that is where the comparison ends!

A SeaCat vessel is 242 feet in length with a beam of 85 feet. It can carry 450 passengers and 80 vehicles on a separate car deck. It is powered by four diesel engines housed in the vessel's side hulls that generate jets of water for steering and for propulsion at speeds of up to 42 knots, making it the world's fastest passenger ferry. Known as a wave-piercing catamaran, it has a narrow hull that is designed to pass through waves rather than ride over them. In 1990, the Hoverspeed *Great Britain* earned its place in history by making the quickest crossing of the Atlantic by a passenger ship since 1952. This record-breaking voyage took just 3 days, 7 hours, and 52 minutes at an average speed of 36.6 knots. It also holds the record for the fastest crossing of the English Channel by a passenger ship.

Because the cabin of the SeaCat is on flexible mounts and the engines are positioned down in the side hulls away from the passenger area, the levels of noise and vibration are greatly reduced. The stylish interior is more like an airliner than a ferry boat. You can stretch your legs by taking a stroll on deck and watch the waves whiz by, pick up a sandwich in the snack bar, or enjoy a drink in the panoramic stern bar. A duty-free shop is also available to help you stock up on bargains.

What we found most amazing about the SeaCat was its maneuverability, which is made possible by having steering and reversing controls on waterjets fitted on both outboard hulls of the craft. On the evening prior to our crossing to Calais, we observed our SeaCat arriving in the harbor in Folkestone, where it turned about on its own length and then docked *sideways!* This same maneuver was repeated as we landed in Calais the following day. Together with fast check-in, boarding, and disembarkment procedures, the SeaCat's maneuverability adds up to an enjoyable, high-speed crossing of the English Channel.

Even with the opening of the English Channel Tunnel, Britain's ferry operators are optimistic about what the future holds in store for them. We are of the opinion that with watercraft like the SeaCat—and even bigger ones are on the drawing board—crossing the Channel by ship will always remain a delightful alternative.

Choosing a Channel Crossing

Since there are various ways of crossing the English Channel and the North Sea en route to Europe, which one should you select? The fastest route from London to Paris or Brussels will be through the tunnel *under* the Channel, utilizing the Eurostar passenger services. Eurostar passenger trains depart London's Waterloo International Eurostar Terminal.

For those who prefer to skim *over* the channel rather than *under* it, the fastest means of crossing the English Channel for direct rail connections between London and Paris is by SeaCat. If time permits, however, you may want to select a Sealink crossing by regular displacement vessel. The ultra-modern fleet of Sealink ferries plies the waters between England and the French port of Calais in an elapsed time of one hour and thirty minutes, compared to the one hour crossing aboard a hovercraft. The slower crossing provides more time for shopping in the ship's duty-free store, however, and time to enjoy a leisurely meal as well.

Duty-free items are also available on the SeaCat crossing, but shopping can get a bit hectic in such a limited time. If the channel is rough, the SeaCat's stores are stowed and you might have to forgo restocking your larder until later—and not at popular duty-free prices, either.

As previously described, London to Paris by Sealink ferry takes you from London's Victoria Station to Dover by special boat train right to the dock. After the crossing, a French National Railroads' train will be waiting in Calais for you to continue your journey on to Paris. You will arrive in the Gare du Nord (North Station) of Paris approximately three hours after you reach the French port.

Other Crossings

Ramsgate–Oostende. The Belgian marine services of Regie des Transports Maritime (R.T.M.), in conjunction with Sally Ferries, cross between Ramsgate and the Belgian port of Oostende with train service connecting with Brussels and Köln (Cologne). A Jetfoil service is also available on this route. A supplementary fare of approximately $14 U.S. is payable for travel by Jetfoil. The ferries and the Jetfoil are one class only; connecting rail services are both first and second class.

Train departures for the boat ferries and Jetfoil leave from Victoria Station. Jetfoil passengers must report to the Jetfoil Lounge at track 14 for a boarding card at least twenty minutes before train departure. This route is the most direct connection with Brussels. By rail and Jetfoil, the average time between London's Victoria Station and Brussels Midi (South) Station is five hours; travel by the rail and ship combination requires eight hours plus forty minutes.

Newhaven–Dieppe. If you are looking for an alternate route between Britain and France, Sealink services are available from the English port of Newhaven, east of Brighton, to the maritime terminal of Dieppe in France. The sea route is seventy-one miles and the crossing takes four hours. Night crossings are made throughout the year.

If the English Channel is not in a huffy mood, this can be a very pleasant crossing. Victoria Station is the point of departure from London. The boat train calls at Gatwick Airport en route to the Newhaven harbor. The French National Railroads' express-train service between Dieppe and Paris takes slightly more than two hours. St. Lazare is the rail terminal in Paris. The entire trip takes approximately nine hours.

Harwich–Hook of Holland. This is an excellent routing for travelers ranging between Britain and the Netherlands. It is the most direct sea link between London and Amsterdam. Convenient connections may also be made from the Hook of Holland (Hoek Van Holland) to Brussels, Belgium.

Both day and night crossings are available on this route. Sleeping accommodations aboard begin at modest prices. Reservations for the night crossings are obligatory and should be made well in advance of your journey. Departure out of London is from the Liverpool Street Station.

In the *Thomas Cook European Timetable,* Table 15 carries schedule information on the service between London and Amsterdam and features EuroCity name trains, the Admiral De Ruyter and the Benjamin Britten. Many famous express trains utilize this North Sea crossing, such as the Warszawa (Warsaw) Express, the Scandinavian Express, and the Loreley Express to Switzerland, as well as regular through-train service to Brussels, Munich, and Moscow. If you are looking for international intrigue, you'll be most likely to find it on the Harwich–Hook of Holland crossing. Running between the Liverpool Street Station and the Harwich harbor takes one hour and twenty minutes. Once aboard, the daytime crossing is completed in six hours and thirty minutes; passage at night requires up to eight hours and thirty minutes.

BritRail Passes are not accepted by Sealink, Hoverspeed, or any of the privately owned shipping companies operating on either the English Channel or the North Sea. In addition, BritRail Passes cannot be utilized for rail travel in Continental Europe. Point-to-point tickets must be purchased for all sea voyages and continuing rail travel once you have departed Britain. If you hold a Eurailpass, you may have it validated at the rail station of the European port upon arrival and then continue your rail trip without the inconvenience of having to purchase point-to-point tickets.

Portsmouth–Cherbourg/Le Havre. Details of this crossing are listed on Table 1030 of the *Thomas Cook European Timetable.* Table 504 provides rail-schedule information between London and Portsmouth; Table 120 describes rail schedules between Cherbourg and Paris. Table 115 should be consulted for train times between Le Havre and Paris. Arriving in Portsmouth, passengers are advised to use the bus service from the Portsmouth Continental Ferry Port to the Portsmouth Harbor rail station. The crossing from Portsmouth to Cherbourg takes four hours and forty-five minutes (eight hours, thirty minutes to nine hours forty-five minutes at night); the sailing to Le Havre requires five hours and forty-five minutes (seven to nine hours at night). Both routes to the French capital pass through Normandy, where the Allies stormed ashore on 6 June 1943 in the invasion of Hitler's "Fortress Europe."

Ramsgate–Dunkerque. (Details of this crossing are given in Cook's Table 1020.) After departing from Ramsgate Harbor at the most easterly point of Kent County in England, the ferries operated by the Sally Line provide two and one-half hours at sea (where the English Channel meets the North Sea) before docking at Dunkerque, the French port where German military forces held off the Allies throughout World War II until VE Day on 9 May 1945. After going ashore, roam the restored streets of Dunkerque before proceeding on to Lille, France, and connections for Brussels, Paris, or Strasbourg.

Sealink's combined fleet of British, French, and Netherlands registries is one of the world's largest passenger-carrying fleets. They link London to Amsterdam, Brussels, Dublin, and Paris. Augmented by catamaran, these shipping services carry passengers and vehicle traffic passing in and out of Britain.

9   CROSSING THE IRISH SEA

Many of the ferry crossings on the Continent of Europe involve loading the passenger-rail cars aboard the ferry. When this occurs, the passengers need not disembark. But at all ferry ports in Britain, passengers are required to leave the train and board the ferry. Then they board another train after landing. You will find that this change of transportation mode is no great hardship. In fact, it can be a very enjoyable experience by including drinks and dinner aboard the ferry, followed by a chat with fellow passengers. The salon of a ferry is a good place for meeting people. Everyone has a common interest in travel, and everyone is going to the same destination.

Crossing the Irish Sea is very much like crossing the English Channel by ferry, except you cannot forward your luggage on to the Republic of Ireland. What you take is what you carry. So again, adhere to our admonition to "go lightly" when it comes to luggage. Porter service is almost nonexistent at the marine terminals, except by prearrangement. It is best not to expect porter service. Furthermore, the trolleys (baggage carts) found in the majority of British Rail stations are missing at the piers because their use is impractical on the sloping ramps and gangways used for access to the vessels.

When you visit Ireland, keep in mind that the Republic of Ireland and Northern Ireland are two separate political states. Northern Ireland is a part of the U.K., while the republic is independent. There are no customs to contend with when arriving in Northern Ireland from England, Scotland, or Wales. On the other hand, customs formalities entering the Republic of Ireland should present no problem for the bona fide traveler. The efficient "declare" or "nothing-to-declare" system is used by Irish Customs.

Duty-free shops are operated on all of the shipping lines crossing the Irish Sea between Britain and the Republic of Ireland. Crossing times are adequate enough to permit shopping at leisure. Except for tobacco and alcoholic beverages, however, there are few bargains. Check with the salespersons to be certain that you are not exceeding the import limits. Duty payments on excesses can be stiff. Tax-free shops are not available on routes to Northern Ireland.

Sealink provides services to Northern Ireland through Stranraer in Scotland to Larne, with train connections from there to Belfast. From Holyhead in England, Sealink ferries cross to Dun Laoghaire, a suburban port of Dublin; from Fishguard in England, Sealink connects with Rosslare, one-hundred miles south of Dublin, for direct train connections to southern points. Fares are listed on page 65.

Sea Links to Ireland

Stranraer–Larne. A short crossing of two hours, twenty minutes port to port, this is the most direct route to Northern Ireland. Access to England, Scotland, and Wales by rail is through Glasgow. Larne to Belfast takes another forty-five minutes on the train. The BritRail Pass is *not* accepted on trains in Northern Ireland because rail services are operated by Northern Ireland Railways, not British Rail. Food and beverage services are available aboard. No customs formalities for entering Northern Ireland from Scotland. No tax-free shops aboard. Train connections from London through Euston Station with overnight-sleeper service are available between London and Stranraer. First- and second-class accommodations are available aboard ship. Direct train service from the Glasgow Central Station to Stranraer Harbor takes two hours, fifteen minutes. Details are found on Tables 591, 620, and 632 of the *Thomas Cook European Timetable.*

Holyhead–Dun Laoghaire. This crossing is from Holyhead in Wales to Dun Laoghaire (a suburb of Dublin). The elapsed time from port to port averages three hours and thirty minutes. Catamaran service is also available, taking one hour, fifty minutes. Connections from the port into Dublin can be made by train, city bus, or taxi. All three transportation modes are available at the pier. The BritRail Pass cannot be used for transportation in the Republic of Ireland. The Eurailpass and the BritIreland Pass are accepted on the railroads. It would not be economical to validate your rail pass for the short ride into Dublin, however, if you plan to spend a few days sightseeing there before traveling to other parts of the country by train. Food and beverage services are available aboard the ferries, and tax-free shops are open during the crossing. Customs formalities are observed upon disembarkation. Train connections from London's Euston Station to Holyhead provide through-coach and sleeper accommodations. The ferries offer first- and second-class accommodations. Consult Tables 555 and 620 of the *Thomas Cook European Timetable.*

Fishguard–Rosslare. This Sealink ferry crossing is recommended for train travelers bound for Cork, Killarney, and the Shannon Airport. Crossing takes three hours and thirty minutes. Catamaran service is also available, taking one hour and thirty to forty minutes. Food, beverages, and tax-free shops are available during the voyage. One-class service only aboard ship. Customs formalities are observed at disembarkation. Daytime train service only from Paddington Station in London. Train time between London and Fishguard is six hours. From Rosslare Harbor, connecting time to Dublin is three hours by train; to Limerick for connections to the Shannon Airport, three hours and fifty minutes. Transportation time to the airport from the Limerick rail station is forty-five minutes. Tables 531, 620, 637, and 643 of the *Thomas Cook European Timetable* have details.

SAILING TO THE CONTINENT

One-way Fares (1994) in U.S. Dollars. 1995 rates not available at press time. Exact rates will be quoted at time of booking.

From London To:	Services Per Day	Approx. Journey Time (hrs)	One-Way Fares First	Standard
Amsterdam† (via Hook of Holland)	2	11-13	$108	$90
Boulogne* (catamaran)	2	3	84	72
Brussels* (via Oostende)	3	8	96	76
Brussels††* (by jetfoil)	3	5½	96	76
Calais* (ship)	2	4	73	61
Dieppe*	2	5½	73	64
Hook of Holland†	2	8-10	86	76
Oostende* (ship)	3	6	73	57
Oostende††* (jetfoil)	3	3½		61
Paris via Calais* (ship)	2	8	121	93
Paris via Dieppe*	2	9½	111	118
Paris* (by catamaran/hovercraft)	2	6½	132	104
Sea Crossing Only To:				
Boulogne/Calais* (catamaran)	31	50 min		49
Calais	18	1½-1¾		38
Oostende* (ship)	3	4		38
Oostende††* (jetfoil)	3	1½		38
Dieppe	2	4		45
Hook of Holland†	2	6-8		55

Notes: Round trip: Double one-way fares. All prices subject to change. Reservations required on all services during peak travel periods; $4.00 per person each journey. Use of TGV in France (Calais to Paris) cuts one hour from the journey and adds $48 (first class) or $34 (second class).

* One-class ship or catamaran or Jetfoil

** First-class train and ship

† Sleeping berth and cabin reservations are essential on Harwich-Hook of Holland overnight service. Cancellation penalty 15%.

†† Via Oostende, both ship and Jetfoil service available; approximately $14 supplement for Jetfoil service. Reservations required.

SAILING TO IRELAND

From London To:	Services Per Day	Approx. Journey Time (hrs)	One-Way Fares First	Standard
Dublin (via Holyhead)	2	10	$169	$128
Rosslare (via Fishguard)	2	9	123	96
Larne (via Glasgow/Stranraer)	1	11	170	124
Sea Crossings Only To:				
Holyhead-Dun Laoghaire	4	3½		42
Fishguard-Rosslare	2	3½		42
Stranraer-Larne	9	2¼		42

Notes: Round-trip: Double one-way fare. Special fares available on some routes upon request. One class on ship. Reservations ($4.00 per person per journey) are required for all port-to-port-only journeys, and for through journeys during peak travel periods. Sleeping berths/cabins available on some overnight services.

65

Big Ben. London's most famous landmark, stands in the clock tower of the Houses of Parliament (officially known as the Palace of Westminster). Actually, it's the bell, not the clock, which is called Big Ben. The thirteen and one-half-ton bell's name honors Sir Ben Hall, Commissioner of Works in 1858.

10   LONDON

"Why, Sir, you find no man, at all intellectual, who is willing to leave London. No, Sir, when a man is tired of London," wrote Samuel Johnson, "he is tired of life; for there is in London all that life can afford." London is a wonderful mixture of ancient elegance and modern technology, of outdated traditions and contemporary inconveniences. While plumed guardsmen mount jet black horses in Whitehall, bankers examine computer printouts on Lombard Street.

London sits astride the Thames River about forty miles inland from its estuary on the North Sea. One of the largest cities in the world, London, like a typically modern megalopolis, has failed to come to terms with the present century yet has managed to preserve many of the virtues of those past. Presumably a consort to kings, London appears to many as being ruled by the Cockneys of the city's east end, and the shouting down of the prime minister in Parliament is observed by visitors in total disbelief that a government could operate in this manner.

It's difficult to get the first-time visitor to Britain interested in anything other than London until he has seen the great city. Although London is Europe's largest city, most of its historical sights are clustered around a compact area. A reasonable stroll will take you past the Houses of Parliament and its clock tower housing Big Ben, Westminster Abbey, Whitehall, Downing Street, Buckingham Palace, and Trafalgar Square. If strolling is not your thing, then take the advice that Prime Minister Gladstone once gave a group of American tourists: "See London from the top of a bus." London Transport makes it very convenient by running buses around a twenty-mile circular tour in about one and a half hours, and they pass most of London's major landmarks.

If you would like a personally guided tour of London, hail a taxi—any taxi. London's taxicab drivers are a special breed. They are not issued a taxi operator's license just because they can drive a car. An extensive knowledge of the city and its history is an important part of their taxi-licensing examination. Cabbies usually have fixed rates for such sightseeing excursions. Hail one and make inquiry. We're sure that you'll be pleased with the outcome.

After you have seen London, see more of this wonderful country where, among many of its advantages, everyone speaks your language—well, almost everyone. You cannot get to know the country without experiencing the charms of its other cities and seeing first-hand the loveliness of the rural areas that separate them. There is no better way to do that than aboard a train, viewing the passing scene and conversing with the British themselves.

Day Excursions

Like the road builders of Rome, Britain's rail builders laid their tracks leading to London—or, more properly, out of London. Picture, if you will, London as the center of a somewhat lopsided spider web with its radials running east and south to the sea on the short side of the web and the longer extensions running west to Wales and north into Scotland. Thirty-two day excursions from London await your pleasure. They have been selected for a variety of reasons. Varied reader interest was the main consideration, but any "mix" should certainly provide the desired cross section of this green and pleasant land.

Like a knight of old, perhaps you would prefer to sally forth on a short sortie or two before departing on a crusade. In that case, you will find the Greenwich, Windsor, and St. Albans day excursions to your liking. Ranging southeast out of London, Kent beckons with its towns of Canterbury, Dover, Folkestone, and Ramsgate. Southward, rail trails lead along the English Channel to the port/resort towns of Hastings, Brighton, Portsmouth, and Southampton and to the Isle of Wight.

Having whetted your appetite with the excursions above, you should be ready now to venture farther afield. Everything you plan to see has been there for quite some time—usually at least a century or two—so relax and enjoy your further travels throughout Britain.

West from London, excursions to Salisbury and Stonehenge, Bath, Gloucester, and Cardiff (Wales) await the train travelers. Ready to crusade? Go farther west to the pilgrims' Plymouth or the pirates' Penzance. You may want to make these "out-and-back" visits. If so, make arrangements with your hotel. If you plan to return, pack light and have the hall porter store your bulky luggage. In the heart of England you will find awaiting you excursions to Birmingham, Stratford-upon-Avon, Coventry, Nottingham, Sheffield, Lincoln, and York. From farther west beckons Chester.

Northeast of London is East Anglia, where historic King's Lynn, Bury St. Edmunds, and Ipswich wait to greet you. East Anglia was the area from where the U.S. Eighth Air Force staged its massive attacks on the Third Reich in World War II. It abounds in museums and memories relating to the conflict. For the academic flavor of the country, you may want to visit Cambridge or Oxford (or both) for the cap-and-gown atmosphere. School-tie types will appreciate Eton, a stone's throw away from Windsor.

Select your day excursions carefully. Don't rush—take time to enjoy the flowers. Time flies when you're having fun, so keep in mind that the land of Scotland to the north is also looking forward to the honor of your visit. Budget your time accordingly.

Arriving and Departing

By Air. London has three major international airports: Gatwick, Heathrow, and Stansted. Stansted opened for international operation during 1992. Be certain to ask your airline which airport you'll be using for your flight.

Heathrow, fifteen miles west of the city, is connected to London's Underground (subway) system. If you are not overloaded with luggage, the Underground provides fast and frequent service between Heathrow and Central London. The journey time is about fifty minutes; trains depart every five to ten minutes. The one-way adult fare is £3.10; children (ages five to fifteen), £1.10. If you are burdened with luggage, consider the airbus system. This fast and frequent door-to-door service by deluxe double-deck coaches between all four Heathrow terminals and Central London offers convenient en route stops in London's major hotel areas. All coaches are equipped for handicapped travelers. Airbus tickets can be purchased from the driver or in the London Transport Tourist Information Centres at Heathrow, Euston, and Victoria stations. One-way fares: adults £5.00; children £3.00. The Airbus travel information number is (071) 222–1234. Taxi journey time to Central London is about one hour; the fare is approximately £30.00–£35.00.

Gatwick, 27 miles south of London, has its own rail station in the airport's South Terminal. The Gatwick Express departs every fifteen minutes from early morning until late evening for Victoria Station. Journey time is thirty minutes. For late arrivals, an hourly night service runs until 0600. One-way fares: adults £8.60 Standard Class and £13.00 Club Class; children £3.50. Bus transport between Gatwick and Victoria Station is provided by Flightline 777 service from both the North and South terminals at Gatwick. Service is hourly from 0642 to 2152 (North Terminal) and from 0650 to 2200 (South Terminal). The en route time is approximately seventy to eighty minutes. One-way fares: adults £13.00; children (ages five to fifteen) half price. Bus services to most points in England depart from the coach station on the ground floor of the South Terminal. Taxi and limousine service from Gatwick to Central London is available—but *expensive.* Rates range from £40 to £60.

Stansted, thirty-one miles northeast of London, has a direct rail link to London's Liverpool Street Station. Trains depart from the airport every thirty minutes between 0600 and midnight; from Liverpool Station, from 0530 until 2300. Travel time is forty minutes. The fare between Stansted and London is £10 Standard Class, £15 First Class. Additional trains run from Stansted via Cambridge and Peterborough to Birmingham, Cardiff, Manchester, and Liverpool. Motorcoach services are operated by National Express and Cambridge Coach to London and many other points throughout England. Airport and tourist information is located in the arrivals area of the terminal, as is a Thomas Cook money exchange.

By Train. London has a plethora of rail stations; however, you need only be concerned with five of the city's major stations when arriving from, or departing to, the Continent, the Irish Republic, or Scotland.

Travelers heading to London from the Continent may choose from a variety of travel options. The newest and fastest method is the Eurostar passenger service, which carries travelers non-stop from Paris or Brussels to London in three hours via the Chunnel. Arrival in London is at the Waterloo International Eurostar Terminal at Waterloo Station.

Ferry service is available from France (Calais or Boulogne) and Belgium (Oostend), where your ferry, catamaran, or Jetfoil will dock at Dover or Folkestone. From there, the boat trains proceed to London's Victoria Station.

The voyage time for crossing by ferry between Dover and Calais is under two hours; the time is the same for ferry crossings between Folkestone and Boulogne. On the other hand, the same crossings by catamaran are made in fifty minutes or less. Catamaran seat reservations are required since space is limited. Ferry crossings between Dover and Oostende take about four hours; a Jetfoil crossing takes one hour plus thirty-five minutes. Reservations are required.

There are several land-sea routes that may be taken between London and Dublin, capital of the Irish Republic. The rail route linking the two capitals through the English port of Holyhead and the Irish port of Dun Laoghaire, however, is the most traveled. The ship crossing takes three hours and thirty minutes. The English terminus is London's Euston Station, which also shares honors with London's Kings Cross Station for rail traffic to Glasgow and Edinburgh in Scotland.

London's Liverpool Street Station is the gateway for rail and ship traffic between the Netherlands, northern Germany, and Scandinavia. Trains departing Liverpool Street bound for that part of Europe proceed to Harwich, where passengers then embark from the Parkeston Quay by ship to Hook of Holland, a small peninsula jutting out into the North Sea. There, trains are waiting to take them to further destinations such as Amsterdam, Hamburg, Berlin, or the Scandinavian capital cities of Copenhagen, Oslo, and Stockholm. The ship crossing is made in eight hours and thirty minutes.

For those who can recall Robert Taylor and Vivien Leigh bidding good-bye in the Waterloo Bridge Station, the same nostalgia can and probably will sweep your imagination whenever you enter a London rail station. The clouds of wet steam are gone, as is the huffing of the coal-burning steam engines at the head of the platform as they stand waiting to take passengers on to their destinies. *But the electricity of the moment still survives.* Sense it. Enjoy it. After all, that's what rail travel is all about!

London taxi stands briefly in front of Eros Fountain in the center of London's most celebrated traffic circle, Piccadilly Circus. The steps of the fountain were at one time the "marketplace" of London's flower sellers. Officially, the fountain is a memorial to the philanthropist Lord Shaftesbury.

London's Railway Stations

If the major cities of the world were to enter a train-station contest, London would win. Perhaps a glance at the London Station Plan on page 294 would be helpful at this point as we try to put things into order verbally. You will note a total of fifteen stations listed in the plan, which looks very much like a quarter-back's option play for the Pittsburgh Steelers. For the sake of brevity, we will reduce the number of station descriptions to the manageable number of eight—those stations of major arrivals, departures, and *Britain by BritRail* day excursions from London. Take heart—at least all of the major train terminals are linked by the London Underground, principally by the Circle Line. For a quick reference, check the Inter-Terminal Plan on page 295 of this edition.

Victoria Station's train services cover the south and the southeast of England in addition to the sea-rail services to Belgium and France. A special Sealink Travel Centre is located in the station, at the head of platform 2, to cater to the more than two million passengers who transit Victoria every year en route to and from the Continent. As the gateway rail station for the Gatwick Airport, Victoria operates a "Next Train to Gatwick Airport" indicator between platforms 9 and 15 to assist air-rail travelers. Train departures for connections to the Continent are also displayed in this area. The International Rail Centre is located to the left of platforms 3 and 4.

Most important to *Britain by BritRail* readers is the London Tourist Board Centre located in the station forecourt. It's in operation 0800–1900 Monday through Saturday and 0800–1600 Sunday. To reach it, follow the corridor running out from train platform 15. This tourist information center is located directly *in* a London rail station. It is also one of the few London stations providing currency-exchange facilities.

Euston Station is closely grouped with St. Pancras and King's Cross stations for rail services to England's Midlands, northern England, and Scotland. One of the most modern facilities in the British Rail system, it is the Sealink terminal for services to Belfast via Stranraer and to Dublin via Holyhead. It is also the London departure point for the all-electric-hauled InterCity trains to Glasgow. Train departures and arrivals are displayed in digital format on an easy-to-read display board over the train entrance doors. As you face the train departure/arrival announcement board in the Euston Station, the travel center will be on your left. In general (although some functions operate at different hours), the travel center is open year-round, Monday through Saturday, 0700–2330, and Sunday, 0800–2330. Waiting rooms, restaurants, and other conveniences are located on the far side of the station hall from the travel center. A Barclays Bank is located on a pedestrian esplanade beyond the restaurants. It is open Monday–Friday, 0930–1530.

The train information windows are 12 and 13; hotel bookings (for Dun and

Bradstreet–rated hotels only) may be obtained at windows 16 and 17. Other windows, according to their signs, provide sleeper and seat reservations, air tickets, special-events reservations—there is even a special information window for travel to Ireland.

St. Pancras Station is the London terminal of the Midland Mainline of the British Rail system serving *Britain by BritRail*'s day excursions to St. Albans, Nottingham, and Sheffield with both diesel and electric service. Directional signs for the Euston and King's Cross stations, as well as the London Underground, are found throughout the station.

Charing Cross Station is London's rail terminal for direct train service to Folkestone, Canterbury, Hastings, Ramsgate, Dover, and other ports for Sealink and Hoverspeed services to Boulogne and Calais on the Continent.

King's Cross Station is the London terminal for InterCity 225 train service to Aberdeen and Edinburgh. The station's travel center provides its major services from 0700–2300 daily, with its hotel-bookings section closing at 1900. Full information, reservations, and advance ticketing services are available. Outside the station, to the left, a Bureau de Change is open daily, 0800–2000.

Paddington Station serves the west with its InterCity 125 service through Plymouth to Penzance. It is also the London terminal for Sealink services to Ireland via the ports of Fishguard and Rosslare. All facilities operated within the station are exceptionally well marked with overhead signs and directional signals. Paddington's travel center stands in front of platforms 1 and 2 and operates 0800–2130 Monday through Saturday and 0900–2000 Sunday. Three banks (Barclays, Midland, and Westminster) are close to the station.

Liverpool Street Station, one of the oldest rail terminals in London, has undergone extensive renovation. There is a map of the station in front of track 11. The ticket windows are in front of tracks 8, 9, and 10 and the Underground (London Transport) Travel & Tourist Centre is in front of tracks 4 and 5 directly behind the stairs.

Waterloo Station is primarily for trains to the south of England, including the Isle of Wight. Its travel center is located at the end of tracks 15 and 16, opposite the Underground entrance. The center is open 0800–2200 seven days a week. A Westminster Bank facility is between tracks 18 and 19. A map is positioned at tracks 3 and 4 and at tracks 15 and 16. The new Waterloo International Eurostar Terminal occupies tracks 20 through 24.

London's Visitor Information Services

"Everything should be made as simple as possible," wrote Albert Einstein, "but not simpler." Apparently, this is the organizational pattern of London's tourist information services. Regardless of the office and the service, you will find that its personnel are trained to respond professionally to the basic ques-

London's Tower Bridge has remained in constant service since its construction between 1886 and 1894. The huge bascule sections of the drawbridge remain in operation, and the footbridge at the top is a major tourist attraction.

tions most visitors ask: "Where can we stay tonight?" "How do we get there?" "What's going on in London?" "Where are the sights?"

The following are the primary points of contact with the London Tourist Board offices and their hours of operation:

Victoria Station: Streetside in the forecourt, outside platform 15. Operating hours are 0800–1900 Monday through Saturday and 0800–1600 Sunday. Services available include visitor information, hotel accommodations, free and saleable publications, and tourist tickets for buses and the Underground. To get there, use the Underground Circle Line to the Victoria Station stop; proceed to street level and the front of the main entrance.

Heathrow Airport: The office is at the bottom of the passenger ramp in the concourse leading to the Underground station in Terminal 2. For directions, inquire at any one of the airport information desks in Terminals 1, 2, 3, or 4. Operating hours are 0800–1800 daily. Services available are the same as those at Victoria Station, except the airport office does not handle tourist ticket sales.

Selfridges Store: This office is located in Selfridges basement services arcade of the Oxford Street store. Open during regular store hours. Services available: visitor information, free and saleable publications, tourist tickets for the bus and the Underground. To get there, exit at the Oxford Circus station of the District or Central lines of the Underground.

Harrods Store: The office is located on Brompton Road in the basement banking hall of Harrods Knightsbridge store. Open during regular store hours. Services available are the same as at Selfridges. Use the Knightsbridge Station of the Underground's Piccadilly line to get there.

Tower of London, West Gate: This information center is in operation from the second week in April through the first week in November. Operating hours are 0930–1800 Monday through Saturday and 1000–1800 on Sunday. From the Tower Hill Underground station of the District or Circle line, follow signs marked TOWER GATEWAY.

London Telephone Information: The London Tourist Board also operates a telephone accommodations and tours reservation service (credit card holders only). Ring up (071) 824–8844. It operates 0930–1730 Monday through Friday. You also may call (071) 730–3488 for general information from Monday through Friday, 0900–1800; Saturday, 0900–1700.

In addition to its tourist information services in London, the London Tourist Board maintains a mail order service for advance hotel reservations provided that you write ahead at least six weeks prior to your arrival date. Direct requests and inquiries to: Correspondence Assistant, Distribution Department, London Tourist Board & Convention Bureau, 26 Grosvenor Gardens, London SW1W ODU, England. A £5.00 booking fee plus a £12.00 deposit must be paid to confirm the reservation. The deposit is deductible from the hotel bill; the booking fee is nonrefundable.

Accommodations may be booked on the day of arrival at the London Tourist Board's information centers at Victoria Station or Heathrow Airport. The same booking fees and deposit are required.

British Tourist Authority Services

Additional tourist information services are provided in London by the British Tourist Authority (BTA). The BTA offices in North America are listed on page 286 of this edition.

BTA British Travel Centre: Located at 12 Lower Regent Street, SW1, just a few minutes walk south of Piccadilly Circus. The center houses the offices of the British Tourist Authority, British Rail, and American Express. Facilities such as Expotel Hotel Reservations, a book store, and a gift shop also are on the premises.

The center books rail, air, and car travel, reserves sightseeing tours and theater tickets, and provides information on all of Britain. A currency exchange also is available. The center is open daily 0900–1830 Monday through Friday, 1000–1600 Saturday and Sunday, with extended Saturday hours from mid-May to September.

The BTA also operates a telephone information service on (071) 730–3400 Monday through Friday, 0900–1830, Saturday from 1000–1600, and Sunday (summer only), 1000–1600.

Expotel will assist you in finding accommodations in London for any date you require (tel: 071–930–0572). Booking fees and room deposit are the same as the London Tourist Board's. Expotel also operates a Book-A-Bed-Ahead service, which enables visitors to reserve their hotel accommodations for any area in Britain.

British Rail Travel Centres

In addition to the office located in the British Travel Centre described above, British Rail has many offices throughout Greater London where you can buy tickets, make seat and sleeper reservations, and obtain information. Locations in Euston, King's Cross, Liverpool Street, Paddington, St. Pancras, and Waterloo stations open daily at 0800. Go to a station in person or call the British Travel Centre on (071) 730–3400 for directions.

Getting Around in London

London has been described as "a whole world wrapped up in a unique city." For sightseeing in London during your visit, London Transport has many convenient, time-saving ways for you to see the city. The fastest get-acquainted mode of seeing London's highlights is London Coaches' "Original London Sightseeing Tour" by red double-decker bus. This one-and-a-half hour tour passes most of London's major landmarks and includes either live commentary by an approved London tourist board guide or recorded commentary available in several different languages. After your "orientation" tour, you can then go back to those places of particular interest for a closer look.

You may start your London sightseeing tour from any one of four points: Piccadilly Circus, the Speakers' Corner at Marble Arch, Baker Street outside the Forecourt Underground station, or Victoria Street outside the Victoria Underground station. The tour covers a twenty-mile circular course. The adult fare is £9.00; children under sixteen years, £4.00. The original London sight-seeing tour, London Plus, allows you to get on and off as you please (£12.00 adults; £5.00 children). Buses run daily except Christmas Day; summer every ten minutes from 1000 to 1700; winter (mid-October–April) every thirty minutes. The tour is not included with the London Visitor Travelcard. Tickets may be purchased at any of the London Tourist Board Information Centres, London Transport Travel Information Centres, or American Express at the British Tourist Authority Office, 12 Lower Regent Street, and from many hotel porters.

A London Visitor Travelcard will make your London visit smoother, faster, and more enjoyable. It gives you three, four, or seven days of unlimited travel on all London red double-decker buses and the Underground. The Travelcard is also good for unlimited round-trips from London to Heathrow Airport on the Underground during the time of its validity.

The London Visitor Travelcard, like the BritRail Pass, isn't sold in London. (The One Day Travelcard is sold in London.) You must purchase it, in conjunction with your BritRail Pass, before leaving home. (In the United States, telephone (800) 722–7151 for ordering information.) You will be issued an airline ticket–style coupon upon purchase, plus a ticket jacket listing the London Transport Travel Information Centres throughout the city where you may exchange the coupon for the Travelcard. At that time, you will also be given a set of discount vouchers to many of London's top attractions and a free Underground map.

"Whilst" in London, you should not deny yourself the opportunity of traveling in one of the city's taxis. The London taxi is an institution in itself. It is designed so that it can virtually turn on its own wheelbase and has an amazing amount of space for passengers and their luggage. Taxis may be hailed if the yellow FOR HIRE sign is illuminated. Fares and supplemental charges are displayed inside the cab. Fares within London are on the meter. Each driver is thoroughly examined before being licensed. Many American cities should take note of this!

Royal Guardsmen, hallmark of Britain's allegiance to her sovereign, stand duty at royal buildings and residences. The regimental identification of the guards, who traditionally wear the bearskin hat, scarlet tunic, and dark blue trousers, is distinguished by badges, buttons, and various insignia.

LONDON–EDINBURGH TRAIN SERVICE
(First- and second-class accommodations for all services listed)

DEPART FROM		ARRIVE IN EDINBURGH		
EUSTON	KING'S CROSS	MON–FRI	SAT	SUN
—	0600	1109	1109	—
—	0700	—	1137	—
—	0800	1215	1242	—
—	—	—	—	—
0825(R)	—	1428	—	—
—	0830	—	1300	—
—	0900	1338	1337	1445
—	0930	—	1402	—
—	1000	—	1909	1535
—	1030	—	—	1612
—	1030	1451	1451	—
—	1100	1530	1530	1639
—	1200	1626	1626	1724
—	1230	—	—	1757
—	1300	1725	1738	1823
—	1330	—	—	1856
—	1330	1809	1806	—
—	1400	1824	1830	1924
—	1500	1906	1934	2022
—	1600	2024	2034	2112
—	1700	2115	2134	2159
—	1730	2218	—	—
—	1800	2223	2240	2311
2115(R)*	—	—	0600 + 1	—
2310(R)*	—	—	—	0620 + 1
2335(R)*	0602	—	—	—

Distance: 393 miles/632 km
References: British Rail Table 26A
                  Thomas Cook Table 570

High-speed, food service available; reservations recommended for all above-listed trains
(R) Reservations required
* Sleeping cars only

Useful Phone Numbers

Tourist Information Centre	*Train Information*
All Scotland: 031–332–2433	London: 071–278–2477
Edinburgh: 031–557–1700	Edinburgh: 031–556–2451

Churchill's War Rooms

Few Americans are aware that a memorial to their World War II president, Franklin Roosevelt, exists in London's Grosvenor Square. Fewer perhaps are aware that the place where Prime Minister Winston Churchill of Britain held telephone conversations with him is now open to the public.

In 1936 when the storms of the war were gathering, the British government began constructing a communications center, or war room, beneath the government offices in Whitehall. Building a ten-foot layer of concrete above a labyrinth of wine cellars and connecting tunnels, workmen toiled at night so as not to arouse suspicions of what was being constructed. Virtually bombproof, facilities for electrical power, water, and air from one primary plus two alternate sources were installed. Anticipating that the prime minister and his staff might be required to spend extended periods of time underground without the benefit of sunlight, a room was equipped with ultraviolet machines.

The Nazis captured Warsaw in September 1939. With the stage set for the ensuing conflict, Churchill's staff moved in. Essentially, the Allies' direction of the war was conducted from this communications center until the war ended. The center was sealed in 1945 and not reopened until it was removed from the British official secrets list in 1975. Today, it is the Cabinet War Rooms Museum. A visit there will place you in the exact location where some of the most dramatic decisions in the history of mankind were made.

In a small, soundproof room, you can see the telephone on the British end of the "hotline" connected with the White House in Washington. It was here that Churchill spoke with Roosevelt over a secure line that was made possible by a scrambler invented in 1943 by the Bell Telephone Laboratories. The clock on the wall was equipped with two sets of hands: one set in black for London time, the other set in red for the time in Washington.

Nearby, Churchill's bedroom is maintained in much the same manner as it was when occupied by the prime minister. Seated at the desk in the bedroom, Churchill delivered many of his famous radio broadcasts that helped so much in maintaining morale throughout the free world. Of equal interest is the Map Room, where information from all over the world regarding the war was collected and displayed. The scene visitors view today depicts the situation during the last few months of the war; it was left in place when the center was closed down and sealed.

The entrance to the Cabinet War Rooms Museum is located at the Clive Steps on King Charles Street, across from St. James Park. Open daily, 1000–1800; admission is £3.80 for adults; children £1.90. For information, call (071) 930–6961.

LONDON–GLASGOW TRAIN SERVICE
(First- and second-class accommodations for all services listed)

DEPART FROM		ARRIVE IN GLASGOW CENTRAL		
EUSTON	KING'S CROSS	MON–FRI	SAT	SUN
0620(R)(0610 SAT)	—	1212	1218	—
—	0700	—	1254	—
—	0800	1319	—	—
0840(0830 SAT)	—	1358	1358	—
—	0900	—	1445	—
0940(R)	—	—	—	1633
—	1000	1519	—	1644
1040(R)(1030 SAT)	—	1539	1539	—
—	1100	—	1645	—
—	1200	—	—	1839
1230(R)	—	1755	1755	—
—	1300	—	1845	—
—	1330	1919	—	—
—	1400	—	—	2039
1430(R)	—	2035	2035	—
—	1500	2012	2047	—
1540(R)	—	—	—	2137
1540(R)	—	2118	—	2140
1640(SUN)	—	—	—	2221
1725(M-F)	—	2229	—	—
1715(SAT)	—	—	2229	—
2120(R)*	—	—	0634 + 1	—
2325(R)*	—	—	—	0640 + 1
2350(R)*	—	0640 + 1	—	—

Distance: 402 miles/647 km
References: British Rail Table 26A
              Thomas Cook Table 550

High-speed trains, food service available; reservations recommended for all above-listed trains
(R) Reservation required
* Sleeping cars only

Useful Phone Numbers

Tourist Information Centre	*Train Information*
All Scotland: 031–332–2433	London: 071–387–7070
Glasgow: 041–227–4880	Glasgow: 041–204–2844

The great Roman bath attracted visitors from all parts of the Roman Empire between the first and fifth centuries. It was constructed around a natural hot spring with waters rising from the ground at 116°. The abbey church tower of Bath looms in the background.

From London . . .

A DAY EXCURSION TO BATH
DISTANCE BY TRAIN: 107 miles (172 km)
AVERAGE TRAIN TIME: 1 hour, 20 minutes

Bath has been in the limelight of social attention during two eras of recorded history—once during the Roman occupation of Britain and again in the eighteenth century when Bath became the "in place" for royalty and other well-to-do's. Development of the only hot spring in Britain is attributed to the Romans soon after the Emperor Claudius invaded the land in A.D. 43.

To the Romans, the city's name was *Aquae Sulis*—literally translated, "the waters of Sul." By the end of the first century, the Romans had established a great bathing facility. The magnificent hot baths were said to have curative powers. Although modern scientists are doubtful of the waters' purported healing properties, there is no doubt that the only hot mineral springs in Britain played a major role in establishing Bath as the "hot spot" for socializing.

The baths made Aquae Sulis famous throughout the empire. Its fame lasted 400 years until the rising sea level and the fall of the Roman Empire brought the city's prosperity to an end. By the end of the seventh century, the city was described as "a ghostly ruin with crumbled masonry fallen into dark pools, overgrown and bird haunted, but still a wondrous sight."

The second revitalization of the city, a cultural one, began in 1705 with the arrival of thirty-one-year-old Richard Nash. Like the Romans, he, too, conquered, but not by force. Nash was Bath's first public relations expert. It was during his "reign" that Queen Anne visited Bath and it again became an elegant and stylish resort for the wealthy. When Nash died at the age of eighty-eight, he had created a kingdom of taste and etiquette over which he reigned as Beau Nash, King of Bath.

Although the hot springs were used again during the Middle Ages, the Roman ruins remained buried even during the times of Beau Nash, when the gilded bronze head of Minerva was uncovered by workmen while digging a sewer in 1727. Although the statues and columns of the present-day Roman bath were added by Victorian restorers, the original bath area still has the lead floor and limestone paving installed by the Romans.

The restoration of Bath's Roman past and the combining of the city's two eras of fame finally began in 1878 when the city engineer, while investigating a water leak, came upon the Roman reservoir and the huge complex of baths that it fed. In other words, someone finally called a plumber.

The Roman baths are one of Britain's major tourist attractions and draw visitors from all points of the globe to their waters. The baths rank a close second to England's number-one attraction, the Tower of London, and are well

BATH—*ROMAN ENGLAND*

A Day Excursion from London

DEPART FROM PADDINGTON STATION	ARRIVE IN BATH SPA STATION	NOTES
0815	0941	(2)
0830	1008	(3)
0915	1041	(2)
0930	1108	(3)
0945	1112	(1)
1015	1141	(2)
1030	1208	(3)

(Plus other frequent service)

DEPART FROM BATH SPA STATION	ARRIVE IN PADDINGTON STATION	NOTES
1427	1600	(2)
1512	1705	(3)
1527	1700	(2)
1612	1800	(3)
1627	1800	(2)
1657	1825 (SUN 1835)	(2)(3)
1727	1855	(2)

(Plus other frequent service)

Distance: 107 miles/172 km
References: British Rail Table 125
                   Thomas Cook Table 530

(1) MON–FRI   (3) SUN
(2) MON–SAT

Train Information: 0225–463075
InterCity Services: 071–262–6767
Bath Tourist Information Centre: 0225–461111

worth the short train ride to see them and the "glory that was Rome"—transposed to England.

The City of Bath abounds in sightseeing opportunities. We suggest that upon arrival in Bath you proceed immediately to the Bath Tourist Information Centre located on Bath Street and let it assist you in your visit. To reach the center on foot, proceed up Manvers Street directly in front of the Bath rail station until you cross North Parade Road. At this point, you will see the Bath Abbey tower to your left. Pass the Abbey on its right side and proceed through the Abbey Church Yard. At the columns, turn left and then take the first right into Bath Street. With the Roman Baths at your back, proceed down Bath Street. The Tourist Information Center will be on the right. Should you want to telephone ahead from the rail station, "ring up" on (0225) 462831. This will connect you with the Inquiries Office of the center.

The center has a wealth of information about the City of Bath and its surroundings. We can recommend purchasing the illustrated *Official Guidebook*. You'll want to show it to the folks back home. The second publication we recommend is the pamphlet "36 Leisure Attractions In and Around Bath." This informative piece contains a city map and lists places of interest. Those interested in the story of fashion over the last 400 years will want to visit the Museum of Costume and Assembly Rooms (No. 27 on the pamphlet map), located on Bennett Street. Then, turn left on Bennett Street and Proceed to nearby No. 1 Royal Crescent (No. 28 on the pamphlet map) to tour the beautifully restored eighteenth-century town house designed by John Wood.

The *Official Guidebook* devotes a part of its pages to "Wandering Through Bath," which will prove most helpful to you when you explore this beautiful city. Bath has won many awards for its floral displays, and its natural beauty makes a walking tour through the city a real pleasure.

On the subject of tours, you should check to see if you may avail yourself of the Mayor's Corps of Honorary Guides. They conduct guided tours at various times throughout the summer season at no charge. These tours, which depart from the Abbey Church Yard, take approximately one and one-half hours. For advance information, ring up (0225) 461111 and ask to be put through to extension 2785. By the way, we'd appreciate having you mention *Britain by BritRail* when the Guides' office asks who recommended their services. We've been mutual admirers for years.

If you are on a tight schedule, the best sights in the city are cloistered about the Roman baths. The baths and the abbey practically adjoin each other. Upstairs from the baths, you may visit the Pump Room and sample its water. During your visit, take time to touch the worn paving. In that moment, you can recall the glory that was Rome.

A stately statue of Britain's Queen Victoria overlooks the plaza fronting Birmingham's Council House. One of the World's great industrial cities, Birmingham has made spectacular strides in developing itself as a beautiful residential city and is no longer England's "ugly duckling."

From London ...

A DAY EXCURSION TO BIRMINGHAM
DISTANCE BY TRAIN: 119 miles (191 km)
AVERAGE TRAIN TIME: 1 hour, 30 minutes

Birmingham has more canals than Venice. This is rather unusual because Birmingham claims to be Britain's "city at the center." Although it is in the approximate geographic center of the British Isles, it was once the center of England's waterways, which carried most of the nation's industrial traffic. With the development of other forms of transportation, particularly rail, canal transportation dissipated. Most of the canals have been developed into recreation areas with walks, pubs, and restored buildings along their right-of-ways.

For decades, Birmingham has been recognized internationally as one of the world's great industrial cities. Along with the recognition came the image of a smoke-filled, grimy Victorian sprawl of a city. Since World War II, Birmingham has made spectacular progress in developing a beautiful residential city. The center of the city has been completely rebuilt. One of the most striking landmarks marking the city center is the Rotunda, a 250-foot tower. Beneath the tower is the "Bull Ring," the world's first under-one-roof-shopping complex. The multilevel, temperature-controlled Bull-Ring shopping center is linked by subways with major shopping streets of the city. It connects directly with the New Street railway station, where you will arrive from London on your day excursion. If you experience difficulty in gaining your bearings in the vast New Street Station, consult the travel center (train information) in the station's main hall on the extreme far right as you exit from the train platforms.

Something unusual in the development of a modern city is Birmingham's National Exhibition Center. For years the exhibition centers in Continental Europe lured the larger trade fairs. Now Britain has its own showcase at Bickenhill, only one hour and twenty minutes from London by InterCity trains. This modern exhibition-and-conference center is on a 310-acre site readily accessible by rail. Rail connections to the exhibition center may be made through the New Street Station on any trains departing in the direction of London. The stop, Birmingham International, is a short, seventeen-to-twenty-minute ride. Obtain full details from the tourist information center. With 1.2 million square feet of air-conditioned exhibition space in nine halls, it is by far the largest complex in Britain, and it's still growing. With the opening in 1991 of the International Convention Centre in the city center, Birmingham can compete with any city in Continental Europe.

To reach the Birmingham tourist information center at 2 City Arcade, make your way to Corporation Street from the station, and behind the Superstore C&A, you will find the tourist information and ticket shop. The office is open

BIRMINGHAM—*HEART OF ENGLAND*

A Day Excursion from London

DEPART FROM EUSTON STATION	ARRIVE IN BIRMINGHAM NEW STREET STATION	NOTES
0715	0857	(1)
0745	0926	(1)
0815	0957	(1)
0845	1026	(1)
0915	1057	(1)
0935	1126	(3)
0945	1218	(4)
1015	1157	(1)
1035	1226	(3)

(Plus other frequent service)

DEPART FROM BIRMINGHAM NEW STREET STATION	ARRIVE IN EUSTON STATION	NOTES
1445	1627	(1)
1515	1659	(1)
1545	1727	(1)
1615	1757	(1)(4)
1645	1845	(2)(4)
1718	1929	(2)(4)
1745	1943	(1)
1818	2039	(2)(4)

(Plus other frequent service)

Distance: 119 miles/191 km
References: British Rail Tables 65 and 68
             Thomas Cook Table 540

(1) MON–FRI	(3) SAT
(2) MON–SAT	(4) SUN

Train Information: 021–200–2700
InterCity Services: 071–387–7070
Birmingham Tourist Information Centre: 021–643–2514

0930–1730 Monday through Saturday; closed on Sunday.

Check with the city tourist information center concerning a sightseeing tour. Despite a massive redevelopment program after World War II, the best of the old has been carefully preserved. The city has an interesting skyline. Historic buildings appear unexpectedly among new ones in a way that emphasizes the quality of both.

Also located in the Victoria Square vicinity and worthy of a visit for its classic elegance and Victorian style is the Town Hall. Opened in 1834, it was designed by Joseph Hansom, the inventor of the Hansom cab. It is the concert hall in which Mendelssohn conducted the first performance of *Elijah* in 1846. Many distinguished musicians have appeared there since, including Sir Edward Elgar.

Other historic buildings in the nearby suburbs include the Sarehole Mill (served by Hall Green Station), an eighteenth-century water mill restored to working order, and Blakesley Hall (Stechford Station), a seventeenth-century timber-framed yeoman's house furnished in period style and with an interesting garden. For rail buffs, a visit to the science museum is a must. It houses the world's oldest steam engine, which was built in 1784, and displays of early machinery, engines, and motorcars. Two and one-half miles north of the city center on Trinity Road is another seventeenth-century gem, Aston Hall (Wilton Station). The magnificent Jacobean mansion was begun in 1618 and took seventeen years to complete.

Birmingham's Civic Centre is a modern contribution to the city's skyline. It includes a repertory theatre and one of the largest and best stocked libraries in Europe, featuring a comprehensive Shakespeare collection. The city's Central Museum and Art Gallery houses paintings and sculpture by Van Gogh, Botticelli, and Gainsborough, and its pre-Raphaelite painting collection is the best.

After all the sightseeing, you may develop a thirst. You came to the right city. Birmingham has long been one of Britain's major brewing centers, and its beer is recommended highly by both locals and visitors. There are plenty of pubs in which you can conduct your own taste tests.

Birmingham is justly proud of its restaurants, which cater to every palate and purse. The city has stylish theater-restaurants with entertainment by international cabaret stars, as well as a wide selection of eateries providing French, Italian, Spanish, Greek, "Balti" cuisine from northern India, Chinese, and traditional English cuisine. There's no reason to leave Birmingham with an empty stomach or an unquenched thirst.

Birmingham has undergone many structural changes in recent years, and, undoubtedly, it is becoming one of Europe's outstanding cities.

Brighton's Royal Pavilion, onion-domed creation and seaside home of England's King George IV, still contains most of its original furnishings. The Banqueting Room is set out with period glass and gold plates in the festive style of an era past.

A DAY EXCURSION TO BRIGHTON
DISTANCE BY TRAIN: 51 miles (82 km)
AVERAGE TRAIN TIME: 55 minutes

Brighton is, and always has been, much more than a traditional seaside resort. Since the earliest days of travel, visitors have been attracted by the resort's unique sense of style and architectural splendor. These special qualities are as strong as ever. But they are only part of a continuing success story that secures Brighton's position as Britain's leading resort area.

Perhaps Brighton would have remained a tiny, humble fishing village originally known as Brighthelmstone if it were not for the efforts of Dr. Richard Russell and the Prince Regent (who later became King George IV). In 1750 Dr. Russell, a Brighton resident, published a book extolling the magical effects of sea air and saltwater. This started a fashionable trend that brought royalty and commoner alike to Brighton. The good doctor prescribed bathing in the sea and drinking a pint and a half of seawater daily as a cure for glandular diseases. Such a prescription, incredible as it seems, must have initiated a whole new series of maladies. Chronicles of that period, however, have failed to note them.

The gifted and wayward Prince Regent first visited Brighton in 1783. Enamored by it all (and well heeled with royal funds), he ordered his Royal Pavilion constructed there. Completed in 1822 from an architectural style taken somewhere east of Suez, it has been termed the most bizarre and exotic palace in all Europe. The Royal Pavilion's ostentatious onion-domed exterior, looking very much like a series of hot-air balloons about to ascend, is only surpassed by its even more amazing interior. It is fully furnished in its original style and open to the public daily. Queen Victoria, not at all amused by the pavilion's architecture, calculatedly was permitting it to fall to ruin when Brighton's citizenry saved it from demolition in 1850. The Royal Pavilion recently underwent a £10 million refurbishment to restore the seaside palace to its original condition.

The city maintains "The Lanes," where you take a step backwards into the old fishing-village days. The buildings in these narrow, twisting passages were fishermen's cottages in the seventeenth century. Today, they are quaint and fascinating antique, jewelry, and high fashion shops; pubs; and cafés.

Part of the changing scene in Brighton has been the introduction during the last twenty years of English-language schools, which attract international students from a score of foreign lands. This youthful input has made it one of the most vibrant resorts in Britain.

Brighton's train terminal was refurbished in 1986. A landmark, the wooden, manually operated dispatch board now rests in York's National Railway

BRIGHTON — *COLORFUL SEASIDE RESORT*

A Day Excursion from London

DEPART FROM VICTORIA STATION	ARRIVE IN BRIGHTON STATION	NOTES
0747	0900	(1)
0832	0945	(1)(3)
0904	1017	(2)
0908	0959	(1)
0932	1049	(1)(3)
1008	1059	(1)
1032	1149	(1)(3)
1108	1159	(1)
1132	1249	(1)(3)

(Plus other frequent service)

DEPART FROM BRIGHTON STATION	ARRIVE IN VICTORIA STATION	NOTES
1550	1643	(1)
1600	1716	(1)(3)
1650	1743	(1)
1700	1816	(2)(3)
1749	1840	(1)
1752	1853	(3)
1949	2040	(1)
2000	2116	(1)(3)
2200	2316	(1)(3)

(Plus other frequent service)

Distance: 51 miles/82 km
References: British Rail Table 186
            Thomas Cook Table 505

(1) MON–SAT   (3) SUN
(2) SAT

Train Information: 0273–206755
InterCity Services: 071–928–5100
Brighton Tourist Information: 0273–323755

Museum. Its digital replacement is at the head of the train platforms. The station's rail information center is located at the entrance.

The tourist information center is located in Bartholomew Square next to the Town Hall, about a ten-minute walk from the station. To reach it, walk directly out of the rail station and down Queens Road to the sea. Turn left at that point onto Kings Road. Where Kings Road becomes Grand Junction, turn left again and proceed to the Town Hall and the tourist information center. If you want to call ahead, the telephone number is (0273) 323755. The center is open every day (except Christmas) from 0900 to 1700, with extended evening hours in summer.

In English-style directions, had you denied yourself the turning at Grand Junction, you would have come quickly upon the gates of the Palace Pier, which extends out into the English Channel like a silent sentinel. Constructed in 1899, the pier has been restored and features free entrance, free deck chairs, and free entertainment. It opens daily at 0900. Have a look. It's free—and quite enjoyable.

If you would like to participate in a guided walking tour of Brighton's "Old Town," obtain details from the information center. From June through mid-September, the tours start at the tourist information center. Or you can pick up the Brighton "Mini Guide" at the information center. The "Mini Guide" features a town plan showing where to go and what to see.

Brighton's shopping center, including the Churchill Square Pedestrian Precinct, is one of the largest in southern England. The kids will love the Sea Life Centre and Peter Pan's playground. Because of the city's number and variety of shopping areas, Brighton is sometimes referred to as "London by the sea." Swank shops can be found in Brighton's east side and the adjoining Regent Arcade. For the more bizarre, shop the Upper Gardner Street junk market on Saturday mornings and the station car park's "carboot" (junk and antiques) sale on Sunday mornings.

Young and old alike should take a ride along the sea front on the Volks Railway, Britain's first public electric railway. Open daily between Easter and Labor Day, the railway travels along the beach on Madeira Drive to Black Rock. Lacking the speed of British Rail's InterCity 125s, the Volks Railway makes up for it with its nostalgia.

Brighton's marina is one of the largest in Europe. Whether you are a boating enthusiast or not, a visit there is well in order. A complete village is now the centerpiece of the marina with an eight-screen cinema, elegant shops, quayside restaurants, and, of course, traditional British pubs on the waterfront. The marina also stages many colorful events, such as boat shows and sailing regattas throughout July and August.

If you're caught up in Brighton's buoyancy, check with the tourist information center for hotel accommodations and catch a morning train back to London.

"Fowl play" in front of the dovecote. In 1327 the Abbey of St. Edmunds was badly damaged by townspeople protesting against monastic control. It is said that in 1214, English barons swore before the abbey's high altar to force King John to ratify the Magna Carta—which he did the following year at Runnymede.

From London . . .

A DAY EXCURSION TO BURY ST. EDMUNDS
DISTANCE BY TRAIN: 74 miles (119 km)
AVERAGE TRAIN TIME: 2 hours

For centuries, the East Anglian town of Bury St. Edmunds has been the scene of a fight for freedom of conscience, speech, worship, and the rights of the individual man.

In his *Pickwick Papers,* Charles Dickens described Bury St. Edmunds as " . . . a handsome little town of thriving and cleanly appearance." So it remains today. A monastery was built on the present site of Bury St. Edmunds in A.D. 633. In 903, thirty-three years after King Edmund of East Anglia was killed by the Danes at Hoxne, his body was brought to the town by Bishop Theodred. Thus, the town became known as Bury St. Edmunds. The abbey church was built soon afterwards to honor the memory of the king. For many, Bury St. Edmunds is regarded as one of the most famous towns in all England. It is said that in 1214, barons gathered at the high altar of the abbey to take a solemn oath to force King John to grant a charter of liberties, one of the events leading to the granting of the Magna Carta in 1215.

The town center is most notable for its pleasant Georgian atmosphere, recalling the days when the town was a leading social center within East Anglia. The great abbey was one of the largest in Europe at one time. It was sacked in 1327 by townspeople protesting against monastic control and again in 1381 during the Peasants' Revolt. In 1465, a severe fire damaged the church, which had to be extensively repaired. It was subsequently robbed of much of its stone for use in building materials in the town. A placard on the abbey gate indicates that the gate was destroyed and the abbey badly damaged by the townspeople in 1327 but was rebuilt in 1347.

Across from the abbey gate is the Angel Hotel, more than 500 years old, known for its association with Charles Dickens. His room, No. 15, is preserved exactly as it was more than a century ago. The hotel was originally one of three East Anglian inns on the site. A unique attraction of the Angel Hotel is its tavern room, dating back to 1433—fifty-nine years before Columbus discovered America.

During World War II, Bury St. Edmunds was ringed with American air bases. Today, the Third Air Force of the U.S. Air Force European Command operates RAF Mildenhall, west of Bury St. Edmunds. Visitors are welcome at the base but are advised to contact the base information office or its community relations advisor before proceeding there. The tourist information center can provide complete details.

The tourist information office is located at 6 Angel Hill, immediately oppo-

BURY ST. EDMUNDS—*MAGNA CARTA*

A Day Excursion from London

DEPART LIVERPOOL STREET STATION	ARRIVE IN IPSWICH	DEPART IPSWICH	ARRIVE BURY ST. EDMUNDS
0625(2)	0731	0806	0833
0830(2)	0933	0943	1014
0830(3)	0940	1005	1042
1030(2)	1135	1212	1249

DEPART BURY ST. EDMUNDS	ARRIVE IPSWICH	DEPART IPSWICH	ARRIVE LIVERPOOL STREET STATION
1405(3)	1437	1445	1557
1556(2)	1628	1645	1758
1722(2)	1759	1845	1953
1705(3)	1737	1745	1857
1843(2)	1922	1945	2053

Distance: 95 miles/153 km
References: British Rail Tables 12 and 15
                      Thomas Cook Tables 580 and 583

Note: Via Ipswich. Service also available through Cambridge.

(1) MON–FRI
(2) MON–SAT
(3) SUN

Bury St. Edmunds Tourist Information Centre
0284–763233
Evenings and Weekends: 0284–764667

site the abbey-gate entrance to the ruins of St. Edmunds Abbey, a short distance from the train station. Station personnel will gladly provide directions. The information office is open during the summer months from 0930 to 1730 Monday through Friday, 1000–1500 Saturday, and 1000–1500 Sunday (June–September only). Winter hours are 1000–1600 Monday–Friday and 1000–1300 Saturday.

Sightseeing in Bury St. Edmunds is, of course, highlighted by the abbey ruins and gardens. St. Mary's Church, which borders the southern boundary of the abbey grounds, is also a popular visiting spot. The Borough Council's Museum of Local History is housed in Moyses Hall. Constructed in the latter part of the twelfth century, it is a fine example of Norman domestic architecture. The Manor House Museum faces the abbey grounds. This restored Georgian mansion houses clocks, paintings, costumes, and objets d'art from the seventeenth to the twentieth century.

There are two distinct parts to the town. As was customary in most medieval towns with a monastic foundation, there was a physical division between the monastery and the townspeople—possibly the first example of separation of church and state. This division resulted in the business section and public buildings standing on a hill to the west of the abbey ruins today.

The Theatre Royal, one of the three surviving Georgian playhouses in Britain, was built in Bury St. Edmunds during 1819 by England's famous architect, William Wilkins. He also designed Downing College on the campus at Cambridge. The Theatre Royal's architecture displays in elegant fashion the style and form for which the Georgian architects were famous. This historical theater's repertoire features a broad scope of entertainment, plays, dance, opera, and every form of music ranging from classical to jazz and rock. In 1892, the Theatre Royal made international headlines by presenting the world premiere of *Charlie's Aunt,* a comedy that is still performed in every major language throughout the world.

Bypassed by time, Bury St. Edmunds is essentially a country town that was spared the industrial expansion of the Victorian Age. But the town stands tall in history. The principles of the Magna Carta, which had their foundation in Bury St. Edmunds and were developed over the centuries by English Common Law, have become the heritage not only of the British Isles but of countless millions throughout the world. As history records, the grant of the Magna Carta by King John is the basic source of the constitutional liberties of English-speaking peoples, forming a common bond of peace between them.

One of Bury St. Edmunds's local products is ale. Although the city boasts numerous pubs, we suggest that you sample a pint in the Nutshell, the smallest pub in England. Its single bar room measures twelve feet by seven feet.

King's College Chapel in Cambridge, universally known as one of the world's finest architectural structures, took seventy years to build.

The "backs," that portion of the River Cam passing the college buildings and gardens, is ideal for a placid boat tour of Cambridge.

From London . . .

A DAY EXCURSION TO CAMBRIDGE
DISTANCE BY TRAIN: 56 miles (90 km)
AVERAGE TRAIN TIME: 1 hour

Oxford graduates often refer to Cambridge as "the other place." Both universities hold one thing in common—organized along the classic federal structure, they house a number of largely autonomous colleges. Comparisons stop here. Cambridge is Britain's "university city." It is said that if you visit only one other English city besides London, it should be Cambridge.

Cambridge is situated on the River Cam around the original bridge over which all trade and communications passed between central England, East Anglia, and Continental Europe 1,000 years ago. It was a natural spot for travelers to pause to exchange news and opinions, thereby preparing the ground for a center of learning.

Several religious orders, including the Franciscans and Dominicans, established monasteries and affiliated schools in Cambridge early in the twelfth century. Students from the University of Oxford and the University of Paris left to study in Cambridge during the thirteenth century. The present-day colleges originated at that time, when students began residing in hostels and halls.

There are daily walking tours of the colleges with qualified guides who can tell you about the university and its colleges. Schedules and tickets for the tours may be obtained from the tourist information center. The main colleges are closed to visitors from mid-April until the end of June. A note of academic etiquette: College members are happy to welcome you to the grounds and their historic buildings, but they ask you to respect their need for quiet and privacy.

Arriving by rail from London, take the bus (No. 1) located immediately in front of the railway station to St. Andrew's Street and Downing. Cambridge is a complex blend of market town, regional center, university, and tourist attraction and defies neat analysis. Consequently, after getting off the bus in St. Andrew's Street, ask for directions to the tourist information center (tel. 322640) on Wheeler Street (behind the Guildhall) a few short blocks away.

The tourist information center is open Monday through Friday, 0900–1900, 0900–1700 Saturday, 1030–1530 Sunday (Easter–September); 0900–1730 (November–February). It opens at 0930 on Wednesdays. Ask for the *Cambridge Mini-Guide* (nominal fee). It provides basic information about the colleges and museums and includes a street plan of the city. Other books and gifts are available for those wanting to know more about the history of Cambridge and places of interest outside the city.

If you plan to see Cambridge on your own, planning an itinerary may be difficult because there is so much to see. King's College Chapel is regarded

CAMBRIDGE—*UNIVERSITY CITY*

A Day Excursion from London

DEPART FROM KING'S CROSS STATION	ARRIVE IN CAMBRIDGE STATION	NOTES
0845	0938	(1)
0945	1038	(1)
0955	1108	(3)
1045	1138	(1)
1145	1238	(1)
1315	1407	(1)

(Plus other frequent service out of King's Cross and Liverpool Street stations)

DEPART FROM CAMBRIDGE STATION	ARRIVE IN KING'S CROSS STATION	NOTES
1554	1649	(1)
1617	1727	(3)
1654	1749	(1)
1707	1810	(3)
1754	1846	(1)
1807	1910	(3)
1824	1916	(1)
2031	2137	(1)

(Plus other frequent service into King's Cross and Liverpool Street stations)

Distance: 56 miles/90 km
References: British Rail Tables 21 and 25
            Thomas Cook Table 581

(1) MON–SAT   (3) SUN
(2) SAT

Train Information: 0223–311999
InterCity Services: 071–928–5100

Cambridge Tourist Information Centre: 0223–322640

universally as one of Cambridge's finest architectural structures. It was constructed in stages over a period of nearly seventy years and was completed in 1536. The chapel, which is open to the public, displays the carved coats of arms of Henry VIII. His initials, along with those of Anne Boleyn, can be seen on the screen. The chapel's stained-glass windows depict stories from the Old Testament and the New Testament. Rubens's *Adoration of the Magi* is the altarpiece.

Trinity College's great court is one of the largest collegiate quadrangles in England. It's so large that much of its detail goes unnoticed. It is said that taking advantage of this situation, Byron bathed nude in the fountain and shared his room with a pet bear, which he claimed he kept for the purpose of taking examinations. Sir Isaac Newton first measured the speed of sound in the great court by stamping his foot in the cloister along the north side.

The admission qualifications to the University of Cambridge are exceptionally demanding. Each year, approximately 8,000 students apply for admission. In the end, however, only about 20 percent are admitted.

The Cam River, the source of Cambridge's being and delightful throughout every season, deserves a portion of your visit. A tour of the city by boat along the "backs," as the placid stretch of the river is called, is an experience not to be missed. You can hire a punt, rowboat, or canoe to boat along the backs. If your selection is the punt—which is propelled with long wooden poles—be aware that these poles frequently stick in the mud and have been known to vault a punter into the river. A "chauffeur punt" service is also available.

Visitors have a wide choice of museums covering a wide range of interests. Allow yourself time to wander in at least one of them. The Fitzwilliam Museum on Trumpington Street features medieval and Renaissance objects of art, arms, and armor. The Folk Museum on Castle Street contains a vast array of domestic articles. Another point of interest is Kettles Yard Art Gallery at Castle Street on Northampton with its fine collection of modern paintings and sculpture.

Steeped in history, Cambridge has a reminder of a more recent historical event—Duxford Airfield, which is located eight miles south of the city. Now the site of the Imperial War Museum, Duxford was one of the many airfields from which Allied aircraft flew raids into Continental Europe during World War II. A visit to the museum is recommended. The American Military Cemetery, four miles from Cambridge, contains the graves of 3,811 American airmen who operated from bases in Britain. The cemetery and the museum may be reached by bus.

The Old Weaver's House in Canterbury owes its name to Flemish and Huguenot weavers who came to the city in the sixteenth century and set up looms in private houses along the River Stour. Now a small but attractive stream, the river played an important role in Canterbury's earlier times.

A DAY EXCURSION TO CANTERBURY
DISTANCE BY TRAIN: 62 miles (99 km)
AVERAGE TRAIN TIME: 1 hour, 25 minutes

Canterbury was originally a huddle of huts that the Romans captured as they penetrated inland from the Kentish coast. They fortified the area and built their roads to London and beyond, and along these roads came the Roman legions of occupation. Although the Romans' domination of England ended in the fifth century, the road between London and Canterbury remains heavily traveled even today.

In early times, the River Stour meandered through the valleys, creating a large boggy area. At Canterbury there was a ford for crossing the watery barrier. The selection of the Canterbury site for settlement probably was dependent on its natural advantage as a ford and on the consequent communications that spread out from it.

Canterbury has had a hectic history. In the year 1011, it was sacked by the Danes. It was again invaded by the Normans, who founded the city of Canterbury as we know it today. The victory of William the Conqueror began an era during which the city developed in an orderly manner until the Reformation. In England, the Reformation lasted several decades, during which time there were martyrs in Canterbury on both sides of the dispute.

Thomas á Becket was made Archbishop of Canterbury in 1162. A close confidant to King Henry II and an advisor in matters of state, Becket chose, upon his ordination, to disregard the wishes of the king and transferred all of his efforts to trying to establish the claims of the Church. Invoking the ire of the monarchy, Becket spent some years in exile, but returned in 1170 to a tumultuous welcome from the populace. On 29 December 1170, he was murdered in his own cathedral after King Henry II mused aloud in the presence of four knights, "Who will free me from this turbulent priest?" Horrified by the murder, Christendom immediately declared Becket a saint.

Becket's murder induced vast pilgrimages to Canterbury, enriching both the cathedral and the city's development during the Middle Ages. These pilgrimages, conducted in a boisterous spirit from all parts of England, have been portrayed by Chaucer in his *Canterbury Tales.*

During World War II, Canterbury was the victim of air raids and bombings, which destroyed about one-quarter of the city. The most severe raid occurred in 1942 in reprisal for British raids on Cologne. The West Gate, however, the only one of seven medieval gates not destroyed more than one-hundred years ago, survived the raids.

Canterbury has two railway stations—West Station and East Station. Trains

103

CANTERBURY—*AND THE CATHEDRAL*

A Day Excursion from London

DEPART FROM VICTORIA STATION	ARRIVE IN CANTERBURY EAST STATION	NOTES
0735	0932	(4)
0805	0931	(2)
0835	1032	(4)
0905	1031	(2)
0935	1132	(4)
1005	1131	(2)
1035	1232	(4)

(Plus other frequent service)

DEPART FROM CANTERBURY EAST STATION	ARRIVE IN VICTORIA STATION	NOTES
1551	1748	(4)
1647	1823	(1)
1649	1817	(3)
1751	1948	(4)
1819	2015	(1)
1849	2017	(3)
2051	2248	(4)
2119	2315	(2)

(Plus other frequent service)

Distance: 62 miles/99 km
References: British Rail Table 212; Thomas Cook Table 500

(1) MON–FRI	(3) SAT
(2) MON–SAT	(4) SUN

Train Information: 0732–770111
InterCity Services: 071–928–5100

Canterbury Tourist Information Centre
0227–766567

departing London's Charing Cross and Waterloo stations arrive at Canterbury West. Those departing London's Victoria Station arrive at Canterbury East. For simplicity, day-excursion schedules are given for Victoria and Canterbury East stations only.

Arriving in Canterbury East Station, use the pedestrian bridge to reach the city walls. There's a taxi queue just outside the station entrance, or you can walk to the city center and the cathedral in about fifteen minutes. From the station entrance, you'll see a sign across the street that says, CITY CENTRE-MARLOWE THEATRE-CATHEDRAL. A blue sign showing a person walking indicates where to cross the highway. Proceed along the city's old Roman walls, which enclose Dane John Park. Climb the mound in the park for a view of the town and the cathedral. Farther along, you'll come to the city bus station. Descend from the wall at this point onto St. George's Street. Turn left and walk until the cathedral is in view on your right through the Christ Church Gate. Passing through the gate will bring you onto the cathedral grounds.

Not far from the Christ Church Gate is the Longmarket, a paved pedestrian area beginning at the intersection of Rose Lane and St. George's Street. Walking directly away from the Christ Church Gate on St. Margaret's Street will bring you to the Canterbury Visitor Information Centre at No. 34 (telephone 766567). The center is open Monday through Saturday year-round and on Sunday in the summer. City tours depart from this point.

From High Street, where it intersects St. Margaret's Street, walk down until you pass over a narrow bridge on the River Stour. On the far right of the bridge you will see the Old Weaver's House, built in 1500. Canterbury was the background for Dickens's novel *David Copperfield*, so your imagination can take over here for a few fleeting moments and transport you back into English history and literature. The structure houses a beautiful collection of English Church brass rubbings from the medieval and Tudor periods. Unfortunately, as of press time it is closed to the public temporarily due to a change of ownership.

Following World War II, Canterbury became an educational center of great importance. In 1962 Christ Church College was opened adjacent to St. Augustine's College. More recently, the University of Kent was established on a hill overlooking the cathedral and city from the west. Its buildings are designed in a modern idiom; in keeping with the theme of Canterbury, however, it was organized on the basis of colleges with emphasis on artistic and cultural development.

Canterbury, proud of its historical past, is nonetheless eager to respond to the demands of present "pilgrims"—visitors who come to see the cathedral and the other historical landmarks. The city of Canterbury has done an excellent job by exhibiting its history as a living part of a modern, living community.

Castle Clock Tower, an outstanding feature of Cardiff, was designed by Victorian architect William Burges. Commissioned by the Marquis of Bute in 1865 to restore Cardiff Castle, Burges replaced a turret of the castle with this magnificent clock tower as part of the restoration.

From London . . .

A DAY EXCURSION TO CARDIFF
DISTANCE BY TRAIN: 145 miles (233 km)
AVERAGE TRAIN TIME: 1 hour, 46 minutes

A triple treat lies in store for those who take this delightful day excursion to the Welsh capital of Cardiff. The first is the opportunity to travel on one of British Rail's "journey shrinkers"—the fabulous InterCity 125 trains. As an example, the 0900 InterCity out of London's Paddington Station will set you down in Cardiff Central Station exactly 117 minutes later, averaging an amazing speed of seventy-nine miles per hour along the 155 miles separating the two capital cities. As an added bonus, you can savor a delicious English breakfast while watching the western English countryside glide by.

Arriving in Cardiff, your second treat is sampling the scenery of a historic city of the empire that has cast off its grim mantle of industrialism to reveal a sparkling center of shopping arcades, a glistening white array of impressive civic buildings, a most memorable museum (well worth the trip), and smack in the middle of town, a genuine 1,900-year-old castle with walls dating back to the Roman occupation of Britain.

If you recover in time, you'll be off on a fifteen-minute train ride from the city's Queen Street Station for the third treat to nearby Caerphilly Castle, second in size only to Windsor Castle. Covering thirty acres and remarkably well preserved, it's crammed with interesting things, including a tower that even Oliver Cromwell's gunpowder couldn't topple—at least not completely.

Cardiff was first developed by the Romans, then by the Normans. Both left their marks in the form of formidable fortifications. The Romans fought their way into south Wales, reaching the area that is now Cardiff about A.D. 76. At first they erected a wooden fort; but as Cardiff grew in importance as a Roman naval base, a stone fortress was erected, parts of which still exist today as a portion of Cardiff Castle. Following the conquest of England in 1066, the Normans arrived in Cardiff in 1091 and established a stronghold on the site of the old Roman fort.

The city as we see it today is largely a creation of the nineteenth century. Cardiff, a seaport ideally located to handle the iron and coal shipments of the region, saw in 1839 the construction of its first dock and, ten years later, its first railroad. Cardiff is accustomed to welcoming visitors and does it well. We're sure you will find yourself returning there again and again.

We suggest that you first visit the Cardiff information center in Cardiff's Central Station to get your bearings, pick up some brochures (including a map of the city), and then begin your sightseeing. The tourist center is on the ground floor in the main concourse next to the main exit.

CARDIFF—*CAPITAL OF WALES*

A Day Excursion from London

DEPART FROM PADDINGTON STATION	ARRIVE IN CARDIFF CENTRAL STATION	NOTES
0645	0856	(1)
0800	0953(A)	(2)
0830	1041	(1)
0900	1103	(2)
0900	1126	(3)
1000	1204	(2)
1000	1230	(3)
1100	1303	(2)
1100	1326	(3)

(Plus other frequent service)

DEPART FROM CARDIFF CENTRAL STATION	ARRIVE IN PADDINGTON STATION	NOTES
1525	1730(B)	(2)
1545	1810	(3)
1625	1835(A)(C)	(2)(3)
1725	1935(C)	(2)(3)
1825	2030(B)(C)	(2)(3)
1925	2140	(2)
2125	2340	(1)

(Plus other frequent service)

Distance: 145 miles/233 km
References: British Rail Table 125
              Thomas Cook Table 530

(1) MON–FRI	(A) Arrives 10 minutes later, Saturdays
(2) MON–SAT	(B) Arrives 5 minutes later, Saturdays
(3) SUN	(C) Arrives 20 minutes later, Sundays

Train Information: 0222–228000
InterCity Services: 071–262–6767

Cardiff Tourist Information and Accommodations Hotline: 0222–395173

It's open during the summer from Monday through Saturday, 0900–1730; Sunday, 1000–1800. Winter hours are Monday through Saturday, 0900–1730; closed Sunday. If you visit Cardiff on a Sunday, you'll find the castle and the museums open, but the train service is much slower.

Lofty Cardiff Castle is a lavishly restored medieval fortress, and, like Mt. Everest, you can't overlook it. The castle provides the background for a series of spectacular events throughout the summer, ranging from a hot-air balloon festival to massed military bands.

The shopping arcades are back on High Street and Queen Street. Many are pedestrian precincts—Cardiff claims to have had them long before the phrase was invented. The city map will help you in your orientation. We specifically recommend the *Cardiff Guide* booklet with the Cardiff Castle's Norman keep on its cover. This booklet is not available in the tourist information center, but you can pick up a copy in the castle bookshop.

Cardiff's civic center lies beyond the castle, as does the National Museum of Wales. The civic center is one of the most impressive buildings in Europe. Separated by wide avenues and parks, the presence in the spring of cherry blossoms and tulip beds create a perfect setting for the white stone buildings. In the National Museum of Wales, you may view, among other art treasures, four recently discovered tapestry cartoons by Rubens. Rodin's bronze statuary, *The Kiss,* is also housed there. The museum is unusual in that it contains a variety of exhibits—from priceless works of art to dinosaurs. It is truly a place where there is something for everyone.

To sample some traditional Welsh dishes served by waitresses in traditional costume, try the Blas ar Gymru (A Taste of Wales) Restaurant at 48 Crwys Road, about a twenty-minute walk from Cardiff Castle. Proceed north through the Civic Centre to Corbett Road, turn right and over the bridge into Cathays Terrace, right onto Woodville Road, and left onto Crwys Road. Reservations advised—telephone (0222) 382132.

Trains depart Cardiff's Queen Street Station for Caerphilly thrice hourly at three, thirty-four, and forty-six minutes past the hour. Trains returning to Cardiff depart Caerphilly thrice hourly at six, fourteen, and forty-seven minutes past the hour. Returning to Cardiff, ride through to the Central Station for connections with InterCity 125 trains back to London. Central Station is three minutes beyond the Queen Street Station.

The world-famous Rows, a double tier of shops with walkways at ground and first-floor levels, is Chester's most distinctive architectural feature. The Rows line streets originally laid down by Roman engineers almost 2,000 years ago. Extensive rebuilding followed the disastrous fire of 1278. (Courtesy City of Chester)

From London . . .

A DAY EXCURSION TO CHESTER
DISTANCE BY TRAIN: 178 miles (287 km)
AVERAGE TRAIN TIME: 2 hours, 30 minutes

"All's well" in Chester, but don't take our word for it. Check personally with Chester's town crier. He appears twice daily (Tuesday through Saturday, April through October) in the center of the city to announce that fact—first at noon and again at 1400. Chester is one of the few cities in England with its encircling walls completely intact. It is a splendid example of a fortified medieval town.

The center of Chester, known as the "Cross," takes its name from the stone "High Cross" standing in front of St. Peter's Church. From this point you may view Chester's distinctive landmarks, the Rows—two tiers of shops (one at ground level, the other immediately above), each with its own walkway. The Rows are unique and justly world famous. The upper levels are great for people watchers who like to linger undisturbed while observing the stream of passers-by in the streets below. The true origin of the Rows has never been satisfactorily explained, but they far exceed any modern day shopping center in utility and beauty. One opinion is that they served as a means of defense against the incursions of the Welsh raiders, who came to plunder their richer English neighbors.

The Romans gave Chester its street plan. Walk today along the four main streets within the city's walls and you will follow the lines laid down by Roman engineers almost 2,000 years ago. Part of the Roman wall survives and is incorporated in the massive tenth-century fortifications enclosing the city. You can find out more about the city's Roman heritage at the Deva Roman Experience, just off Bridge Street (tel. 0244–343407). A walk on the walls provides an opportunity to enjoy the vista of the surrounding countryside.

Restoration has thrived on a large scale in Chester. Entire blocks were renovated in massive programs. The city's famous "black and white" Tudor buildings survived the ravages of time but did not escape alterations to their facades by Victorian architects. In all, however, Chester has managed to preserve its pleasant medieval appearance.

The railway station in Chester is about a twenty-minute walk from the city's center. City Road, at the front of the station, will get you started in the right direction. Change at the pedestrian underpass onto Foregate Street, which turns into Eastgate Street and brings you to the center of the city's historic area. Or you can board a bus at the side of the Queen Hotel, just across the street from the station. The bus arrives at the town hall in approximately five minutes for a charge of sixteen pence. Taxi meters click off between £1.50 and £1.70 for the ride.

111

CHESTER—*MODERN "MEDIEVAL" CITY*

A Day Excursion from London

DEPART FROM EUSTON STATION	ARRIVE IN CHESTER STATION	NOTES
0850	1130	(3)
0850	1213	(4)
1020	1249	(1)

DEPART FROM CHESTER STATION	ARRIVE IN EUSTON STATION	NOTES
1514	1802	(4)
1647	1931	(2)
1720	2014	(4)

Distance: 178 miles/287 km
References: British Rail Table 65
                 Thomas Cook Table 555

(1) MON–FRI   (3) SAT
(2) MON–SAT   (4) SUN

Train Information: 0244–40170
InterCity Services: 071–387–7070

Chester Tourist Information Centre: 0244–318356
0244–313126 (24 hours/day)

Your first call should be at the Chester Visitor Centre, which is located on the Inner Ring Road, just outside the city walls in Vicars Lane. It is open from 0900 to 2100 seven days a week. The center operates an accommodations booking service, a licensed restaurant, and a reconstruction of a Chester street in Victorian times—complete with sights, sounds, and smells. In addition, the center has a video presentation of Chester's history and a money exchange. Regular guided walks of the city depart from the center from 1030 to 1930 daily.

The tourist information center at the town hall is on Northgate Street across from the entrance to Abbey Square. It is open 0900–1730 Monday through Saturday and 1000–1600 Sunday from November through April; between May and October, weekday hours are 0900–1930 and Sunday, 1000–1600. It offers a wide range of facilities including a national room-finder service and ticket agency. Special guided walks are also available: "Pastfinder" tours depart daily year-round at 1045; the "Ghosthunter Trail" departs at 1930 on Thursday, Friday, and Saturday from May through October; and the "Roman Soldier Patrol" sets forth at 1130 and 1430 on Thursday, Friday, and Saturday from June through September. Opposite the town hall is Abbey Square, an island of quiet in the center of the city. By entering the square through its massive fourteenth-century gateway, you will find various buildings constructed anywhere from the sixteenth to the nineteenth century.

Chester also boasts a cathedral, which is within sight of the town hall. An abbey was founded on this site in the tenth century. It remained as a monastery until its dissolution in 1540, when the building was made a cathedral. The bell tower of the cathedral is a concrete structure that was finished in 1974, the first freestanding bell tower for a cathedral built since the fifteenth century.

An interesting observation point that provides a splendid view of the city, the River Dee, and the locks of the Chester canal is located at the north end of the city walls. A spur wall connects there with the water tower, which was built to protect the port of Chester. Another vantage point is from Bonewaldesthorne's tower, about one-hundred feet from the water tower. If you participate in the Roman Soldier Wall Patrol tour, you will be able to enjoy this view.

Also in view at a bend in the River Dee is Roodee, home of the Chester racecourse, one of the oldest in Britain. The main racing season is held in May and its richest prize, the Chester Cup, was first awarded 1824. As a matter of interest to sportive North Americans, the Roodee was, before horse racing, a football field. But due to the violent nature of the football matches, the city assembly members voted to terminate the sport in 1540.

Stark ruins of Coventry's Cathedral of St. Michael stand alongside the city's fine new cathedral. Totally destroyed in a 1940 air raid, an altar of broken stones surmounted by a charred cross stands at the eastern end of the ruins, backed by the words, "Father, forgive."

From London . . .

A DAY EXCURSION TO COVENTRY
DISTANCE BY TRAIN: 100 miles (161 km)
AVERAGE TRAIN TIME: 1 hour, 10 minutes

Explore the legend of Lady Godiva! Did she actually put everything on a horse—or has this tale, retold through the ages, changed with the telling? Was there a "Peeping Tom?" Was he late for the show? Coventry holds the answers.

Coventry is best described as a modern city with ancient roots. Among its tall office buildings, new streets and attractive shops, there is a scattering of old homes and churches, Coventry's remnants of its far-reaching past. The city was devastated in 1940 by Nazi bombers, but after careful and patient rebuilding, a bright new city emerged.

Coventry's new cathedral, consecrated in 1962, stands as visible proof that today's craftsmen can, in fact, create memorable works of supreme beauty, as did their medieval counterparts. In the new cathedral you will see outstanding examples of the finest modern works of art, including the Baptistery Window, the largest piece of modern stained glass in the world. The tapestry *Christ in Glory* hangs behind the altar. Weighing nearly a ton, it is the largest tapestry in the world; ten men worked for three years to complete it. The cathedral, open from 0900–1930 in summer, closes at 1730 in winter.

Alongside the new stands the old Cathedral of St. Michael, reduced to ruins by one dreadful air raid in November 1940. An altar of broken stones surmounted by a charred cross stands at the eastern end of the ruins, backed by the words, "Father, forgive." In the nineteenth century John Ruskin wrote, "The sand of Coventry binds itself into stone which can be built half-way to the sky." Attesting to this, the tower and spire of the old cathedral survived intact after the bombing. Built in the fifteenth century, it is the third highest spire in England. A visit to both cathedrals should not be missed.

Coventry's rail station lies outside its "ringway," a circular super highway surrounding the city. At the bus stop, you'll find a city map and information regarding Coventry's information center. Buses marked "Pool Meadow" (No. 17 or 27) will take you to the center of town in five minutes along a route that requires about twenty minutes to walk. Dismount at the shopping square by the Leofric Hotel. Lady Godiva's statue stands in a park immediately opposite the hotel, silhouetted against the spires of the cathedrals. Be certain to read the inscriptions on the east and west sides of the statue's pedestal. They were written by Alfred Tennyson, England's poet laureate.

The bus stop at the Leofric Hotel is Broadgate. The tourist information center is located at Bayley Lane and may be found via well-placed direction signs.

COVENTRY—*LADY GODIVA LAND*

A Day Excursion from London

DEPART FROM EUSTON STATION	ARRIVE IN COVENTRY STATION	NOTES
0715(5)	0827	(1)
0745(5)	0857	(1)
0845(5)	0957	(1)
0915(5)	1027	(1)
0945(5)	1057	(1)
1015(5)	1127	(1)
1045(5)	1157	(1)

(Plus other frequent service)

DEPART FROM COVENTRY STATION	ARRIVE IN EUSTON STATION	NOTES
1507	1627(3)	(1)
1537	1659(3)	(1)
1627 (1623 SUN)	1757(3)	(2)
1707	1827(3) (1845 SUN)	(1)(2)
1807	1929(3) (1943 SUN)	(1)(2)
1935	2059(3)	(1)
2037	2202 (2222 SAT)	(1)
2107	2241	(2)

(Plus other frequent service)

Note: Sunday service begins at 1445

Distance:	100 miles/161 km
References:	British Rail Tables 65 and 68
	Thomas Cook Table 540

(1) MON–SAT   (3) Arrives 10 minutes later on Saturday
(2) SUN

Train Information: 0203–555211
InterCity Services: 071–387–7070

Coventry Tourist Information Centre: 0203–832303

The center operates Monday through Friday, 0930–1700; Saturday and Sunday, 1000–1630. It remains open on bank holidays (except Christmas), 1000–1600.

Among many informative publications, be sure to acquire the *City of Coventry Mini Guide*. It contains a plan of the city's central area, along with a brief description of places of interest. It will lead you from Broadgate to a number of interesting places, including the two cathedrals. For the more ambitious visitor, a two-hour walking tour accompanied by a guide leaves the information center Saturdays at 1400. The tour passes Fords Hospital, a fine example of sixteenth-century almshouses, several sections of the remaining city wall, and Cook Street Gate, one of the twelve ancient gates erected in the fourteenth century. You will also be able to see some of Coventry's new buildings, including the Retail Market and the Belgrade Theatre. The price of the tour is £1.50 per person. When returning to the rail station, board the bus at the shelter directly in front of the Holy Trinity Church, opposite the hotel.

Lady Godiva was the wife of Leofric, the "grim" Lord of Coventry. Evidently, she bugged him about the heavy tax burdens he had levied on the townspeople. Legend says Leofric, weary of her nagging, agreed to decrease the tax rate if Her Ladyship would increase the town's morale by riding naked through its streets. Modern historians seriously doubt that Godiva made her gallop without benefit of even a riding crop. They believe her husband challenged her to ride *stripped of her finery and her jewels* and to ride humbly as one of his people and in full sight of them. Stripped of her rank—or just plain stripped—Her Ladyship *did* make the ride and taxes *were lowered*, but she commanded the people to remain indoors with windows barred. Legend says that one town resident called "Tom" unbarred his window to peep as she rode by. Before he could satisfy his gaze, he was struck blind, poor man!

In modern versions of the ride, Lady Godiva now rides her horse through Coventry wearing a body stocking—which is a considerable improvement of the event as conducted in Victorian days, when she was dressed up in petticoats.

Oddly enough, the Godiva story was told for some 500 years before the "Peeping Tom" version was added. In any case, a stunning bronze statue worthy of a *Playboy* centerfold perpetuates Her Ladyship's memory in Broadgate Park as Tom peeps out at her on the hour from the Broadgate clock. We can't help but wonder what effect Lady Godiva's ride would have on our modern-day Internal Revenue Service.

Famous white cliffs, probably Dover's best known landmark, attract thousands of sightseers. Dover Castle, standing guard atop the cliffs, boasts a fine keep, a lighthouse of Roman origin, and a church dating back to Saxon times. Dover's importance as a port began during the Roman invasion of England. Today, Dover is still a principal British maritime port for passenger traffic to and from Europe.

From London . . .

A DAY EXCURSION TO DOVER
DISTANCE BY TRAIN: 77 miles (124 km)
AVERAGE TRAIN TIME: 1 hour, 30 minutes

For centuries Dover has been one of Britain's major channel ports. In theory, this is where England ends and the Continent begins. Here is where countless Englishmen have been parted from, or united with, their homeland. Here stand the white cliffs of Dover. Below, on the beaches, the legions of the Roman Empire stormed ashore in 55 B.C., only to be repelled and to land again, successfully, at Deal.

Atop the cliffs broods Dover Castle. Initially constructed in the 1180s by Henry II to repel invaders, it has been reinforced at every threat to England's shores, including Hitler's in 1940. From its ramparts, on a clear day you can look across the twenty-one miles of the English Channel and see France. Approaching from the sea, a dramatic panorama unfolds as the white cliffs slowly rise from out of the horizon.

You cannot deny it—Dover is dramatic. Brooding hangs over it on a rainy, windswept day; grandeur surrounds it on a clear one when, for example, Boulogne in distant France becomes discernible. The deafening ramjets of the World War II German V-2 "buzz bombs" have been replaced by the humming vacuums of the hovercraft. But the screams of the gulls and the relentless crashing of the sea continue on, unchanged by time. If you are one to "stand in history," Dover becomes a must visit during your stay in Great Britain. Few other places on earth swell the imagination as do the "white cliffs of Dover."

Train service from London to Dover follows two routes. Departures from Victoria Station split destinations at Faversham. Part of the train goes to Dover, the other part to Margate and Ramsgate. As a precaution against "splitting," our schedule is based on direct train service to Dover from London's Charing Cross Station. Readers can, however, avail themselves of either rail route. As a suggestion, depart Charing Cross and return via Faversham to Victoria Station. This way, you will be "joined" by the Ramsgate train instead of being "split" by it.

Leave the train at Dover Priory Station. If you remain on the train, you could find yourself being loaded aboard a Sealink ferry for France, because the next (and last) station on the line is Dover Marine, where that sort of thing takes place. It's a short walk from Dover Priory to Townwall Street, where you will find the tourist information center next door to the Dover Moat House Motel. It's all downhill from the station and in the direction of the sea, so you may walk easily and arrive at the center in about twelve minutes.

The information center is extensive, since Dover is a major debarkation

DOVER—*ON THE WHITE CLIFFS*

A Day Excursion from London

DEPART FROM CHARING CROSS STATION	ARRIVE IN DOVER PRIORY STATION*	NOTES
0730	0917 (0928 SAT)	(1)
0830	1028	(1)
0900	1044	(2)
0930	1128	(1)
1100	1244	(2)
1130	1228	(1)
	(Plus other frequent service)	

DEPART FROM DOVER PRIORY STATION	ARRIVE IN CHARING CROSS STATION	NOTES
1550	1738	(1)
1621	1807	(2)
1651	1835	(1)
1849	2035	(1)
1921	2007	(2)
1949	2106	(1)
2107	2311	(2)
	(Plus other frequent service)	

Distance: 77 miles/124 km
References: British Rail Table 212
                   Thomas Cook Table 506

* Dover Priory is the last stop before the train arrives at the train-ferry docks for transport to Continental Europe.

(1) MON–SAT   (2) SUN

Train Information: 0732–770111
InterCity Services: 071–928–5100
Dover Tourist Information Centre: 0304–205108

point for visitors from the Continent. The center can provide information on all of Great Britain, as well as the local area. The center is open daily, 0900–1800.

Ask for information on Dover Castle and how to reach it. No doubt you will also be interested in visiting the Roman-painted house, Britain's buried Pompeii. It was discovered by an archaeological unit in 1971. Roman legions took over the structure about A.D. 300 for shore-defense purposes. It gains its name from the brilliantly painted plaster of its walls, the oldest and best preserved painted walls in Britain. Incredible as it seems, the Romans even installed an elaborate under-the-floor heating system in the house. The house is a permanent museum, open every day, except Monday, from 1000 to 1700 (April through October). Admission is £1.00 for adults and 50 pence for children.

Legend has it that if Romans are left alone long enough, they will build something. Apparently, this was the case in the second century, when the Roman legions constructed two lighthouse beacons on Dover's cliffs for the purpose of guiding their galleys into the sheltered anchorage below. The surviving lighthouse, reaching to a height of more than forty feet, is the tallest surviving Roman structure in Britain.

Dover can hardly be compared with the Continent's Riviera. Its beaches are small, tiny enclaves in the rugged face of the looming cliffs. And the height of the surf frequently becomes more than the average bather cares to contend with. Dover and its environs, however, lend themselves well to sunbathing, walking, and viewing. It is a point that more people pass through than pause to enjoy, but there is no other point in all of Britain more majestic than Dover. It is the very cornerstone of Britain.

During World War II, Dover was subjected to long-range artillery shelling from the Pas de Calais German gun emplacements. Dover's residents dug cellars deep into the cliffs as sanctuaries from the shelling. The surviving structures, most of which are small hotels, still maintain the shelters for use as wine cellars, bars, and boutiques.

Have you ever been to France? If not, now's your chance! Take the train to Folkestone, a short distance to the west of Dover. From there you can whisk across the English Channel to Calais in about fifty catamaran minutes; to Boulogne, in fifty-five minutes. Day trips from Dover to the Continent are very popular. Stock up on wine and cheese, plus a yard or so of crusty French bread during your visit, and load up with duty-free tobacco and booze on the return journey. Plan ahead by asking any train information office for information on Sealink or catamaran service.

Small boat harbor provides protected haven for Folkestone's fleet of fishing and recreational craft. As a cross-channel port, Folkestone stands second only to Dover in passenger traffic aboard Sealink vessels, which call at the city's harbor–train station pier and the Continent.

A DAY EXCURSION TO FOLKESTONE
DISTANCE BY TRAIN: 70 miles (113 km)
AVERAGE TRAIN TIME: 1 hour, 20 minutes

Folkestone is a "multiple treat" seaside resort. You may either stay within its confines for a delightful day of sightseeing and seafood, ply between Folkestone and Boulogne in France aboard Sealink, go *under* the English Channel via the Chunnel, or elect to survey the thirteen-and-one-half miles of right of way on the world's smallest public railway—the Romney, Hythe and Dymchurch Light Railroad. Each of the four options should take a full day to enjoy, so perhaps you had better plan on making several trips out of London to Folkestone during your visit—or even stay over in Folkestone for a day or two.

The Chunnel is scheduled to begin full commercial operation in mid-1995. With the British terminal at nearby Cheriton, Folkestone now has yet another attraction to offer—the Eurotunnel Exhibition Centre. The history of this exciting engineering project—one of the biggest in this century—can be followed at the center. You can see how the rail traffic through the tunnel operates. A scale model, one of the biggest N–gauge model-railway layouts ever constructed, shows the English and French terminals and the tunnel in-between in action. Check with the Folkestone tourist office or call the Eurotunnel Exhibition Centre (0303) 270111 for details. The center is closed on Monday.

With so many possibilities, we suggest that you make your way to Folkestone's tourist information center immediately on arrival. It can be reached by walking from the Folkestone Central Station down the pedestrian center to Old High Street. Sealink operates a free shuttle bus between Central Station and Harbor Station for the convenience of cross-channel passengers only. It leaves from the left of the Central Station entrance. A schedule is posted nearby explaining the shuttle-bus service, which operates 1000–2310 daily. The shuttle bus passes the information center but cannot stop until it reaches the Harbor Station, where passengers board the next outbound Sealink vessel.

The scenery along the seawall of Folkestone's outer harbor is enjoyable, to say the least. From there, you will have a commanding view of the harbor. The Sealink ferry passage to Boulogne takes one hour and fifty minutes; Hoverspeed's SeaCat catamaran service takes just fifty-five minutes. So if you are tempted to set foot on French soil, the Sealink or Hoverspeed office will provide you with current fares and schedules if you choose to cross the Channel "topside" rather than go under it. You can obtain tickets at the pier office or at the tourist information office. Fares are listed on page 65.

Folkestone has a dual distinction. As a cross-channel port, it is second only to Dover in total passenger traffic and may even surpass it when the Chunnel

FOLKESTONE—*TRADITIONAL SEASIDE RESORT*

A Day Excursion from London

DEPART FROM CHARING CROSS STATION	ARRIVE IN FOLKESTONE CENTRAL STATION*	NOTES
0730	0904	(1)
0755 (0800 SAT)	0930	(2)
0830	1016	(2)
0900	1033	(3)
1000	1129	(2)

(Plus other frequent service)

DEPART FROM FOLKESTONE CENTRAL STATION	ARRIVE IN CHARING CROSS STATION	NOTES
1601	1738	(2)
1633	1807	(3)
1703	1835	(2)
1802	1936	(2)
1833	2007	(3)
1902	2035	(2)
2033	2207	(3)
2215	2358	(2)

(Plus other frequent service)

Note: Eurostar Passenger Services schedule not available at press time.

Distance: 70 miles/113 km
References: British Rail Table 207
                    Thomas Cook Table 506

* See page 300 for Folkestone station plan.

(1) MON–FRI   (3) SUN
(2) MON–SAT

Train Information: 0732–770111 (24-hour service)
InterCity Services: 071–928–5100
Folkestone Tourist Information Centre: 0303–258594

passenger services are in full swing. For beauty of location, it probably stands second to none. The Leas, Folkestone's famous cliff-top promenade, served as an inspiration for some of H. G. Wells's finest works. It surveys the town's beach from a vantage point more than 200 feet above. From there, one can view the landscape from Dover to Dungeness. Stretching behind the Leas are the spacious, well-planned business and residential quarters.

One side of the Leas promenade is lined with large hotels, the other with hanging gardens through which winding paths lead down to the beach. A route for the less hearty is the charming one-hundred-year-old "cliff lift," which plies between the Leas promenade and the picturesque harbor area.

Below the Leas, at harbor level, lie the city's marine gardens and the busy harbor pier, an endless source of interest to visitors. There are regular guided walks organized by the White Cliffs Countryside Project (tel: 0304–241806).

The harbor area has been redeveloped extensively. Only a few of the quaint, old, narrow streets remain. Nevertheless, the area has a marked nautical flavor that sets it apart from the rest of the town. With the increased interest in sail boating, more of these small craft may be seen in the harbor. If you happen to be in the harbor area at 1300 hours on a Thursday or a Sunday, you will see the Orient Express.

Sandgate, on the western outskirts of Folkestone, has become one of the major antiques centers of England. Numerous antiques and curio shops beckon to shoppers from Sandgate's narrow High Street. Also competing for shoppers' attention are several old-world inns and the Sandgate Castle.

Trains meeting the Hoverspeed's SeaCat catamarans at the Harbor Station proceed to London via Dover and *do not stop at Folkestone Central Station.* This, of course, makes possible a circuitous train trip back to London. But it could also lead to embarrassment if you boarded a London-bound train at the Folkestone Harbor Station but had friends or family waiting to join you at the Folkestone Central Station.

A bus from the city station will take you to the town of Hythe, west of Folkestone, in about twenty-two minutes. There, the young—and those not so young—may board the fascinating Romney, Hythe and Dymchurch Light Railroad for a delightful run by steam traction to New Romney, with stops in Dymchurch and St. Mary's Bay. Service is generally every hour, so you can stop en route at Dymchurch, England's "children's paradise," or at St. Mary's Bay, where boating and fishing are two highlights of that holiday center. The RH&D Railroad terminates its service at Dungeness, another five-and-a-half miles down the RH&D "road," where you'll find great contrast between its fishermen's shacks and its atomic plant.

Gloucester Cathedral, originally of Norman design (1089-1260), was remodeled (1331–1370) to house the tomb of King Edward II. The east window of the cathedral, one of the largest in England, was erected as a memorial to those who fought for England at Crécy in 1346.

From London ...

A DAY EXCURSION TO GLOUCESTER
DISTANCE BY TRAIN: 114 miles (184 km)
AVERAGE TRAIN TIME: 1 hour, 50 minutes

Gloucester is steeped in history. First to arrive were the Romans, following their invasion of the British Isles. A legion fort was erected at the site of the present city center, and by A.D. 96–98, the Roman city of Glevum (now Gloucester) was established and flourishing. Little remains of the Roman presence in modern Gloucester. None of the Roman wall is now visible above ground, but its line is still followed by the principal streets of the city.

Although Gloucester is situated some distance from the open sea, by the construction of a ship canal in 1805, Queen Elizabeth I granted the city a charter and declared it a "port." Ocean-going ships of up to 5,000-ton capacity are able to dock at Sharpness, the terminal dock of the city's port system. The entire dock complex is being given a new "lease on life"; an ambitious redevelopment program is converting the site into a haven of recreation, education, and commerce.

The National Waterways Museum is the principal tourist attraction in the dock complex. Two hundred years of history, which shaped the fortunes of Britain, may be viewed there, housed in an imposing seven-story building. In the main basin of the dock area, you can inspect an authentic canal maintenance yard that has been re-created to display and demonstrate the traditional crafts and skills needed to operate the canals. Following this, you may ride in a horse-drawn wagon around the dockland area. The museum is open daily, 1000–1800 (1700 in winter), and admission is £3.75 for adults; children and senior citizens, £2.75.

Gloucester's showplace is, of course, its cathedral. It consists of a Norman nucleus (1089–1260) with additions in every known style of Gothic architecture. Topped by a towering fifteenth-century pinnacle that rises 225 feet above ground level, Gloucester's cathedral is judged to be one of the six most beautiful buildings in Europe. If you have a limited amount of time to spend sightseeing in Gloucester, you will make the best use of it by concentrating on the cathedral and its surroundings.

The cathedral's origins began in 679, when the Saxons founded the monastery of St. Peter on the site. In the year 909, Alfred the Great's daughter gave relics to the priory, making it the Church of St. Oswald. The cathedral is the oldest building in Gloucester. It is a magnificent example of medieval architecture with its great Norman piers still in the cathedral nave. Since the fifteenth century, craftsmen have continued to work on the structure, gracing it with an elegant exterior of later architectural designs, but basically it remains a Norman edifice.

GLOUCESTER—*ON THE RIVER SEVERN*

A Day Excursion from London

DEPART PADDINGTON STATION	ARRIVE SWINDON STATION	DEPART SWINDON STATION	ARRIVE GLOUCESTER STATION	NOTES
0740	0836	0845	0931	(1)
0845	—	—	1028	(1)
0915	1016	1054(A)	1141(A)	(2)
0930	1035	1045	1148	(4)
1100	1158	1205	1252	(3)
1125	—	—	1308	(1)

DEPART GLOUCESTER STATION	ARRIVE SWINDON STATION	DEPART SWINDON STATION	ARRIVE PADDINGTON STATION	NOTES
1522	1608	1627	1735	(2)
1617	—	—	1810	(1)
1628	—	—	1830	(4)
1748	1834	1855	2000(B)	(2)
1900	1946	1955	2105	(1)
1906	—	—	2105	(4)

Distance: 114 miles/184 km
References: British Rail Table 127
              Thomas Cook Table 529

(1) MON–FRI   (3) SAT   (A) 10 minutes later on Saturday
(2) MON–SAT   (4) SUN   (B) 15 minutes later on Saturday

Train Information: 0452–29501
InterCity Services: 071–387–7070
Gloucester Tourist Information Centre: 0452–421188

The city's tourist information center is located in St. Michael's Tower at the city's major intersection, "The Cross." Its hours of operation are 1000–1700 Monday through Saturday. City bus transportation from Gloucester's Central Station to the tourist information center requires a transfer, and the taxi fare varies.

To reach the tourist center on foot, walk toward the cathedral from the Central Station until you reach Northgate Street. Then turn left to where it intersects Eastgate Street at The Cross. Northgate and Eastgate streets take their names from the ancient city routes through the Roman wall.

Sightseeing in Gloucester has been made easy by the "Via Sacra," a walkway around the city center that follows the lines of the original city wall. It is described in several publications that are available in the information center. It can be recognized by the pattern of dark paving placed in the sidewalk to keep visitors from going too far astray. The "Via Sacra" information sheet, the "Historic Gloucester" folder, and *The Gloucester Mini Guide* brochure all describe this suggested walk in good detail and make seeing Gloucester on foot an easy accomplishment.

At the beginning of the walking tour, you can observe a considerable variety of early English architecture, ranging from fifteenth-century timber-frame structures to the Tudor facades of the present county offices. You will pass Blackfriars, the best preserved medieval Dominican friary in Britain. Although it is under restoration, a portion is open to the public. Greyfriars is also on the route. Unlike Blackfriars, however, most of it stands in ruins.

Stopping in the city museum and art gallery affords the opportunity to examine many archaeological items, including a part of the original Roman city wall. The museum is open 1000–1700 Monday through Saturday. It is also open 1000–1600 on Sunday from July through September.

The tour passes not only the old points of interest in Gloucester, but many of its new ones as well. Just beyond the city museum, for example, you will see the Eastgate Shopping Center, which provides traffic-free areas at ground level. The tour ends at the cathedral in St. Lucy's Garden, the approach to the college green.

Gloucester abounds with interesting eating establishments ranging from McDonald's to such ancient eateries as the New Inn on Northgate Street. But don't let the name fool you. The New Inn was built by St. Peter's Abbey to accommodate pilgrims in 1450. The inn courtyard was used for staging plays during the time of Queen Elizabeth I, and in the eighteenth century, the inn became renowned for its association with traveling menageries and exhibitions of "curiosities." It is said to be the finest medieval open-gallery inn in England, and the food served there today matches the excellence of its medieval decor.

Cutty Sark, built for the China tea trade, rests in dry dock at Greenwich. One of the fastest of sailing ships, she once logged 363 nautical miles in twenty-four hours! Launched at Dumbarton, Scotland, November 1869, the dry-docked ship was opened to public view by Her Majesty Queen Elizabeth II in 1957 following refit.

130

From London . . .

A DAY EXCURSION TO GREENWICH
DISTANCE BY TRAIN: 5 miles (8 km)
AVERAGE TRAIN TIME: 15 minutes

Greenwich is the cradle of Britain's maritime history and the home of time. Henry VIII and Elizabeth I were born in the Royal Palace of Greenwich. It was here that Elizabeth greeted Sir Francis Drake upon his return from sailing around the world in 1580. In 1967, Queen Elizabeth II knighted Sir Francis Chichester for his solo circumnavigation of the world at a public ceremony at the Royal Naval College, which now stands on the site of the Royal Palace.

The clipper *Cutty Sark*, one of the fastest of sailing ships, lies in dry dock at Greenwich. The world's largest maritime museum, the National Maritime Museum of Greenwich, has in its fascinating collection the paddle tug *Reliant*, often described as "the world's largest ship in a bottle." At the Old Royal Observatory, visitors can stand astride the strip marking the Prime Meridian for Greenwich Mean Time (GMT), with one foot in an east longitude and the other one in west longitude. If time permits, you can walk *under* the Thames River to the Isle of Dogs and treat yourself to a panoramic view of Greenwich from that vantage point. Greenwich has much to offer.

Upon arrival in the Greenwich railway station, use the pedestrian subway (underpass) to the main station and the street. Turn left and walk along the road into the town. Follow the signs guiding you to the National Maritime Museum and the *Cutty Sark*. Where they split, continue to follow the CUTTY SARK signs until the ship's masts come into view. The local Greenwich information center is just before the entrance of the *Cutty Sark* Gardens at 46 Greenwich Church Street. The center is open 1015–1645 daily throughout the year. Of the various publications available, we recommend the brochure, *Greenwich Visitors' Guide*.

The *Cutty Sark* was launched in 1869 and served in the China tea trade, as well as the Australian wool trade. Her curious name, which means "short chemise," originated in "Tam o'Shanter," a poem by Robert Burns in which the witch Nanny appeared in a *cutty sark*. The ship's figurehead represents the witch Nanny.

A short distance away stands the fifty-four-foot ketch, *Gypsy Moth*, which Sir Francis Chichester sailed solo around the world. Sir Francis sailed from Plymouth on 27 August 1966. He completed his circumnavigation of the world on 28 May 1967, when he sailed into Plymouth harbor to a tumultuous welcome. In his voyage, he covered a distance of 28,500 miles.

While at Greenwich, you can take the opportunity of viewing it from the Island Gardens on the Isle of Dogs, located on the opposite bank of the River Thames. To get there, take the Greenwich foot tunnel under the river. It takes

GREENWICH — *ON THE PRIME MERIDIAN*

A Day Excursion from London

DEPART FROM CHARING CROSS STATION	ARRIVE IN GREENWICH STATION	NOTES
0812	0826	(3)
0823	0840	(1)
0844	0901	(1)
0913	0929	(1)
0942	0957	(1)
0957	1011	(4)

Additional trains depart at fourteen and forty-four minutes past the hour through 1944.

DEPART FROM GREENWICH STATION	ARRIVE IN CHARING CROSS STATION	NOTES
1531	1548	(2)
1608	1626	(2)
1731	1748	(3)
1830	1845	(4)

Additional trains depart at eight and thirty-eight minutes past the hour through 2338.

Plus frequent service serving Waterloo (East), as well as Cannon Street station.

Distance: 7 miles/11 km
References: British Rail Table 200

(1) MON–FRI	(3) SAT
(2) MON–SAT	(4) SUN

For a circuitous rail trip to or from Greenwich, inquire regarding The Docklands Light Railway (DLR) running between its London terminals, Tower Gateway or Bank, and the Island Gardens Station on the Isle of Dogs, with access to Greenwich via the foot tunnel under the Thames. Information is available by ringing up (071) 918–4000. *BritRail Pass not accepted.* One-way fare, Tower Gateway to Island Gardens, adults £1.10; children under sixteen, 60 pence. The London Underground station, Tower Hill on the District Line, is within walking distance of the DLR's Tower Gate terminal.

Train Information: 071–928–5100

only about four minutes to walk through the tunnel to the opposite bank. From this vantage point, it is possible to photograph the entire Greenwich complex. The domed entrance to the tunnel lies in front of the *Cutty Sark*.

A few yards beyond the *Cutty Sark*'s stern is the entrance to the Royal Naval College. Built on the original site of the old Tudor Palace at Greenwich during the seventeenth-century reign of William and Mary, the present buildings were used as a hospital for disabled and aged naval pensioners. In 1873, it became the Royal Naval College to provide for the higher education of naval officers.

Visitors are admitted to the Royal Naval College's Painted Hall and Chapel daily except Thursday from 1430 to 1700. (Admission is free.) The Painted Hall is now used as the officers' mess of the college. After the Battle of Trafalgar, the body of Lord Nelson lay in state in the Upper Hall. The interior decorating, by Sir James Thornhill, took nineteen years to complete. (You'll find out why when you see it.) Benjamin West's painting of the shipwrecked *St. Paul* in the college chapel is one of the highlights of that beautiful structure.

There is an admission charge for the *Cutty Sark* and the National Maritime Museum. To reach the museum, turn left on King William walk, leaving the Naval College. Walk past the Seamen's Hospital to Romney Road. Cross it and turn left. The museum entrance is a few yards beyond. The National Maritime Museum tour leads you through its west wing where you can view the *Reliant* and the state barges once used on the River Thames. The museum houses an amazing display of old ship models and features naval history of the nineteenth and twentieth centuries. Also included are two galleries of Victorian paintings and Arctic exploration exhibits.

Adjacent to the National Maritime Museum stands The Queen's House, a royal villa from the time of Charles I. Reopened by Queen Elizabeth II in May 1990, the palace has been restored to its former glory with sumptuous furnishings and rich silk hangings reflective of its heyday when Henrietta Maria, wife of Charles I, was in residence there. It is the earliest example of English Palladian architecture. The admission charge is £3.95.

In Greenwich Park, next to the museum, you may enter the Old Royal Observatory, an integral part of the museum. There is an admission charge of £3.95. The Prime Meridian marking the line of zero degrees longitude on which GMT (Greenwich Mean Time) is calculated is located in the courtyard of the observatory's meridian building.

Hastings Castle beckons to visitors from atop the city's west hill, where it was built by William the Conqueror in 1067 following the Battle of Hastings the previous year. Among the castle ruins, you'll find an eleventh-century siege tent. Enter and you will be transported back to the most famous date in English history—1066! Below the fortress in the old city's narrow streets are many eighteenth-century houses. (Courtesy Tourism and Leisure Department, Hastings/Chris Parker)

A DAY EXCURSION TO HASTINGS
DISTANCE BY TRAIN: 63 miles (101 km)
AVERAGE TRAIN TIME: 1 hour, 30 minutes

Undoubtedly, 1066 is one of the most well-known dates in history. When dusk fell at the field of Senlac near Hastings on 14 October 1066, William the Conqueror, Duke of Normandy, had defeated the Saxon army of slain King Harold and had become the new king of England. Hastings holds the lore of the Battle of Hastings plus the lure of its ancient fishing village and Norman castle.

In addition to its rich historical heritage, Hastings has been an attractive seaside resort since the mid-eighteenth century, when London physicians began prescribing sea air and saltwater as a panacea for all their patients' ills. Three miles of promenades line its beaches, many of them two-tiered with sun-trapped shelters overlooking the English Channel. Sun is more sought after in Hastings than surf because the water is very cold. Examine any photo of an English seaside resort and you'll see that the majority of the bathers are on the beach, not in the sea!

There are four railway stations within the Borough of Hastings. Use the Hastings Central Station as a focal point. The tourist information center is at 5 Robertson Terrace. Leaving the Central Station, walk downhill to the seaside and orient yourself on Carlisle Parade. The information center is on the west end. The office operates Monday through Friday, 1000–1700; Saturday, 1000–1300. The sign on the center entrance reads TOURIST INFORMATION. During summer, the center is open longer hours during the week and on Sunday as well.

Contrary to popular belief, the Battle of Hastings was not fought in Hastings, nor was the Norman castle in Hastings involved. After landing, the Norman army marched northward about six miles, where they engaged the Saxons on the field of Senlac. The castle in Hastings, formerly a timber fort, was converted to stone in 1067, a year after the battle.

Harold's troops were not pushovers. Nineteen days prior to the Battle of Hastings, his men had put a Norse army to rout at Stamford Bridge near York. In the initial onslaught at Senlac, the Normans retreated with the Saxons in hot pursuit. In so doing, the Saxons had to break the tight formation of their Saxon wall of shields, and the Norman cavalry quickly took advantage of the hole opening up in the line and inflicted heavy losses upon the Saxons. This tactic was twice repeated and the conflict ended. Today's Super Bowl tactics may have developed in Hastings! To go sightseeing at the battleground, board any "Battle Abbey" bus.

During the Roman occupation, Hastings was one of the famous Cinque

HASTINGS—*FAMOUS BATTLE SITE*

A Day Excursion from London

DEPART FROM CHARING CROSS STATION	ARRIVE IN HASTINGS STATION	NOTES
0810	0937 (0947 SUN)	(3)(4)
0815	0943	(1)
0910	1038	(2)(4)
1010	1139	(2)(4)
1110	1238	(2)(4)
1210	1338	(2)(4)

DEPART FROM HASTINGS STATION	ARRIVE IN CHARING CROSS STATION	NOTES
1610	1755	(2)
1652	1822	(2)
1711	1851 (1901 SUN)	(3)
1740	1921	(1)
1752	1921	(3)
1811	1954	(2)(4)
1911	2051 (2101 SUN)	(2)(4)
2111	2257	(4)

Distance: 63 miles/101 km
References: British Rail Table 206
                  Thomas Cook Table 501

(1) MON–FRI   (3) SAT
(2) MON–SAT   (4) SUN

Train Information: 0732–770111
InterCity Services: 071–928–5100

Hastings Tourist Information Centre: 0424–718888

(five) Ports where the caesars moored their galleys. Later in history, however, the harbor was silted up by a series of violent storms, culminating with the great tempest in 1287. As a result, Hastings was reduced to the status of a small fishing community during the following four centuries.

The tourist information center has an excellent brochure entitled "Hastings 1066 Country." With it in hand, you can easily visit the Norman castle via the West Hill lift. After visiting the castle, venture a few more paces to St. Clement's Caves for the "Smugglers' Adventure." The Smugglers' Adventure is set in a labyrinth of caverns and secret passageways beneath West Hill, where the smugglers are brought to life.

After drinking in the panoramic sights from atop the hill, you can drift back toward the sea and Hastings' "Old Town." On Hill Street, observe the two cannonballs on either side of St. Clements Church belfry. The right one was shot into the tower by the French; the one on the left was added by the locals to balance things off.

The French artillery attack in 1337 also leveled the All Saints Church in the Old Town. Undaunted by the French shelling, the locals got busy and re-erected the church in 1436. The interior of the church contains a well-preserved fifteenth-century mural depicting the Last Judgment, with the devil casting souls into hell. The mural was intended to portray a lesson in morality for illiterate people of the Middle Ages. Today, television is utilized for the same purpose.

You'll pass many interesting points on your walk. Stop for a closer examination of the Old Town Hall on High Street. It is now a museum. Drop by the Stables Theatre opposite the Old Town Hall. It originally served as the stables for the Old Hastings House, which was spared demolition by being converted into a cultural center. Your next stop should be the Shovells, circa 1450, reputedly the oldest house in town. If you're desperate for a libation, you might try the Stag Inn opposite the Shovells, where remains of mummified cats and rats decorate the bar. Nearing the end of the Old Town walk, you will pass an unusual wedge-shaped house called the "piece of cheese," no doubt the funniest house in town. If you have time, head out on Rock-A-Nore Road to Hastings Sea Life Centre and take an incredible 3-D voyage from outer space to the depths of the earth's seas.

Don't miss the 243-foot embroidery in Hastings' town hall on Queens Road. It depicts eighty-one of the greatest events of British history since 1066, including the Battle of Hastings, the Boston Tea Party, and the first television broadcast.

The city of Hastings celebrates the famous battle every year by staging a program of events and attractions over a full week, encompassing the fourteenth day of October, to commemorate the battle day in 1066.

Station Hotel is a relatively new addition to Ipswich, considering the city was chartered in A.D. 1200. The hotel stands opposite the town's rail station, and its memorabilia of railroading provide a pleasant decor for luncheon, dinner, or a pint of ale while waiting for your train.

A DAY EXCURSION TO IPSWICH
DISTANCE BY TRAIN: 63 miles (101 km)
AVERAGE TRAIN TIME: 1 hour, 10 minutes

The architecture of Ipswich reflects its history. By-passed by the Romans, this town does not display the former grandeur of Rome. A seafaring community long before King John granted the town's first charter in 1200, Ipswich has always been engaged in commerce and has risen or declined along with the fortunes of its citizens' enterprises. The lack of Georgian buildings in Ipswich is evidence of the town's decline during that period, caused by the loss of its famous Suffolk cloth trade. A revitalization of its harbor by the mid-nineteenth century brought new prosperity to Ipswich and accounts for the number of splendid public buildings erected then, as well as the Victorian architecture of its homes.

Ipswich has withstood the onslaughts of the Vikings and other seaborne raiders down through the ages. Starting with World War I, the town's docks became the targets of a new type of raider coming from the sky rather than from the sea. From 1915 to the end of the conflict, there were a number of zeppelin attacks, but damage was light. During the years 1943–45, Ipswich was rimmed by no fewer than sixty-five air bases of the U.S. Eighth Air Force, from which were launched a staggering 3,000-plus bomber raids against the Third Reich.

Today, with a population of 120,000, Ipswich has a developing port and is an important industrial and commercial center with fine shopping, sports, and entertainment facilities. Ipswich considers its Tudor Christchurch Mansion, set in sixty-five acres of parkland, only a five-minute walk from the center of town, to be its finest attraction. The information office will gladly point out the way to you.

The tourist information center is easy to reach. It is located in St. Stephen's Church on Falcon Street. Departing the rail station proceed straight ahead down Princes Street to Friars Street and turn right. Friars Street curves and turns into Falcon Street. St. Stephen's Church will be on your left. If the weather is inclement, catch the "City Centre" bus or hail a taxi immediately in front of the station. Obtain a map at the information center before going off to explore the endless streets and enticing alleyways leading off Ipswich's Cornhill. Office hours are 0900–1700 Monday through Saturday, closed Sunday.

The town's Leisure Services Department has devised the excellent brochure *Tourist Town Trail.* The trail is signposted by black-and-white signs that are numbered to correspond with the descriptions in the brochure. No

IPSWICH—*CHARTERED IN A.D. 1200*

A Day Excursion from London

DEPART FROM LIVERPOOL STREET STATION	ARRIVE IN IPSWICH STATION	NOTES
0800	0900 (0924 SAT)	(2)
0830	0934	(2)
0850	1036	(4)
0930	1036	(2)
1000	1122	(2)
1010	1148	(4)
1030	1134	(2)
1130	1234	(2)

DEPART FROM IPSWICH STATION	ARRIVE IN LIVERPOOL STREET STATION	NOTES
1445	1552 (1611 SUN)	(2)(4)
1545	1652	(2)
1645	1758 (1811 SUN)	(2)(4)
1745	1853	(2)
1845	1952	(2)
1945	2050	(1)
2000	2158	(3)
2025	2158	(4)

Distance: 69 miles/111 km
References: British Rail Table 11
Thomas Cook Table 580

(1) MON–FRI	(3) SAT
(2) MON–SAT	(4) SUN

Train Information: 0473–690744
InterCity Services: 071–928–5100
Ipswich Tourist Information Centre: 0473–258070

doubt the trail was laid out for British walkers, for it is much too ambitious a course for the average Yank to complete within the prescribed period of one hour—at least it was for us! The route is circular, so you can join (or leave) at any point.

Places along the Tourist Town Trail that may be of interest to you include the junction of Butter Market, St. Stephens Lane, and Dial Lane. As you can probably guess, the Butter Market was once a marketplace for many products, one of which was butter. If you enter the Ancient House in the Butter Market, you'll be reminded of its age (more than 500 years old), for its windows represent the known world during its time—and Australia is missing because it had not yet been discovered. A seventeenth-century merchant, Robert Sparrow, added the exquisite, ornate plasterwork to the exterior.

Dial Lane is a traffic-free pedestrian area that gets its name from a clock that was once on the St. Lawrence Church. Although most of the church dates back to the fifteenth and early sixteenth centuries, its tower was rebuilt in 1882 to reflect its original design.

By passing the church and turning left into St. Lawrence Street and then right into Tavern Street, you'll come upon the Great White Horse Hotel. It is the only surviving inn that can be traced in the city records before 1571. Its Georgian brick facade, completed in 1818, covers a basically timber-frame structure from the sixteenth century. A young London news reporter, sent to Ipswich to cover an election, stayed in the Great White Horse and later wrote his recollections in a comic novel that changed the course of his life. The reporter was Charles Dickens; the novel, *The Pickwick Papers*.

Near the end of your walking tour, take time to pause at the junction of Tavern Street and Dial Lane. The view down Dial Lane to the Ancient House is one of the most photographed areas in Ipswich. The Tudor-style buildings reflect the detail and attention of the city's craftsmen. From this point, a left turn will take you to the Cornhill, the end of your Tourist Town Trail walk.

As you stand at Cornhill, it may be sobering to consider that only 400 years ago, nine people were burned at the stake on this hill for heresy. Before becoming too sober, however, we suggest you visit one of the bars in the Great White Horse Hotel. Distinguished visitors of the past, who, besides Charles Dickens, included such notables as King George II, Louis XVIII, and Lord Nelson, have quaffed many a draft there. A toast to these gentlemen would seem only proper. So have a go at it, mate, if you can get there before they call "time!"

Thatched roofs of Shanklin's old village area attract visitors to the resort town where poet John Keats once resided.

Hovercraft skims between the mainland and the Isle of Wight, augmenting catamaran service between Portsmouth and Ryde for residents and holiday makers on England's vacation isle.

A DAY EXCURSION TO THE ISLE OF WIGHT
DISTANCE BY TRAIN: 88 miles (142 km)
AVERAGE TRAIN TIME: 2 hours, 40 minutes

"Britain's miniature" is a term often employed to describe the Isle of Wight. Shaped like a diamond, the island is a veritable jewel of every feature of the mainland condensed into a mere 147 square miles. It is dotted with historic spots, sandy beaches, thatched villages, rolling countryside—and discotheques, too, if that's your pleasure. There is fun for everyone on the Isle of Wight, and getting there can be fun, too.

The majority of trains departing Waterloo Station in London for Portsmouth Harbor are InterCity trains. As they glide through the scenery of southern England bound for the coast, you'll be treated to a delightful kaleidoscope of England's landscape from the wide-vision train windows. Stay aboard when the train halts briefly in the Portsmouth and Southsea Station. Your destination is the Portsmouth Harbor Station, five minutes farther on.

Board the Portsmouth-Ryde catamaran at the end of the harbor station. Your BritRail Pass does not cover the passage. The fare is about £5.40 one way. The crossing takes only about fifteen minutes.

Docking at the Ryde pier head, you have three options of sightseeing on the island by train. The trains, by the way, run right onto the pier and look every bit like those of the Bakerloo Underground Line in London. All the coaches are one class, but try to select one with ventilators at the top of the windows. It can get a bit stuffy aboard the train in summer. The three options? They are Ryde, Sandown, or Shanklin. All three lie along the nine miles of track extending from the Ryde pier head to the terminal in Shanklin.

Ryde is the Isle of Wight's gateway. Set picturesquely on a hillside, it becomes a wonderful grandstand from which to watch the great ships of the world sailing by. The pier at Ryde is more than 2,300 feet long, so board the train after disembarking from the passenger ferry and ride the train to its first stop, Ryde Esplanade, where you will find a tourist information kiosk ready to assist you during summer season. The pier has a pedestrian walk, if you elect to make your way to the shore in a more leisurely manner. Ryde has six miles of sandy beach backed by pleasant, wooded gardens. The town is also noted for its Regency and Victorian buildings and for its Royal Victoria Arcade shopping center.

Sandown is the next railway stop after passing the Brading Station. It has all the facilities for a summer holiday, including a new pier complex that offers a modern theater, licensed bars, cafés, and a restaurant. The theater offers a musical review, which opens in May and runs through the beginning

ISLE OF WIGHT — *THE HOLIDAY ISLAND*

A Day Excursion from London*

DEPART FROM WATERLOO STATION	ARRIVE IN SHANKLIN STATION	NOTES
0715	0945	(3)
0723	0945	(1)
0815	1045	(2)
0825	1107	(4)
0915	1145	(2)
0925	1206	(4)

DEPART FROM SHANKLIN STATION	ARRIVE IN WATERLOO STATION	NOTES
1552	1838 (A)	(2)
1625	1855	(4)
1652	1935 (A)	(2)
1752	2033 (A)	(2)
1832	2136	(1)
1912	2155	(4)

Distance: 88 miles/142 km
References: British Rail Table 167
                  Thomas Cook Table 504
(Above service through September 25. Inquire in station for off-season schedules.)

* Via ferry service between Portsmouth-Ryde to Shanklin on the Isle of Wight. One-class service between Portsmouth Harbor and Shanklin. Buffet and bar service is available en route. BritRail Pass *not* accepted on ferry crossing. Purchase tickets at pier.

(1) MON–FRI	(3) SAT	(A) Arrives at 32 minutes past the hour
(2) MON–SAT	(4) SUN	on Saturdays

Catamaran service between Portsmouth/Southsea and Ryde runs frequently throughout the day. Purchase tickets at pier.

Shanklin Tourist Information Centre
0983–862942

of October. The sheltered Sandown Bay has more than five miles of attractive, sandy beaches, where you may find such diversions as miniature golf and a canoe lake. Motor-launch trips are popular. Check at the pier or the tourist information center on the esplanade for details.

Sandown and Shanklin are considered the twin resorts on the Isle of Wight. Because the distance between the two rail stations is exactly two miles, you should select one or the other for your day excursion. There is much to see and do in either resort.

Shanklin frequently holds the British annual sunshine record. It is built on a cliff with a sheltered mile-long beach lying below. It is the end of the line for rail travel. It is easy, however, to transfer to the buses operated by the island's bus company, Southern Vectis, for farther points such as Ventnor, Newport, and Cowes. Check with the Southern Vectis Travel Office on Regent Street, two blocks from Shanklin's train station.

Our personal selection of the Isle's options would be Shanklin. It is certainly one of the prettiest towns in Britain. Shanklin's Old Village on Ventnor Road is world-famous for its quiet beauty. From there, you may descend to Shanklin's beach esplanade via a walk through Shanklin's Chine, a cleft in the town's cliff with overhanging trees, plants, ferns, and a cascading stream. Passage through the Chine costs £1.10 for adults; for children, 50 pence. Check first with the town's information center at 67 High Street for all details.

One of the most gifted and appealing of England's nineteenth-century poets, John Keats, found Shanklin's climate congenial to his health and the town's scenic beauty so inspiring that he resided there for a long period of time. Keats Green, a spacious promenade on the cliff top of Shanklin, commemorates his loving association with the town.

Queen Victoria spent her holidays on the Isle of Wight and died there in Osborne House in 1901. This house, built by order of the queen in 1845, is maintained in good order with the queen's furniture still in place. In a shed on the Osborne House property, you can see the gardening tools of the royal children from more than a century ago. Each tool and wheelbarrow is marked with the small owners' initials. The Queen and Prince Albert used Osborne as a country residence, and it is said that the prince had a considerable influence on the design of the residence. The main rooms and many of the private apartments are open to the public between Easter Monday and early October. Situated at East Cowes, which is the northern one of the island's twin peaks, you can reach the Osborne House by bus from Ryde Esplanade Station.

Checker-work front graces the fifteenth-century Trinity Guidhall, located between the Victorian town hall and the sixteenth-century Old Gaol House, in King's Lynn. It houses an eighteenth-century card room and assembly rooms.

From London ...

A DAY EXCURSION TO KING'S LYNN
DISTANCE BY TRAIN: 97 miles (156 km)
AVERAGE TRAIN TIME: 2 hours, 5 minutes

King's Lynn, once "Bishops' Lynn" and renamed when Henry VIII took over the bishop's manor, is one of the most historic towns in England. The old section of town still seems medieval, complete with narrow streets, guildhalls, and riverside quays, where the gulls reel and scream overhead. The town's former prosperity has left it with a rich heritage of architecture. Set along the east bank of the wide and muddy Ouse River, King's Lynn is the northern terminal of the London-Cambridge-Ely rail line.

King's Lynn came into being during the eleventh century on the middle of three islands, where four streams ran into the Ouse River. Water highways became vital to the commerce of the town. With these waterway connections to the English Midlands, the town of Lynn became an important trading port, bustling with the romance of foreign cargoes, sailing ships, and foreign accents. By the thirteenth century, the town found prosperity in the wool trade between England and the Continent. This aura of a wealthy medieval town still prevails. Today, the town is a thriving, modern port, an essential link between Britain and the rest of the Common Market.

Streets and alleyways in King's Lynn twist and wind about on a grand scale, so a town map will be an invaluable aid. We suggest you make your way immediately from the train station to the King's Lynn Heritage Centre and Tourist Information Centre. To do so, walk directly away from the front of the train station (which faces the west) down Waterloo Street. The street undergoes a name change at every intersection—Market, Paradise, New Conduit, Purfleet—but if one continues walking toward the west, one will come to King Street. Turn left onto King Street, which immediately becomes Queen Street. But don't despair—the tourist information center is a mere 200 yards away on the lefthand side in the Old Gaol House in Saturday Market Place.

You will be tempted to wander about in Queen Street with its lovely merchants' houses, each with a character all its own. Proceed to the information center and equip yourself with a copy of the *King's Lynn Town Walk* booklet. With it, you'll know where you are. The information center operates on a variety of schedules. We suggest that you telephone ahead: (0553) 763044. Walking from the train station to the town hall takes about ten minutes.

The previously mentioned town-walk booklet is a masterpiece of simplicity. It is packed with facts about the town and its buildings. The trail follows a circular route, so you may start and finish wherever it is most convenient for

147

KING'S LYNN—*RICH IN ARCHITECTURE*

A Day Excursion from London

DEPART FROM KING'S CROSS STATION	ARRIVE IN KING'S LYNN STATION	NOTES
0652	0853	(1)
0743	0935	(2)
0845	1021	(1)
0911(5)	1116	(4)
0945	1126	(2)

DEPART FROM KING'S LYNN STATION	ARRIVE IN KING'S CROSS STATION	NOTES
1605	1749	(2)
1718	1910	(4)
1805	1946	(3)
1909	2046	(1)
1918	2110	(4)
1942	2137	(2)
2042	2239	(2)

Distance: 97 miles/156 km
References: British Rail Table 22
                   Thomas Cook Table 581

(1) MON–FRI   (4) SUN
(2) MON–SAT   (5) Departs from Liverpool Street station
(3) SAT

Train Information: 0553–772021
InterCity Services: 071–928–5100

King's Lynn Tourist Information Centre: 0553–763044

you. We suggest starting at the town hall, which was rebuilt in 1421 after a fire. There is an admission charge to view its treasury. There you will see the magnificent King John Cup and the Red Register, purported to be one of the oldest books in the world.

A focal point in King's Lynn is the Tuesday Market Place, into which King Street leads. True to tradition, a country market is conducted there every Tuesday in the shadow of the Duke's Head Hotel, a most impressive seventeenth-century structure. The market is everything that one would expect it to be—stalls packed with the agricultural and manufacturing products of the area, augmented by absolutely free entertainment as the hucksters bid for attention.

If you miss the Tuesday market, there's another one on Saturday at a location appropriately named the Saturday Market Place. It is just opposite the town hall. A newer shopping center has been established in the center of town, on the site of the old cattle market, which was moved to one of the industrial estates outside of the town.

Visit St. George's Guild Hall at 27 King Street. It's the largest surviving medieval guild hall. When not in use as a theater, it is open Monday through Friday, 1000–1700, and 1000–1230 on Saturday. Built about 1410, it has been used as a theater, a court house, and an armory, and it is now a cultural center housing a theater and an art gallery.

King John, who ruled England between 1199 and 1216, granted the town its charter in 1204. The king came to Lynn in October 1215 in pursuit of rebellious barons. One story relates that after he was wined and dined by the burghers of Lynn, the king and his entourage set off in hot pursuit of the baronial rebels. Heading west out of King's Lynn towards Newark, the king and his entourage crossed the Norfolk tidal flats, where the River Ouse empties into The Wash, a shallow bay known for the treachery of its tides.

During the crossing, a high tide from The Wash wiped out the king's baggage train. King John reached the safety of higher shores, but he lost the crown jewels and everything else that went with such a collection in those days. King John was so distraught that he contracted dysentery (a bad "burger" perhaps?) and died a few days later. No one questioned the burghers as to exactly what they fed the king before he left Lynn. We have our suspicions, however, because reportedly all of the burghers felt fine the following morning.

The lost treasure has never been found. Somewhere near King's Lynn, buried under centuries of silt, lies King John's treasure. None of it has been recovered, and no one knows where to look for it. If you have any ideas, perhaps Robert Stack from television's *Unsolved Mysteries* show would be interested.

Magnificent Lincoln Cathedral has withstood fire, earthquakes—even Cromwell's artillery. Each of its three towers had a lofty spire, but because one fell during a storm in 1547, the other two were removed in 1807.

A DAY EXCURSION TO LINCOLN
DISTANCE BY TRAIN: 135 miles (217 km)
AVERAGE TRAIN TIME: 2 hours, 10 minutes

Lincoln's landmark is its cathedral. It stands on a ridge overlooking the city. Dominating the skyline, the cathedral appears as though it might be half church, half stronghold. There are actually two Lincolns—one, the cathedral and castle standing politely on the hilltop; the other, the city below girding the River Witham and buzzing with commerce. We suggest you scale the heights first and later return to the lower level by a dizzy descent down Steep Hill.

On arrival in Lincoln's Central Station, go to the city bus station, which is in front and to the right of the main station entrance (use the designated pedestrian walkways, because the vehicular traffic can be heavy at times). From the bus station, take city bus 1, 8, or 9 up the hill to the cathedral and ask the driver to let you off at the corner of Eastgate and Castle Square. The tourist information center is at No. 9 Castle Hill.

On the other hand, if you abound with energy, bear to the left when leaving the station and walk a short distance on Mary Street to where it intersects with High Street. Turn right at this point, and, keeping the cathedral in sight, start walking in its direction up High Street. Disregard the fact that the street changes names several times. When you reach an area where a ski lift or a cable car would be most welcome, you'll be on Steep Hill—and it's appropriately named. Now gain the high ground (and your breath), and you will find yourself in Castle Square. With a right turn at the Exchequer Gate, you may enter the cathedral grounds.

Walking up the Lincoln ridge from the railway station to the cathedral can give one a sense of accomplishment. It can also be hazardous to your health. Use discretion—take the bus or a taxi if there's any doubt in your mind about the climb.

Walking or riding up Steep Hill, you will pass the House of Aaron the Jew, a money lender from the twelfth century who reportedly became the richest man in England at that time. Halfway up Steep Hill, and turning off at Danesgate, your visit will be well rewarded by an inspection of the Usher Gallery. You can view an assortment of personal property belonging to England's poet laureate, Alfred, Lord Tennyson, born in a Lincoln suburb in 1809. The gallery also houses an extensive collection of paintings by Peter de Wint (1784–1849). Should you arrive at Castle Square in need of lunch or a libation, seek out the Wig & Mitre, a licensed restaurant with a Dickensian atmosphere.

The tourist center atop Lincoln's ridge is between the castle and the cathe-

LINCOLN—*HILLTOP CATHEDRAL*

A Day Excursion from London

DEPART KING'S CROSS STATION	ARRIVE LINCOLN CENTRAL STATION	NOTES
0700	0919	(1)(5)
0810	1005	(3)(5)
0910	1110	(2)(5)
1010	1236	(4)(5)
1030	1310	(1)(6)
1110	1313	(2)(5)
1210	1504	(2)(6)
1210	1448	(4)(5)

DEPART LINCOLN CENTRAL STATION	ARRIVE KING'S CROSS STATION	NOTES
1500	1743	(4)(5)
1524	1731	(2)(5)
1657	1912	(3)(5)
1717	1957	(1)(5)
1858	2111	(3)(5)
1915	2143	(4)(5)
2032	2259	(2)(5)
2104	2333	(4)(5)

Distance: 135 miles/217 km
References: British Rail Table 30
             Thomas Cook Tables 569 and 570

Note: All trains are standard class only.

(1) MON–FRI   (4) SUN
(2) MON–SAT   (5) Change trains in Newark Northgate
(3) SAT   (6) Change trains in Peterborough

Train Information: 0302–340222
InterCity Services: 071–387–7070

Lincoln Tourist Information Centre
0522–529828

dral. This office is open 0900–1730, except Friday, when it closes a half hour earlier. On Saturday and Sunday, it is open 1000–1700 in the summer and 1100–1500 in winter. There is a wealth of information available in both offices. The *Official Guide, City of Lincoln,* is published by the Lincoln City Council and is worth its purchase price. There is an abundance of other saleable and free literature available as well.

The cathedral is the main point of interest in Lincoln. When you view its exterior and examine the spacious areas under its roof, it becomes rather difficult to comprehend that it was built by medieval craftsmen in only twenty years. The Normans began construction of the cathedral in 1072. In 1141 the roof was destroyed by a fire, and in 1185, the main structure crumbled into ruins as a result of an earthquake. But it survived.

Reconstruction, which began in 1186, returned the cathedral to its original conforms, and, through the ensuing centuries, it was altered frequently. The central tower was completed around 1311. In more modern times, Lincoln's greatest attraction has withstood Cromwell's artillery and Hitler's bombs. If you have but a short period of time to visit in Lincoln, the cathedral *must* take priority over all else. In the summer, the cathedral is open 0715–2000 weekdays and 0715–1800 Sunday. In the winter, it closes at 1800 weekdays and at 1700 on Sunday. A contribution of £2.50 for adults and 50 pence for children is appreciated.

Lincoln Castle was built by William the Conqueror in 1068. It became the Normans' military stronghold in the area. Its construction is unusual in that it has two mounds: one crowned by the twelfth century Tower of Lucy, the other with Norman structures on which in the nineteenth century an observatory tower was constructed. From either of these points of vantage, there are beautiful views of the cathedral and the surrounding countryside. Today the Lincoln Castle is a huge, walled enclosure of lawns and trees. The crown courts and the old county jail are located in the castle yard. On permanent exhibition is one of only four surviving originals of King John's Magna Carta.

If you wish to visit the "other Lincoln," start by descending (or plunging down) Steep Hill with its bow-fronted shops until you again reach High Street. You will find interest in the twelfth-century High Bridge, which crosses the River Witham. It is the oldest one in Britain to still carry a building on its structure, in this case, a sixteenth-century timber-framed house. The route leading from the cathedral down Steep Hill is studded with other interesting structures such as numerous public houses and restaurants. Modern Lincoln blends easily with its historical counterparts.

Ye Olde Trip to Jerusalem, one of Britain's oldest inns, crouches on the hillside below Nottingham Castle. It was so named because many crusaders stayed at the inn before setting off for the crusades. Its chimney, which runs about sixty feet through solid rock, is swept once every thirty years.

154

From London ...

A DAY EXCURSION TO NOTTINGHAM
DISTANCE BY TRAIN: 127 miles (204 km)
AVERAGE TRAIN TIME: 2 hours

Nottingham is famous for many things, among them the legend of Robin Hood. Many tales of Robin and his band of merry men have been passed down through the ages by ballad and legend, though only scattered fragments remain of his origin. It appears that one Robert Fitzooth, reputed to be the Earl of Huntingdon, was born in 1160 during the reign of Henry II. Of noble birth, he squandered his inheritance at an early age; so either by necessity or by choice, he sought refuge in the forest. Here he was joined by men in similar circumstances, such as Little John, Will Scarlet, Friar Tuck, and—to add the love-interest angle to the legend—Maid Marian.

Robin Hood reigned in the forest, defying the powers of government, protecting the poor, and giving to the needy. The king's deer provided food and the king's forest provided fuel. Other necessities were obtained through barter. Taking the king's property was, of course, illegal and it drove the Sheriff of Nottingham "bananas," to the point where he offered a substantial reward for Robin's capture—dead or alive. Robin Hood eluded capture and supposedly lived to be eighty-seven years old. Records show his death occurred on 18 November 1247. This man, who lived in an age of feudal tyranny, endeared himself to countless generations and became the legendary hero of Nottingham. A fine statue to his memory stands in the courtyard of Nottingham Castle. Perhaps in the future there will be one of Kevin Costner, too.

Nottingham is also famous for its lace. For centuries it has been the center for lace making in England. The ale that Robin Hood quaffed so copiously is still a local specialty. Why not quaff some yourself in England's oldest inn, Ye Olde Trip to Jerusalem? It has been in Nottingham since 1189 waiting for you. A portion of the inn was dug into the almost vertical rock formation supporting Nottingham Castle above. Legend has it that Robin Hood scaled this rock in his invasions of Nottingham Castle.

The castle was built as a fortress in 1068 by William the Conqueror. It was destroyed during the English civil war, rebuilt, and again destroyed by an angry mob in 1831. Following its second restoration, the castle was transformed into a museum and art gallery late in the nineteenth century. There are a series of underground passages beneath the castle. Naturally, there are many tales of intrigue relating to their purpose. The castle is open to the public daily; the underground passages can be seen only on conducted tours.

The train trip from London's St. Pancras Station passes through England's Midlands en route to Nottingham, passing St. Albans, where Britain's first

NOTTINGHAM—*TALES OF ROBIN HOOD*

A Day Excursion from London

DEPART FROM ST. PANCRAS STATION	ARRIVE IN NOTTINGHAM STATION	NOTES
0700	0847	(1)
0730	0927	(3)
0800	0953	(1)
0900	1048	(1)
0915	1104	(3)
1030	1312	(4)
1100	1255	(1)
1215	1402	(3)

DEPART FROM NOTTINGHAM STATION	ARRIVE IN ST. PANCRAS STATION	NOTES
1438	1629	(1)
1533	1725	(1)
1552	1742	(3)
1636	1826	(4)
1733	1928	(1)
1803	2001	(4)
1903	2101	(2)

Distance: 127 miles/204 km
References: British Rail Table 27
             Thomas Cook Table 560

(1) MON–FRI	(3) SAT
(2) MON–SAT	(4) SUN

Train Information: 0332–32051
InterCity Services: 071–387–7070

Nottingham Tourist Information Centre
0602–470661

Christian martyr was executed, and Bedford, where John Bunyan wrote *Pilgrim's Progress*. For variety, you might want to return to London via Peterborough, transferring there to a train for King's Cross Station. Consult the train information office in Nottingham's station. It is located to your right as you exit from the trains. It is open Monday through Saturday, 0800–1830, and Sunday, 1000–1900.

The tourist information office in Nottingham is located at 1–4 Smithy Row at the Old Market Square, telephone 470661. The office is within walking distance of the train station. But if your time is limited, you can hail a cab at the station and save some time as well as your shoe leather. Otherwise, take Carrington Street on your right leaving the station to where it intersects Canal Street. A left turn at this point, followed by a right turn onto Maid Marian Way, will have you pointed in the right direction. When you reach Friar Lane, turn right again and walk to where Friar Lane meets Wheeler Gate and South Parade. The Old Market Square will be on your left. You can't miss it—but if you do, just inquire at one of the taxi queues in that area.

Nottingham's tourist information center lies astride the city's two huge shopping centers—the Victoria and the Broad Marsh. Both are somewhat mind-boggling in size, and they are linked together by wide pedestrian avenues as well as a free bus service running between the two establishments every eight minutes throughout the day, Monday through Saturday.

If your time in Nottingham is limited, no doubt you should first see the historic castle area and return another day to see modern, downtown Nottingham. To visit the castle, turn right as you exit the rail station onto Carrington Street. It intersects Canal Street. Turn left onto Canal Street, and three blocks farther along in the same direction, you will come to Castle Road running up the hill to your right. Following it a short distance brings you to Ye Olde Trip to Jerusalem pub, where we suggest you rest before continuing up Castle Road to the Nottingham Castle entrance, just off Castle Place. The pub's "grub" isn't bad—in fact, it's downright good—so you might want to arrive there about lunchtime. Books about Nottingham and the lore of Robin Hood are on sale in the Ye Olde Trip to Jerusalem pub and in Nottingham Castle.

Meanwhile, back at the Old Market Square, the tourist information center is open Monday through Friday, 0830–1700; Saturday, 0900–1700; and Sunday, 1000–1600 during the summer. It has a wide selection of literature, souvenirs, and details of walking tours of Nottingham that take you, among other places, along one of the city's main thoroughfares, Maid Marian Way.

Tom Tower of Christ Church dominates St. Aldate's in Oxford. The tower houses the Great Tom Bell, which traditionally tolls at five minutes past nine to signify the closing of the gates to its original 101 scholars. The student body now numbers about 13,500.

A DAY EXCURSION TO OXFORD
DISTANCE BY TRAIN: 64 miles (103 km)
AVERAGE TRAIN TIME: 1 hour

The first glimpse of Oxford as you approach it by train from London confirms its title, "the city of spires." Towers, domes, and pinnacles soar on its skyline. It is impressive. Oxford is one of the great architectural centers of the world, with the double distinction of being not only a university city but an industrial one as well. Oxford contains examples of practically every style of architecture since the time of the Saxons. In the less-than-one-half-square-mile area comprising the city center, you may see some of the finest ancient buildings in the world.

Oxford is the oldest university in Great Britain. It had its beginnings in the twelfth century. Between the thirteenth and fifteenth centuries, it became an established national institution. It has a history of 800 years of continual existence. Oxford's student body has doubled in the past thirty years to about 14,000 students, of which some 10,000 are undergraduates. There is no separate campus; the majority of its buildings lie within the center of the city. Basically, the university is a federation of independent colleges. Visitors coming to Oxford during the summer miss the normal sight of students passing between classes and the student sporting activities, but the buildings alone are worth the trip.

Apparently, there is no single explanation as to exactly how and when the university actually began. One theory claims that it was founded by English students who were expelled from the University of Paris in 1167. Others claim it came about from a gathering of various groups of students from monastic institutions in and around the growing city. From whatever origins, by the end of the twelfth century, Oxford was the established home of the first center of learning in England.

In addition to being a seat of learning, Oxford has a strong industrial segment. Unlike Cambridge, Oxford has made a compromise between scholarship and industry. Foremost in this area is car assembly for Austin Rover, the inheritors of the automobile empire founded by William Morris. Printing and paper making have become Oxford's second industry. In addition to its longstanding industrial and academic base, Oxford has world-famous hospitals and science parks.

Like many other cities, Oxford's major problem since World War II has been traffic. Daily, thousands of automobiles pour into the city, clogging the streets and spoiling the view of its many fine buildings. Admittedly, transitions are rather abrupt when you step from a bustling byway into the tranquillity of

159

OXFORD—*ANCIENT CITY CAMPUS*

A Day Excursion from London

DEPART FROM PADDINGTON STATION	ARRIVE IN OXFORD STATION	NOTES
0820	0925	(1)
0845	0945	(3)
0848	0942	(2)
0918	1021	(1)(4)
1005	1055	(1)
1020	1110	(4)
1048	1153	(1)

DEPART FROM OXFORD STATION	ARRIVE IN PADDINGTON STATION	NOTES
1515	1616	(2)
1615	1718	(2)
1640	1730	(4)
1727	1834	(4)
1815	1915	(2)
1915	2015	(2)
2015 (2017 SUN)	2118	(2)(4)
2130 (2126 SUN)	2238	(1)(4)

Distance: 63 miles/102 km
References: British Rail Table 116
                  Thomas Cook Table 525

(1) MON–FRI	(3) SAT
(2) MON–SAT	(4) SUN

Train Information: 0865–722333
InterCity Services: 071–928–5100

Oxford Tourist Information Centre
0865–726871

a college quadrangle, but this typifies Oxford. The city fathers are urging everyone to return to the traditional Oxford method of propulsion—the bicycle. By the way, be on the lookout for bicycles propelled by students pedaling themselves from their college to lectures or laboratories.

The Oxford Tourist Information Centre is on Gloucester Green, just a short walk from the rail station. The center is open year-round, Monday through Saturday, 0930–1700; Sunday and summer bank holidays, 1030–1530. To reach the Tourist Information Center turn right from the station, then turn left along Botley Road. Turn left at Hythe Bridge Street, and follow it until you reach Wourcester Street. Turn left and the Tourist Information Center will be on your right.

Every day throughout the year, the information center organizes guided walking tours of the colleges. These tours, which explore the heart of ancient Oxford, last about two hours and are an excellent value. There are open-top bus tours of the city which depart from the information center every fifteen minutes throughout the summer. The center also has pamphlets that detail walking tours of Oxford's historic buildings, gardens, and rivers. The walking tour takes about two hours. With the apparent differences in the length of stride between the British and their cousins from "the Colonies," Americans should allow at least another half hour to complete the course.

Less than half of the students come to Oxford University from exclusive schools such as Eton, founded by Henry VI in 1440. Students are only required to meet their tutor once or twice a week, either alone or perhaps with one other student. This seemingly free and easy system, which builds on individuality and confidence, is the hallmark of an Oxford education. All students live in the college for their first year and one subsequent year prior to graduation. Students are usually housed in single rooms, the restrictions on coming and going or on having guests are few.

A renaissance of reconstruction and rebuilding in Oxford during the eighteenth century destroyed much of the old street system and the houses inhabited by many religious groups. From this, the city that emerged was more spacious than before. Notwithstanding this urban renewal program, Oxford still has a certain organized clutter about it that becomes readily discernible as you move from the rail station to the city center.

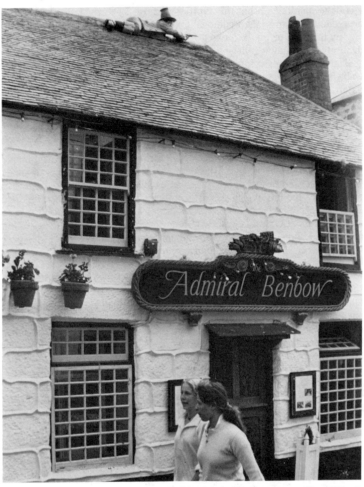

Penzance pirate is portrayed on the roof of the Admiral Benbow Inn on Chapel Street in Penzance. The interior of this 400-year-old tavern is decorated with genuine ship figureheads. Its nautical theme and low-beamed ceilings add to the inn's charm.

From London . . .

AN "OUT-AND-BACK" EXCURSION TO PENZANCE
DISTANCE BY TRAIN: 303 miles (488 km)
AVERAGE TRAIN TIME: 5 hours, 25 minutes

Penzance lends itself more to an "out-and-back" excursion than to a day excursion—although with British Rail's InterCity 125 trains, it is now possible to visit England's westernmost town in the course of a day and still be back in London that evening. An excellent way to visit Penzance is to board the sleeper that departs from London's Paddington Station at one minute before midnight. You can board about an hour before departure time, have the attendant make a nightcap for you, and be well into dreamland by the time the train rolls out of London's suburbs. At 0819 you arrive in Penzance Station after being awakened by the attendant bringing your morning tea or coffee and biscuits. After a full day's sightseeing in Penzance, you can board either the sleeper for your return to London or the InterCity 125 at 1630 and return to London by 2210 the same evening.

Penzance also offers a diversion. When you feel it's time to move on from London to the north and Edinburgh, check out of your London accommodations and take the sleeper to Penzance. Go sightseeing in Penzance, then arrive back in London as described above at 2210 and transfer leisurely to London's Euston Station to board the Night Scotsman at 2335. You'll arrive in Edinburgh the next morning at 0602. Passengers may remain aboard until 0800.

Sleeper reservations should be made well in advance—don't wait until the last minute or you may be disappointed, especially during holidays and peak summer travel periods. Don't forget to check the second-class-sleeper availability if first class is filled. Sometimes if you show up on the departure platform about half an hour before the train leaves, you can pick up a berth cancellation, but don't count on it.

When you arrive in Penzance, you are literally at "the end of the line" insofar as rail travel is concerned. Geographically speaking, you are also at the western end of England. A mere ten miles more would bring you to Land's End, where a road sign pointing to the west cryptically states, AMERICA 4,000 MILES. It is difficult to find a grander coastline. This is Land's End Peninsula—the sightseeing opportunities are endless. The tourist information center in Penzance is located on Station Road, immediately outside of the rail station. Upon arrival in the center, the first item of information you should collect is a Penzance & District map. This graphic presentation of the peninsula will help you put the area into the proper perspective for your visit.

Two additional publications which are available in the information center

PENZANCE—*WESTERN END OF THE LINE*

An "Out-and-Back" Excursion from London

DEPART FROM PADDINGTON STATION	ARRIVE IN PENZANCE STATION	NOTES
0735	1250	(3)
0740	1320	(1)
0903	1420	(3)
1015	1555	(4)
1035	1535	(2)
1235	1740	(3)(5)
1335	1910	(1)
2355 (sleeper)	0819+1	(1)(4)

DEPART FROM PENZANCE STATION	ARRIVE IN PADDINGTON STATION	NOTES
0800	1315	(3)
0837	1415	(4)
0847	1350	(1)
0938	1503	(3)
0941	1455	(1)
1039	1630	(4)
1445	1945	(1)
2215 (sleeper)	0610+1	(1)(4)

Distance: 305 miles/491 km
References: British Rail Table 135
               Thomas Cook Table 515

(1) MON–FRI   (4) SUN
(2) MON–SAT   (5) Summer only
(3) SAT

Train Information: 0736–65831
InterCity Services: 071–262–6767
Penzance Tourist Information Centre: 0736–62207

will prove to be extremely helpful to you as a visitor to Penzance. The first, *Penzance Town Trail,* will guide you on a grand tour of the town and its seacoast. It is available for a nominal fee.

When you leave the tourist information office fully armed with the publications needed to explore this most interesting area, we are certain that you will be immediately attracted to the harbor area lying to the left just beyond the rail terminal. We suggest that you make it your first "port of call," since it can readily put you in the proper adventurous mood to see the rest of the area.

At harbor side you will want to inspect the old warehouse and granary overlooking Battery Rocks. It has been converted to a craft center and art gallery and contains a saltwater aquarium specializing in local species of marine life. Next door is the Dolphin Inn, formerly a smugglers' hideaway and said to be haunted by an old sea captain's ghost. From there, a walk up Chapel Street away from the harbor brings you to a part of Old Penzance filled with Georgian town houses, fishermen's cottages, and the Museum of Nautical Art. This unusual museum, which takes the form of an eighteenth-century battleship with gun decks and life-size figures manning muzzle-loading guns, is filled with displays of actual navigational gear from former times. The museum is well worth a visit. It is a delight to young and old alike.

Termed the "Capital of the Cornish Riviera," Penzance occupies an unusually well-sheltered position on England's western coast. Because the town faces due south and is protected from all other points of the compass by a ring of hills, its climate is ideal year-round. Winter is mild and virtually without frost, followed by an early spring and a temperate summer. Botanically, Penzance is noted for its early flowers and produce.

You need not confine yourself to the limits of Penzance, although you'll find it almost impossible to get away from its magnetic attractions. Local bus service can take you to Land's End, and, as we have indicated on the schedule, rail connections can be made to other equally interesting points on the peninsula such as Falmouth, Newquay, and St. Ives. The tourist information center can give you the background on these interesting places, and you can ask the British Rail Travel Centre in the train station to work out the needed schedules.

Sir Francis Drake statue gazes seaward from atop Plymouth's Hoe, claimed to be the finest natural promenade in Europe. It was from this spot that Drake spied the Spanish Armada. Not overly impressed, he decided to continue his game of bowls—later defeating the Spanish in running naval engagements.

From London . . .

A DAY EXCURSION TO PLYMOUTH
DISTANCE BY TRAIN: 224 miles (361 km)
AVERAGE TRAIN TIME: 3 hours

Plymouth has one of the finest natural harbors in Europe. From Plymouth Hoe (a Saxon word meaning "high place"), there are magnificent views over Plymouth Sound and the harbor. Stand on this huge brow of a hill, which is claimed to be one of the world's finest natural promenades, and you stand in the midst of history. It was here that Sir Francis Drake continued his game of bowls before setting out to deal with the Spanish Armada in 1588. Earlier, in 1577, he set sail from the same harbor in the *Golden Hind* on a three-year voyage around the world. Here, too, in 1620 the Pilgrims embarked on the *Mayflower* for the New World. Too few remember that the first airplane to cross the Atlantic Ocean, the U.S. Navy seaplane NC4, touched down in Plymouth Sound. This spot is indeed steeped in historical heritage—much of it related to America. Stand here proudly!

Check in with the Plymouth tourist information office at 9 The Barbican, Plymouth's Elizabethan quarter. You can reach it on foot from the train station in about fifteen minutes through short underground passages and a pedestrianized area. There are streams, fountains, and gardens which form part of an outstanding display. You can also take a bus. Board any bus stopping at the shelter to the right of the station entrance. Pay your fare and ask to be "deposited" at the Barbican. Folks who are in a real hurry can hail a taxi for the trip. There is a taxi queue just outside of the rail station; the bus stop is a few steps beyond.

The Plymouth Tourist Information Centre is open Monday through Friday, 0900–1700; Saturday, 0900–1600; and bank holidays, 1000–1600. Train information is best obtained in the station's travel center, on the extreme right as you pass the ticket barrier. The travel center is open Monday through Friday, 0830–1745, 0830–1730 on Saturdays, and 1000–1730 Sundays.

While at the tourist information office, you should ask for a copy of the pamphlet, "The Attractions of Plymouth." It contains an easy-to-read map of the attractions within and near Plymouth that are of interest to visitors. For an introduction to Plymouth, we suggest visiting the city's latest attraction, Plymouth Dome. Situated on Plymouth's famous Hoe, the Dome is one of the most up-to-date centers of its kind in Britain. Here you can take a journey through time, use high-resolution cameras to zoom the shoreline, and do many other exciting things. We can guarantee that you won't run out of things to do while in Plymouth.

The Plymouth of today is a city of two distinct parts—the original

PLYMOUTH—*PILGRIM'S PROGRESS PORT*

A Day Excursion from London

DEPART FROM PADDINGTON STATION	ARRIVE IN PLYMOUTH STATION	NOTES
0725	1121	(3)
0740	1121	(1)
0840	1239	(4)
0945	1400	(1)
1030	1407	(4)
1035	1340	(1)

DEPART FROM PLYMOUTH STATION	ARRIVE IN PADDINGTON STATION	NOTES
1535	1905 (1915 SAT)	(2)
1635	1945 (2005 SUN)	(2)(4)
1640	2005	(4)
1835	2210 (2215 SAT)	(2)
1905	2240	(4)

Distance: 226 miles/363 km
References: British Rail Table 135
             Thomas Cook Table 510

(1) MON–FRI
(2) MON–SAT
(3) SAT
(4) SUN

Train Information: 0752–221300
InterCity Services: 071–262–6767

Plymouth Tourist Information Centre: 0752–264849

Elizabethan section called the "Barbican" and the modern city center that has risen from the devastation and debris of the last world war. If your time in Plymouth is limited, we suggest you concentrate on visiting the Barbican area of the city.

The harbor area, where the old town of Plymouth nestled, derived its title, Barbican, from the fact that at the entrance to the harbor stood an outpost of the ancient Plymouth Castle. According to castle phraseology, such outer fortifications were called *barbicans*. The Barbican was spared much of the damage that Plymouth suffered during the bombardments of World War II. Consequently, there are still many old buildings and narrow streets in this area that recapture the Elizabethan atmosphere.

One Barbican landmark of particular interest to Americans is a memorial stone that marks the place on the harbor pier from which the *Mayflower* sailed. The Barbican's historic Elizabethan buildings include the Black Friars Distillery, home of Plymouth Gin since 1793. The distillery is still operating in buildings formerly used as a monastery and dating back to 1425. Visitors are welcome. The Merchants House on St. Andrews Street is the largest and finest structure remaining from the sixteenth and seventeenth centuries. Restored recently, it features displays of Plymouth's history with the theme, "Tinker, Tailor, Soldier, Sailor . . ." It is open daily, except Mondays, and there is an admission charge.

Towering over the Barbican, the Royal Citadel, built in the 1660s by Charles II, was erected as a warning to the citizens of Plymouth. Many of the fortress cannon still point toward the town and not out to sea, as one would normally expect them to do.

If you have ever sung a chorus or two of "The Eddystone Light," you are a likely customer for the engrossing book *The Four Eddystone Lighthouses* by Robert Sanderson. Additional information on the lighthouses may also be found in the booklet *Smeaton's Tower and the Plymouth Breakwater*. The first Eddystone lighthouse was blown down in a storm. The second lighthouse withstood the elements but was destroyed by fire. Smeaton's Tower stood on the Eddystone Reef from 1759 to 1884 and subsequently was reerected on Plymouth Hoe. The tower is open to the public daily, from the end of April to the end of October, from 1030 to 1700.

If your urge "to go down to the sea in ships" overwhelms you, take a boat trip on Plymouth Sound. The information center has the details, including how to view the nearby Royal Naval Base at Devonport. If your call to the sea is more limited, browsing in the Barbican area will suffice if you throw an occasional glance seaward to impress the locals.

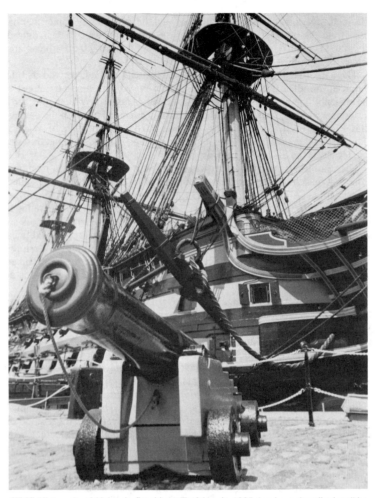

HMS *Victory*, Lord Nelson's flagship at Trafalgar in 1805, has been described as "the proudest sight in Britain." She lies, meticulously preserved, at the Portsmouth Naval Base. One of the ship's cannon partially shields the *Victory*'s starboard sheet anchor.

From London . . .

A DAY EXCURSION TO PORTSMOUTH
DISTANCE BY TRAIN: 74 miles (119 km)
AVERAGE TRAIN TIME: 1 hour, 30 minutes

A visit to Portsmouth requires priorities—priorities involving the choice of what to see there. The city abounds in vast quantities of history, architecture, amusements, and literature. Portsmouth has variety, contrasts, and veneration. Here are a few choices.

If the sea is "your thing," Portsmouth is flanked by natural harbors, east and west. It is the home of one of the world's greatest naval bases, and its resort area, Southsea, offers the largest amusement complex on England's south coast plus four miles of beaches, promenades, and gardens.

Old Portsmouth is for those who relish fine buildings. Lombard Street boasts a host of splendid seventeenth- and eighteenth-century houses, many with distinctive Dutch gables. On adjoining High Street, the motif is primarily eighteenth century, but this gives way as you approach the ultramodern, "new" Portsmouth with its traffic-free shopping precinct, "Cascades," on Commercial Road.

The literary greats of Portsmouth—Charles Dickens, H. G. Wells, Conan Doyle, Rudyard Kipling, and Neville Shute, to name a few—have left their mark on the city in birthplaces, residences, and museums. Resting in the world's oldest dry dock in Portsmouth's naval yard is Lord Horatio Nelson's flagship, HMS *Victory*. Alongside the ship stands the Royal Naval Museum with relics of England's naval hero, ship models, and an outstanding collection of marine paintings. For priority, our first selection is HMS *Victory*. It has been described as "the proudest sight in Britain," and well it is! Meticulously preserved, it stirs the imagination as you relive the events of the Battle of Trafalgar that "made all England weep."

Portsmouth has a total of four tourist information centers. The one you should contact first is located on the main street, The Hard, right next to the Portsmouth Naval Base and the Harbor Rail Station. Trains call first at the Portsmouth and Southsea Station, so stay aboard to the end of the line. Then, instead of moving straight ahead to the ferry dock, exit the station on the right-hand side of the platform to The Hard, from where you will be able to see the gate of the naval base to your left. The tourist information center on The Hard is open daily throughout the year (except December 25 and 26) from 0930 to 1745 during the summer and 0930 to 1715 during winter (telephone 826722). The other centers are located outside the Sea Life Centre, the Continental Ferryport, the Civic Offices, and Commercial Road. The Harbor Centre can direct you should you need their services.

PORTSMOUTH—*BRITAIN'S NAVAL PORT*

A Day Excursion from London

DEPART FROM WATERLOO STATION	ARRIVE IN PORTSMOUTH HARBOR STATION*	NOTES
0723	0849	(1)
0745	0927 (Southsea Station)	(3)
0755	0944 (Southsea Station)	(4)
0815	0943	(2)
0825	1000	(4)
0845	1033	(2)

DEPART FROM PORTSMOUTH HARBOR STATION	ARRIVE IN WATERLOO STATION	NOTES
1602	1733	(2)
1620	1755	(4)
1702	1832	(2)
1720	1855	(4)
1802	1935	(2)
1820	1955	(4)
1902	2033	(2)
1920	2055	(4)
2050	2244	(1)
2122 (Southsea Station)	2315	(3)
2120	2301	(4)

Distance: 74 miles/119 km
References: British Rail Table 156
                    Thomas Cook Table 504

* Portsmouth has two railway stations—Portsmouth Harbor and Portsmouth & Southsea. Portsmouth Harbor should be used for departures to the Isle of Wight as well as visits to Portsmouth Royal Navy Base. Consult British Rail Table 156 or make inquiries with train information personnel for Portsmouth & Southsea train service.

(1) MON–FRI   (3) SAT
(2) MON–SAT   (4) SUN

Train Information: 0703–229393
InterCity Services: 071–928–5100

Portsmouth Tourist Information Centre
0705–826722

In addition to visiting the HMS *Victory* in the Portsmouth naval yard, you may also inspect the hull of Henry VIII's *Mary Rose*, which is undergoing restoration in a special dry-dock workshop. Launched in 1510, *Mary Rose* went down while sailing against a French invasion fleet in 1545; the remains were raised in 1982. The story of the *Mary Rose*—her loss and her dramatic recovery—is related in an audiovisual presentation, and the objects salvaged from the ship are on exhibit.

Some vital statistics in history regarding HMS *Victory* may be beneficial while you are waiting to go aboard. The ship was launched on 7 May 1765. (Lord Nelson was a mere child of six on that date.) She is a vessel of 3,500 tons with an overall length of 226.5 feet. All totaled, *Victory* carried 104 guns and a complement of 850 officers and men. In 1801, the ship was rebuilt extensively and given the appearance she has today. Recommissioned in April 1803, she became Nelson's flagship. On 21 October 1805, the English fleet under Nelson's command vanquished the combined fleets of France and Spain off Cape Trafalgar. Lord Nelson was killed aboard *Victory* in the final moments of what has been termed "the most decisive battle ever fought at sea."

Newcomer to the scene at the Portsmouth Naval Base is the Victorian iron-clad, HMS *Warrior*. Launched in 1860, she was the largest, fastest, and best-armored warship of her time. She has been restored throughout to her appearance during her first commission of 1861–64; when you step aboard you can catch a unique glimpse of life as it was experienced on a nineteenth-century British warship.

The Royal Navy Museum supports these famous ships with displays that set them in their historic context and continues the story of the British Navy into the twentieth century, up to the Falklands Campaign of 1982.

In the resort department, Portsmouth offers the Pyramids Centre, a giant leisure attraction built by the sea next to King Henry VIII's Southsea Castle. A true tropical paradise, where the temperature never drops below 84 degrees Fahrenheit, the center features four areas of entertainment, ranging from swimming pools, top-name entertainment, and a patio bar to a supervised "Fun Factory" where Mom and Dad can park the kids.

Close by the Southsea Castle and the Pyramids Centre, Portsmouth's D-Day Museum and Overlord Embroidery Museum tells the story of that historic event through pictures, plans, and the re-creation of wartime scenes, along with exhibits of various weapons and vehicles. A special audiovisual presentation relates the events leading to the recapture of Normandy. More history unfolds in the castle where an audio-visual show reconstructs scenes of "Life in the Castle."

Portsmouth bears the title "The South's Historic Maritime Resort City." We are certain that you will agree with this entitlement.

Foy Boat Inn stands behind cannon on the site where a watch house stood in eighteenth-century Ramsgate. In the days of sails, foy boats took provisions to ships anchored off Ramsgate. The original inn was destroyed in World War II.

A DAY EXCURSION TO RAMSGATE
DISTANCE BY TRAIN: 79 miles (127 km)
AVERAGE TRAIN TIME: 1 hour, 50 minutes

This day excursion to Ramsgate encompasses the northeast tip of England's Kent County, which is called the Isle of Thanet. Although the sea inlets have all been drained, it still bears the semblance of an island with clusters of seaside towns known as Kent's Leisure Coast, each with its own character. Londoners were attracted to Thanet early in the nineteenth century, and it has been a thriving resort area ever since. The attraction of sandy beaches, safe bathing, and entertainment are the assets the area has to offer.

Ramsgate has been selected as the primary point for the day excursion, for it is the terminal stop for trains departing London's Victoria Station on the North Kent line. En route stops at other Isle of Thanet towns are made on this rail line at Margate and Broadstairs. More comments about them follow. It should be noted that it is possible to return to Victoria Station via another rail route from Ramsgate through Ashford, or yet another route calling at Dover and Folkestone. With so many possibilities, you should consult the timetables posted in all three of the previously mentioned Thanet towns for possible variations of your own itinerary. The train schedule shown on the following page gives details for the London Victoria Station-Faversham-Margate-Ramsgate-North-Kent rail line only.

This frequent train service departs from the first bay (platforms 1–8) of London's Victoria Station. *A word of caution:* The first cars (usually four) closest to the ticket barrier will go to Dover. The balance of the cars (usually eight) at the head of the train will terminate in Ramsgate. The train "splits" at Faversham. You will be reminded of this again by a train announcement when the train stops briefly in the Bromley South Station after leaving Victoria Station and crossing the Thames. Stay alert and board one of the proper cars.

There are tourist information centers in all three Thanet towns touched by rail service—Margate, Broadstairs, and Ramsgate. The Margate information center is on Marine Terrace, east of the railway station near the Dreamland Whiteknuckle Theme Park. In Broadstairs, its center is relatively near the station in Pierremont Hall. A left turn on High Street out of the railway station will bring you to Pierremont Park and the information center. Ramsgate's information center is in the district-council offices on Queen Street, some distance from the railway station, which lies west of the town's center. Buses from the station will take you there, or you can hail a taxi.

All three centers operate on similar schedules: Monday through Thursday,

RAMSGATE—*SEASIDE RESORT*

A Day Excursion from London

DEPART FROM VICTORIA STATION	ARRIVE IN RAMSGATE STATION	NOTES
0805	0947 (1002 SUN)	(1)(3)
0905	1047 (1002 SUN)	(1)(3)
1005	1147 (1102 SUN)	(1)(3)
1105	1247 (1202 SUN)	(1)(3)

(Plus other frequent service)

DEPART FROM RAMSGATE STATION	ARRIVE IN VICTORIA STATION	NOTES
1632	1823	(1)
1652	1849	(3)
1732	1916	(1)
1757 (1825 SUN)	1947 (2020 SUN)	(2)(3)
1852	2046	(1)
1952 (2005 SUN)	2146 (2220 SUN)	(1)(3)

(Plus other frequent service)

Distance: 79 miles/127 km
References: British Rail Table 212
            Thomas Cook Table 500

(1) MON-SAT
(2) SAT
(3) SUN

Train Information: 0227–454411
InterCity Services: 071–928–5100

Ramsgate Tourist Information Centre
0843–591086

0900–1730; Friday, 0900–1700. During summer periods, they also are open on Saturday and Sunday, 1000–1600.

Margate is the Thanet town that has been conjuring up visions of holidays for years. Its biggest drawing card is the famous amusement park, Dreamland Pleasure Park, set on a twenty-acre complex. The municipality of Margate owns nine miles of seafront with sandy beaches and promenades running practically its full distance. The atmosphere of the area differs somewhat from that of England's south coast in that it is more sedate in mood and tempo. Perhaps the presence of the North Sea is one of the contributing factors.

Arriving at Margate Station, the first sight to greet you is the golden sand of the beach. The promenade paralleling the beach is a length of souvenir shops, restaurants, confectioneries, and amusement halls, terminating at the gates of Dreamland Theme Park. Beyond the park lies Margate's main shopping center, where courteous Kentish clerks are most eager to assist you in your shopping. Extending from the promenade, Margate's Old Town of narrow streets and houses clusters around the town's harbor.

Broadstairs has a Victorian atmosphere about it and became a fashionable "watering hole" during the regency of King George IV. Victorians, one of the most eminent being Charles Dickens, favored holidays in Broadstairs. A leaflet from the information center will permit you to follow in his footsteps and see many interesting points within the town. Every June, townspeople remember Dickens by appearing in costume while attending a series of plays, readings, parades, and parties set against the backdrop of Victorian Broadstairs.

Ramsgate, being strong on regency flavor, centers its activities around its royal harbor and marina. Annual events include the May Spring Festival, August Harbor Heritage celebrations, and September Model Ship Ralley. The harbor is a source of constant interest, as is the model village at West Cliff, a charming miniature of England's Tudor countryside. Permanently moored on the clifftops at Pegwell Bay in Ramsgate is a Viking ship commemorating the original Viking landing in 449. Ramsgate harbor has seen Wellington's troops embark for the Continent, where they continued on to defeat Napoleon at Waterloo. The harbor also received thousands of battered British troops during the evacuation from Dunkerque in 1940.

Many recall memories of their travels through their senses of sight and sound. In the case of Ramsgate, we recall our visits there by our sense of taste. Most memorable was our dining experience at Harvey's Crab & Oyster House located on Harbour Parade. Walk down to the harbor area—you can't miss it. As the name indicates, seafood is the house specialty. The restaurant's card states: "Open 12–2:30 P.M. & 8 P.M. till late. Booking advisable. Tel: (0843) 591110."

Fifteenth-century clock tower standing in St. Albans's French Row was originally a curfew tower, the bell dating back to 1335. To the left of the tower stands the Fleur-de-Lys Inn on a site where King John of France was held prisoner after the Battle of Poitiers in 1356.

A DAY EXCURSION TO ST. ALBANS
DISTANCE BY TRAIN: 20 miles (32 km)
AVERAGE TRAIN TIME: 25 minutes

St. Albans takes its name from Britain's first Christian martyr, a Romano-British citizen who was beheaded for his faith on a hilltop outside Verulamium, one of the most important towns at that time in the western Roman Empire. A magnificent fifteenth-century Norman cathedral now stands on the hilltop, and Verulamium has become a parkland on the western side of the city.

St. Albans has much to offer its visitors. Tucked away in various corners of the city are old coach inns, many with a fascinating history. The White Hart Inn, built in the fifteenth century, was restored in 1930. The Fleur-de-Lys Inn on French Row was erected between 1420 and 1440 on the site where King John of France was held prisoner after the Battle of Poitiers. Another inn, the Fighting Cocks, claims to be the oldest licensed house in England. It derived its name from the cock fights that were held there for many years. All three of these ancient "watering holes" are open to the public during licensed hours. St. Albans has always had an open mind concerning alcoholic beverages—Elizabeth I granted the city permission to issue wine licenses in 1560.

French Row in St. Albans, a narrow street of medieval appearance, is fronted by a clock tower built between 1402 and 1411 from the flint and rubble of Verulamium. Its original curfew bell was cast in 1335. Across from the bell tower stands the Wax House Gate, where once candles and tapers were made and sold to pilgrims visiting the shrine of St. Albans. The path through the gate is still the shortest route for pedestrians en route to the cathedral, proving that the ancients had a sharp eye for customer traffic flow. The St. Albans Cathedral contains traces of an eighth-century Saxon church. It has one of the largest Gothic naves in Europe. The cathedral tower was built largely of stone from Verulamium.

Arriving in St. Albans, leave the train station by walking uphill towards the city center on Victoria Street. At the junction of St. Peters and Chequer streets, the tourist information center can be seen opposite, in the town hall. Office hours are 0930–1730 Monday through Saturday. The uphill walk takes about fifteen minutes. The alternative is city bus transportation, which departs from a bus shelter in the station area. The bus stop for returning to the station is at the top of Victoria Street.

Many of the points of interest in St. Albans must be reached on foot. The information center has a pamphlet describing a walking tour, *St. Albans's Town Trail,* which includes the cathedral and the abbey. The tour (two and

ST. ALBANS—*FROM ROMANS TO ROSES*

A Day Excursion from London

DEPART FROM KING'S CROSS THAMESLINK	ARRIVE IN ST. ALBANS STATION	NOTES
0800	0822 (0835 SUN)	(2)(4)
0830	0858 (0905 SUN)	(2)(4)
0915 (0900 SUN)	0937 (0935 SUN)	(2)(4)
1000	1022 (1035 SUN)	(2)(4)
1030	1052 (1056 SUN)	(2)(4)
1100	1122 (1126 SUN)	(2)(4)
1130 (1129 SAT)	1152 (1156 SUN)	(2)(4)

(Plus other frequent service)

DEPART FROM ST. ALBANS STATION	ARRIVE IN KING'S CROSS THAMESLINK	NOTES
1430 (1428 SUN)	1453 (1457 SUN)	(2)(4)
1500 (1458 SUN)	1523 (1527 SUN)	(2)(4)
1530 (1528 SUN)	1553 (1557 SUN)	(2)(4)
1610	1635	(1)
1615	1638	(3)
1632	1657	(4)
1710	1735	(1)
1715	1738	(3)
1732	1757	(4)

(Plus other frequent service)

Distance: 20 miles/32 km
References: British Rail Table 52
Note: To reach King's Cross Thameslink, follow directions to the underground Piccadilly Line from King's Cross.

(1) MON–FRI	(3) SAT
(2) MON–SAT	(4) SUN

Train Information: 071–387–7070

St. Albans Tourist Information Centre: 0727–864511

one-half miles) may prove a bit too ambitious for the less-experienced, less-conditioned walker, but both lead past one or more of the previously described inns, where a libation will probably instill a desire to press on—or stay at the inn until "time" is called.

Helpful publications to take on the trails are *A Historical Map* of St. Albans and *Mini Guide*. The center has them available for a small fee. The information center is close to the marketplace. Markets are held in St. Albans every Wednesday and Saturday. If you are in town on these days, be sure to "go to market" and enjoy the opportunity of watching the locals barter back and forth with the tradesmen. Everything from apples to zinnias, including the weather and current prices, will become subjects of discussion.

The Roman city of Verulamium is engrossing. You can spend an entire day at the site visiting its 200-acre grounds, which include a temple, forum, museum, hypocaust, and theater. The museum houses an impressive collection of Roman antiquities. From the center of St. Albans, you can reach Verulamium in about twenty minutes on foot, or you can opt for a local bus. The tourist information office will give you the directions.

At the Verulamium Museum, artifacts taken from the ruins are displayed in an environment of natural surroundings. The small items from the houses and shops range from iron hinges, latches, and locks to personal ornaments worn by the inhabitants. A full range of pottery and glassware, both for table and kitchen use, are on exhibit.

Exploratory excavations of the site have taken place from time to time, but experts estimate that only one-third of the area within the Roman town walls has been uncovered. Modern techniques such as aerial photography continue to reveal additional features.

The gardens of the Royal National Rose Society are in St. Albans. The rose trial grounds is the place to see the future "greats" of the rose world. The society made its first award for a new rose in 1883 and subsequently established its own trial grounds. New varieties from all over the world are sent to St. Albans to undergo a comprehensive, three-year assessment. The twelve acres of gardens, a spectacle for the casual visitor, are a total fascination to rose enthusiasts. Open from June through October, the gardens are accessible to the public 1000–1800 daily.

The range of history in St. Albans extends from A.D. 43 and the first evidences of the Roman enclosure at Verulamium to the moment you arrive to enjoy the vitality of this timeless city. To step over St. Albans's threshold is to step into a land of enchantment and history.

Tight squeeze hinders a tour bus negotiating the High Street Gate in Salisbury. The gate marks the boundary between the two distinct areas of Salisbury—the "close" around the cathedral and the city's marketplace. Traditionally, the gate is closed and locked every night.

From London . . .

A DAY EXCURSION TO SALISBURY
DISTANCE BY TRAIN: 84 miles (135 km)
AVERAGE TRAIN TIME: 1 hour, 25 minutes

Salisbury holds the distinction of being one of the few English cities *not* originally founded by the Romans. The old town, Old Sarum, had been in existence since the Iron Age. The Romans fortified it, and the Saxons later developed it into an industrial town. All went well in Old Sarum until arguments between the occupants of the church and the castle caused a new church to be built in the valley below the original town site. This new location proved to be more popular than the old. Consequently, although known as Salisbury, the town's official name is New Sarum.

The center of Salisbury has traditionally been divided into two distinct areas, the cathedral and the marketplace. This tradition still exists, and the gates leading to the cathedral and the buildings in the "close" surrounding it are locked every night. Beautiful houses of medieval and Georgian architecture overlook the green.

The marketplace has a history all its own. In the original Charter of 1227, the town was authorized to hold a Tuesday market. This got out of hand and grew into almost a daily market until protests from nearby towns resulted in a reduction of market days in Salisbury to Tuesdays and Saturdays only. Today, Salisbury maintains those traditional market days. The cattle market, once an integral part of the market, was a cause of some congestion in the city center. It is now housed at its new site off Ashley Road. Perhaps moving the cattle market was a step in the right direction, since tourists and cow slips don't go well together.

Salisbury boasts a brace of historic inns that have given rest and refreshment to travelers down through the centuries. The fireplaces in the King's Arms Inn have the same stone as that used in the construction of the cathedral. The Haunch of Venison, an old English chop house, was built about 1320. The Red Lion Hotel, dating back to the same era, was the starting point for the Salisbury Flying Machine, the nightly horse-drawn coach to London.

In Salisbury, you will find many impressive examples of architectural styles, ranging from the town's thirteenth-century cathedral to a modern pedestrian shopping district known as the Old George Mall. The most unexpected structure is the foyer of the movie theater on New Canal Street. Once the banqueting hall of the merchant John Halle, four-time Mayor of Salisbury, it is now a splendid example of fifteenth-century black-and-white timbering.

Salisbury's tourist information center is situated at the rear of the Town Guildhall where Market Square corners on Fish Row. Telephone ahead from

183

SALISBURY—*MAGNA CARTA ARCHIVE*

A Day Excursion from London

DEPART FROM WATERLOO STATION	ARRIVE IN SALISBURY STATION	NOTES
0709	0837	(1)
0735	0906	(3)
0835	0956	(2)
0855	1033	(4)
0935	1110	(1)
1012	1133	(3)
1035	1155	(1)
1055	1238	(4)
1135	1302	(1)

DEPART FROM SALISBURY STATION	ARRIVE IN WATERLOO STATION	NOTES
1429	1618	(4)
1523	1646	(1)
1615	1745	(5)
1725	1845	(1)
1815 (1818 SUN)	1949	(1)(4)
1835	1953	(3)
1953	2118	(1)

Distance: 84 miles/135 km
References: British Rail Table 160
                    Thomas Cook Table 511

(1) MON–FRI   (4) SUN
(2) MON–SAT   (5) Departs 1620 on SAT, 1612 on SUN
(3) SAT

Train Information: 0722–327591
InterCity Services: 071–928–5100

Salisbury Tourist Information Centre
0722–334956

the rail station (334956) for directions, or proceed on foot down Fisherton Street, which you will find to your far left as you exit the station. After crossing the River Avon, the street will narrow and change names several times until it becomes Fish Row.

The tourist center's hours vary seasonally: July–August, 0930–1900 Monday–Saturday and 1100–1700 Sunday; June and September, 0930–1800 Monday–Saturday and 1100–1600 Sunday; and October–May, 0930–1700 Monday–Saturday (Sundays in May from 1100 to 1600). The center operates a booking service for local hotel accommodations as well as the popular "Book-A-Bed-Ahead" program.

From May through September, you can join a daily guided walking tour of Salisbury at 1100 and 1830 from in front of the tourist information center on Fish Row. The tour lasts one and a half hours.

The cathedral has a unity of design that no doubt is attributable to the fact that, unlike most other cathedrals, which took centuries to complete, the Salisbury Cathedral was constructed in only thirty-eight years. In other words, it wasn't affected by several different periods of architecture. Its foundation stones were laid in 1220, during the heyday of Gothic design. One of its greatest treasures is its ancient clock mechanism, which dates from 1386 and is one of the oldest pieces of operating machinery in the world. It originally stood in a detached belfry.

The cathedral contains a library founded in 1089. Seventy of the books installed in the library at that time are still there. The great treasure of the library is the *Magna Carta,* written at Runnymede on 15 June 1215. It was brought to Salisbury by William, Earl of Salisbury, who placed it in the cathedral for safekeeping. It remained there until 1940, when it was hidden for five years in a quarry. Among its many historical achievements, Salisbury made its mark in the annals of medical care. Of the four hospitals currently in or near the city, the Trinity Hospital, on Trinity Street, has a rather interesting story concerning its founding in 1379 by Agnes Bottenham. Chronicles relate that Ms. Agnes ran a "house of ill repute" on the site, and when it prospered, she built a hospital and almshouse there as an act of penitence.

Visitors interested in seeing Old Sarum, one and a half miles north of the new town, can do so by city bus or taxi. Excavations and reconstruction have been under way for some time. Oddly enough, even after the old city was abandoned, the owner of the estate continued to send two members to the Parliament, despite the fact that the city had no inhabitants. It was a case of representation without taxation.

Sheffield's Town Hall on the left and its modern extension (right) aptly depict the changing attitudes of the city. The original building was opened (by Queen Victoria) in 1897; the latter, in 1977. Both buildings were constructed from stone taken from the same quarry in an attempt to blend the two contrasting architectural styles. Another extension to the Town Hall (not visible) was opened by the Prince of Wales in 1923. It bears a strong resemblance to a French chateau.

A DAY EXCURSION TO SHEFFIELD
DISTANCE BY TRAIN: 165 miles (265 km)
AVERAGE TRAIN TIME: 2 hours, 10 minutes

The name of England's cutlery city, Sheffield, is synonymous with quality. Sheffield also has the reputation of being a typical industrial center, dotted with smoke-belching chimneys and all the atmospheric nightmares that go with that sort of environment. *Not so.* Visitors to Sheffield will be surprised to find the city quite different from its reputation. Today, though the city is proud to be one of the world's largest industrial complexes, Sheffield's environment has changed entirely—only the "Made in Sheffield, England" quality remains. Initiated in 1959 and completed in 1972, the city's clean-air programs have paid magnificent dividends. Sheffield now is virtually smokeless and is probably the cleanest industrial city in Europe.

The art of metal working began more than eight centuries ago in the Sheffield area when monks built furnaces there for the purpose of making iron implements. By the fourteenth century, a Sheffield *thwitel* (knife) was so well known that Chaucer referred to one in his Canterbury tales. Formed in 1642, the Company of Cutlers has guarded the reputation of its craftsmen and maintained the high standards necessary to allow cutlery to bear the trademark "Sheffield."

Sheffield's history is not devoted entirely to the development of her major industries. A chapter in royal intrigue records that Mary Queen of Scots was held captive in the Sheffield Castle for fourteen years by the Earl of Shrewsbury.

Charles Dickens probably would never recognize the town he visited to gather material for his novel *Hard Times.* He found Sheffield's fog thick enough to compare with thick soup. Nor when the fog cleared would he recognize Sheffield's skyline. Slums have been swept away, and some of the boldest architecture in Britain has emerged since the city's ambitious building programs and town planning took shape at the end of World War II. A striking example is the award-winning Castle Square in the city center, which blends a vehicular round-about (traffic circle) with a pedestrian underpass and a shopping center.

For a quick look at "new" Sheffield, you can ride the "city clipper," which is a minibus that cuts a circular swath through the center of Sheffield. Serving the railway station, as well as other central points, the city-clipper service runs on weekdays, 0930–1730. The bus-service cost is nominal, so just hop aboard, pay up, then lean back and enjoy Sheffield's scenery.

Sheffield's tourist information center invites visitors to use its many ser-

187

SHEFFIELD—*TRADEMARK OF QUALITY*

A Day Excursion from London

DEPART FROM ST. PANCRAS STATION	ARRIVE IN SHEFFIELD STATION	NOTES
0830	1053	(1)
0830	1057	(3)
0915	1301	(4)
0930	1154	(1)
1000	1226	(3)
1030	1251	(1)

DEPART FROM SHEFFIELD STATION	ARRIVE IN ST. PANCRAS STATION	NOTES
1524	1750	(1)
1554	1825	(3)
1624	1858	(4)
1624	1855	(1)
1724	1952 (1954 SAT)	(2)
1924	2205 (2209 SAT)	(2)

Distance: 165 miles/265 km
References: British Rail Table 53
            Thomas Cook Table 560

(1) MON–FRI   (3) SAT
(2) MON–SAT   (4) SUN

Train Information: 0742–726411
InterCity Services: 071–278–2477

Sheffield Tourist Information Centre
0742–734671/2

vices during their stay. The office is open Monday through Friday, 0930–1715, and Saturday, 0930–1615. The office is located in the city's Town Hall Extension Building, accessible on foot from the train station. Use the pedestrian subway (underpass) directly in front of the station and walk until you reach the far end. Exit the subway by using the stairs leading off to the right. Back at ground level, walk straight ahead, following the tourist information and town hall directional signs.

If you need more explicit directions, you may inquire at the travel center (train information office) in the station. It is located on the far left of the station hall as you exit from the trains. Hours of operation are 0930–2000 daily. The personnel there will be glad to point the way. Taxi service is also available from the station to the tourist information center. Ask to be taken to the Town Hall Extension Building, Union Street entrance.

The free city map that you may obtain from the information center in Sheffield is nicely augmented by *Walk About*, which sells for a small fee. The aim of the publication is to act as a guide to visitors for a walking tour of central Sheffield. Taking just over an hour to complete, the walk is designed to show some of Sheffield's past as well as the improvements that have taken place more recently. The tour begins in front of the town hall, a short distance from the Town Hall Extension Building. The town hall was officially opened by Queen Victoria on 21 May 1897.

For an expanded overview of Sheffield and its environs, ask for a copy of the color brochure, *Sheffield Visitor*. It is packed with photos and facts that touch on the city's history, entertainment, sports, shopping, and a number of places to visit. Churches, parks, and homes also are included in this descriptive publication.

Although Sheffield is an industrial city, it is of great interest to tourists. Sheffield boasts extensive recreation facilities in fifty-four parks and open spaces within the city. More than sixty different kinds of recreational pursuits are made available to all who choose to participate.

A stone's throw from the town hall on Church Street you will find Cutlers' Hall. Erected in 1832, the hall houses the Cutlers' Company silver collection and is the scene for the annual Cutlers' Feast. Arrangements to view the silver collection can be made through the city's tourist information center. The City Museum in Weston Park houses the world's largest collection of Sheffield Plate. Another section of the museum is devoted to a collection of fine cutlery.

Southampton's Bargate, one of four medieval gates in the wall surrounding the original city, has not lost its character despite numerous alterations since its construction in the twelfth century.

From London ...

A DAY EXCURSION TO SOUTHAMPTON
DISTANCE BY TRAIN: 79 miles (127 km)
AVERAGE TRAIN TIME: 1 hour, 10 minutes

In the minds of many, Southampton conjures visions of the great transatlantic ocean liners, for it is Britain's prime ocean-passenger port and home of many of the world's greatest passenger ships, including Britain's flagship, the *Queen Elizabeth II* (*QE2*). Many visitors, however, know little about Southampton's span of centuries, which has given it a rich heritage in the history of England and of Europe. Southampton's museums, classic buildings, and ancient ruins help reveal this rich and interesting heritage.

Southampton is best seen on foot, with the possible assistance of a city bus now and then. From the railway station, you can board any "City Centre" bound bus and ask the driver to "deposit" you at the Above Bar Shopping Precinct, where you will find the city tourist information center. The center is open for business Monday through Saturday, 0900 (1000 on Thursday)–1700 throughout the year. It is closed on Sunday.

The center can make hotel and bed-and-breakfast reservations in Southhampton and its surroundings. Written and telephone requests for reservations may also be made. Write to the Southampton Tourism Unit, Civic Centre, Southampton S09 4XF, England, telephone (0703) 832712, or fax (0703) 631437.

There is a map outside the Southampton railway station showing the route to the center. Pick up the free *Southampton's Visitors Guide*. It contains suggestions for sightseeing. Visitors from the United States will take special interest in the sailing of the *Mayflower* from Southampton in 1620. Persons proving descent from original *Mayflower* passengers can have their names entered on the memorial.

As mentioned in the official handbook, there are many places of interest within easy walking distance of the city information center. A visit to them will gradually unfold a picture of Southampton's past. To catch Southampton's seagoing flavor, a visit to the Ocean Village or the Town Quay Marina would be in order. Similar to the harbor renovation of Baltimore, Maryland, Southampton's Ocean Village has transformed some of its old docks into a cosmopolitan playground with a bevy of specialty shops and eateries overlooking a yacht basin. The Town Quay Marina plays host to the cream of the yacht-racing world. Both areas are close to the terminal used by the *Queen Elizabeth II*. Check with the information center concerning walking directions and the possibility of the *QE2* being in the harbor.

Next in line is the Tudor House Museum, where the costumes, paintings,

SOUTHAMPTON—*AN IMPOSING HERITAGE*

A Day Excursion from London

DEPART FROM WATERLOO STATION	ARRIVE IN SOUTHAMPTON STATION	NOTES
0745	0915	(1)
0750	0916	(3)
0845	1030	(4)
0850	1017	(2)
0930	1041 (1100 SUN)	(2)(4)
1030	1200	(4)
1032	1141	(2)

DEPART FROM SOUTHAMPTON STATION	ARRIVE IN WATERLOO STATION	NOTES
1615	1740	(4)
1615	1729	(2)
1715	1829	(2)
1815	1936	(4)
1815	1928	(3)
1915 (1915 SUN)	2028 (2036 SUN)	(2)(4)
2015	2136	(4)

Distance: 79 miles/127 km
References: British Rail Table 158
             Thomas Cook Table 502

(1) MON–FRI   (3) SAT
(2) MON–SAT   (4) SUN

Train Information: 0703–229393

Southampton Tourist Information Centre
0703–832615
0703–832712 for accommodations

and furniture of centuries past are displayed against the oak beams and stone carvings of Tudor House itself. The Tudor House is one of the few surviving examples in Southampton of a large town house from the early Tudor period. It contains a banquet hall and is surrounded by an authentic Elizabethan herb garden. Don't miss the tunnel entrance to the remains of a twelfth-century merchant's home. The kids will love it.

Next on the agenda is Wool House, once a medieval warehouse and now a showplace for the city's involvement with the sea. Since early times, Southampton has been an important port of call. Its docks have been piled high with luxuries from the Mediterranean and the East, brought there by Genoan and Venetian fleets. If you are not fortunate enough to see the *QE2* during your Southampton visit, Wool House will make up for it with its history of the "Queens," highlighted by a scale model of the *Queen Mary* from the board-room of the Cunard Shipping Company.

If you never expected to see a marine museum in a wool house, you'll be equally surprised to find an archaeological collection in a museum bearing the name God's House Tower. It started out as a gunnery store, changed its use many times, and finally opened as a museum in 1950. It currently houses the most extensive collection of post-Roman European pottery to be found in Europe.

Also in Southampton's repertoire is the Hall of Aviation on Albert Road. The museum is a memorial to R. J. Mitchell, Southampton's famous aircraft designer of the Spitfire, the fighter that valiantly defended the country during the Battle of Britain. The exhibits include a Spitfire Mark 24, possibly one of the last of 24,500 Spitfires produced by the Supermarine Aircraft Company in nearby Woolston, a quarter mile from the museum. The museum's collection also includes a Sandringham Flying Boat as well as hundreds of photographs, plans, and models connected with inventor R. J. Mitchell and the Supermarine factory.

The route between the museums, by the way, is dotted with historic buildings, such as the Duke of Wellington Pub and the Red Lion Pub. Pausing for a pint may provide a pleasant period for pondering Southampton's past and present.

Free guided walks through medieval Southampton depart from the Bargate at varying times throughout the year. Ask for complete details at the tourist information center.

Quay side at Southampton's port, you stand in history. Four-hundred years before the pilgrim fathers departed on their journey to the new world, Richard the Lion-Hearted embarked on the Third Crusade.

A unique wonder of the world, Stonehenge is viewed annually by more than a million visitors. The monument stands on a bed of solid chalk. Because it has been constantly robbed of stone and defaced throughout the centuries, visitors are no longer permitted to enter the stone circle.

A DAY EXCURSION TO STONEHENGE
DISTANCE BY TRAIN: 84 miles (135 km)
AVERAGE TRAIN TIME: 1 hour, 45 minutes

"Observatory, altar, temple, tomb, erected none knows when by none knows whom, to serve strange gods or watch familiar stars . . ." wrote the poet Sir John Squire about Stonehenge. Stonehenge is unmatched—truly one of the wonders of the world. There are many opinions regarding the use and purpose of the monument. Whatever the reason for its existence, however, Stonehenge remains an awe-inspiring reminder of the past.

The landscape for a few miles around the Stonehenge monument reportedly contains more prehistoric remains than any other area of the same size in Britain. There are earthworks, burial sites, erected stones, and hill carvings. Because they belong to the prehistoric period, long before any written records were made, there are many questions about them all that we shall never be able to answer. Through technology, modern man has been able to tell *how* they were made and, in some cases, *when* and *by whom*. The unanswered question is *why*.

Stonehenge sits on the Salisbury plain, an almost treeless, windswept plateau. With its origins dating from 2700 B.C. to about 1400 B.C., Stonehenge comprises a circular group of stones roughly 110 feet in diameter that stand in an area surrounded by a low earthen rampart and ditch approximately 200 feet in diameter. The largest stones, some weighing as much as fifty tons, were brought to the site from quarries some twenty miles distant. The stones are placed accurately to record the position of the sun on the four main dates of the seasons, possibly for an agricultural or a religious purpose.

The monument stands on 300 feet of solid chalk, of which only twelve inches have eroded in the past 4,000 years. Unfortunately, Stonehenge has been robbed constantly of its stone throughout the centuries. In Victorian times, it was common practice for visitors to bring hammers and chisels to chip off souvenir sections of the temple stones.

Deodorus Ciculus, historian to Julius Caesar, described Stonehenge as a temple to the sun god Apollo. Modern Britons have marked the area with small clumps of trees to commemorate the Battle of Trafalgar in 1805. The Order of Druids gathers annually at Stonehenge on the longest day of the year to celebrate the sun's zenith and watch it rise over the heel stone of the temple. One theory relates that Stonehenge was built by the druids as colleges of philosophy, theology, and science. The theory has been discredited by the revelation that the original druids arrived in Britain long after Stonehenge was built.

There are several means by which you can proceed to Stonehenge from the

STONEHENGE—*MYSTERIOUS PAGAN SHRINE*

A Day Excursion from London

DEPART FROM WATERLOO STATION	ARRIVE IN SALISBURY STATION	NOTES
0735	0906	(3)
0835	0956	(2)
0855	1033	(4)
0935	1110	(1)
1012	1133	(3)
1035	1155	(1)
1055	1238	(4)
1235	1357	(1)

DEPART FROM SALISBURY STATION	ARRIVE IN WATERLOO STATION	NOTES
1429	1618	(4)
1523	1646	(1)
1612 SUN	1743 SUN	(4)
1725	1845	(1)
1815 (1818 SUN)	1949	(1)(4)
1835	1953	(3)
1953	2118	(1)

Distance: 84 miles/135 km
References: British Rail Table 160
Thomas Cook 511

(1) MON–FRI   (3) SAT
(2) MON–SAT   (4) SUN

Train Information: 0722–327591
InterCity Services: 071–928–5100

Salisbury Tourist Information Centre
0722–334956

Salisbury railway station. If time is of the essence, a taxi can get you there in about twenty minutes. Buses, operated by Wilts & Dorset, depart from the station for Stonehenge via Salisbury and Amesbury on a daily basis, Sundays and public holidays included. The adult round-trip fare is £3.85; admission to the Stonehenge site (£2.85) is not included. The Wilts & Dorset bus schedule is arranged so as to connect with all express trains to and from the Waterloo Station in London. If you plan to linger at the site, this will provide you with ample time to do so.

In conjunction with Wilts & Dorset, Guide Friday, one of Britain's leading operators of town and city tours, offers a combined tour of both Stonehenge and Old Sarum, the ancient site of Salisbury, for an adult fare of £9.00 (senior citizens £8.00; children under the age of twelve, £4.50). Fares include entrance to Stonehenge, and you are accompanied by a guide throughout the tour. Tour time is just under two hours. For complete details and bus schedules, we suggest that you call ahead to the Wilts & Dorset travel office in Salisbury (0722) 336855.

Time permitting, upon arriving back in Salisbury, you may want to explore the city prior to boarding your London-bound train. If so, stay aboard the bus returning from Stonehenge until it arrives at the Salisbury bus terminal approximately five minutes after its arrival at the rail station. You will note on both the Stonehenge and Salisbury rail schedules that three later train departures to London will still be available to you.

We recommend that you use one of the special excursion buses. If you use the regular public bus system between Salisbury and Amesbury, you will be obliged to walk or take a taxi for the two miles between Amesbury and the Stonehenge site.

From Good Friday or April 1 (whichever is earlier) until September 30, the Stonehenge site is open daily between 1000 and 1800. During the balance of the year, the site opens daily at 1000 and closes at 1600. A gift shop, refreshments, and public toilets are available. All facilities at the site provide access for the disabled.

A sad note: Because of damage to the monument, visitors are no longer permitted to enter the stone circle but can view it only from a distance. Now, visitors are required to remain behind a fence built around the Stonehenge temple to protect it. "Time," as the announcement observes, "is taking its toll."

The Royal Shakespeare Theatre, built in 1932 to replace the original theater destroyed by fire in 1926, employs both decorative and structural brickwork.

Anne Hathaway's Cottage, two miles from the center of Stratford, attracts tens of thousands of visitors annually during visits to Shakespeare country.

From London . . .

A DAY EXCURSION TO STRATFORD-UPON-AVON
DISTANCE BY TRAIN: 121 miles (195 km)
AVERAGE TRAIN TIME: 2 hours, 30 minutes

Visitors—"pilgrims," as many term themselves—began trickling into Stratford-upon-Avon soon after the first folio of Shakespeare's plays was published in 1623. That "trickle" has increased through the centuries. Today, it is a torrent. Swept up in the bardolatry, admirers of William Shakespeare make the pilgrimage to Stratford-upon-Avon regardless of the consequences. It is said that half a million visitors pass through the narrow corridors and down the twisting staircases of his birthplace every year. Sometimes, it seems like they are all there at the same time that you are. Stratford-upon-Avon is crowded during the month of July. Spring and fall are the least crowded times to go there.

BritRail Pass holders may travel from Paddington Station in London directly to Stratford-upon-Avon on the Thames-Avon Express. The Paddington–Stratford train service has two drawbacks: There is no service on Sundays and weekday schedules on this route do not permit both attendance at the evening theater performances in Stratford and a return to London the same evening.

The best route is available between London's Euston Station to Coventry, where you connect with a special Guide Friday Shakespeare Connection motor coach service to and from Stratford-upon-Avon. BritRail Pass holders may use this service by paying a supplementary charge to the motor-coach driver for the road portion of the journey. With a BritRail Pass, travelers pay £6.50 for a single journey and £8.00 for a round-trip. Without a BritRail Pass, the Shakespeare Connection fare from London's Euston Station is £22.00 single journey and £25.00 for a round-trip.

The British Rail link through Coventry makes it possible to attend an evening performance at the Royal Shakespeare Theatre in Stratford-upon-Avon and return to London the same evening. Check with British Rail for complete details. You can pick up schedules in London's Euston Station; telephone (071) 387–7070 or telephone Guide Friday (0789) 294466. Many hotels have the same schedule information available at the porter's desk.

Passengers arriving in Coventry from Euston Station should look for the special motor-coach connections to Stratford-upon-Avon in the bus lanes on the right-hand side of the station. The 0915 (0905 Saturday) train from London arrives in Coventry at 1027, connecting with the coach that departs at 1035 and arrives in Stratford-upon-Avon at 1110. To assure coach-train connections returning to London, take either the 1715 or the 2315 coach. Check

STRATFORD-UPON-AVON—*SHAKESPEARE COUNTRY*

A Day Excursion from London

DEPART FROM EUSTON	ARRIVE IN COVENTRY	DEPART COVENTRY	ARRIVE IN STRATFORD-UPON-AVON	NOTES
0905(A)	1026	1035	1110	(1)
1005(A)	1126	1200	1235	(1)
1655(C)	1803	1815	1850	(1)(3)
1705	1826	1835	1910	(2)
1740	1858	1905	1940	(3)
2135(A)	2316	2345	0015+1	(1)

DEPART STRATFORD-UPON-AVON	ARRIVE IN COVENTRY	DEPART COVENTRY	ARRIVE IN EUSTON	NOTES
0915	0950	1007	1127(B)	(1)
1115	1150	1207	1326(B)	(1)
1715	1750	1807	1929(B)	(1)(3)
1755	1825	1841	2017	(3)
2315	2345	0034+1	0237+1	(1)(3)

Distance: 121 miles/195 km
References: British Rail Tables 65, 68; Thomas Cook Table 540

(A) Departs 10 minutes later, Monday-Friday	(1) MON–SAT
(B) Arrives 10 minutes later, Saturday	(2) SAT
(C) Departs 10 minutes earlier on Sundays, 20 minutes earlier on Saturdays	(3) SUN

The Shakespeare Connection is the fast and comfortable way to travel from London to Stratford-upon-Avon. Relax in your InterCity train to Coventry and then board a dedicated Guide Friday coach link from Coventry to Stratford. Holders of rail passes covering rail travel to Coventry can use the coach link by paying the driver £6.50 one-way, £8.00 round-trip. Those who do not have rail passes pay £22.00 one-way and £25.00 round-trip.

To confirm train times and fare information, telephone Euston Station, (071) 387–7070, or Guide Friday at (0789) 294466

Train Information in Stratford-upon-Avon: 021–643–2711
Stratford-upon-Avon Tourist Information Centre: 0789–293127

with the travel centers (train information office) in the stations for full details and schedules.

Stratford's tourist information center is at Bridgefoot. It's open 0900–1800 Monday through Saturday and 1100–1700 on Sunday. Telephone (0789) 293127, fax (0789) 295262.

Our advice is to take a guided tour of Stratford-upon-Avon. A popular one is the "Stratford and Shakespeare Story Tour," operated by Guide Friday Limited, located in Stratford Civic Hall. On this tour, you are transported by open-top, double-decker buses along a thirteen-mile route and visit all five of the Shakespeare properties: Shakespeare's birthplace on Henley Street; the Nash's House, in which Shakespeare spent his retirement years before his death in 1616; the Hall's Croft Home of Shakespeare's daughter Susanna; Shakespeare's mother's house; and Anne Hathaway's Cottage.

William Shakespeare, the superb English poet and playwright recognized universally as the greatest of all dramatists, was born in Stratford-upon-Avon in 1564. His mother was the daughter of a local farmer; his father was a glove maker and a wool merchant who entered politics to become mayor of Stratford. Although Shakespeare lived throughout his professional career in London, he kept his home ties with Stratford. In 1597 he purchased New Place, one of Stratford's largest houses. He died there in 1616 and was buried in Stratford's parish church.

A visit to the Royal Shakespeare Theatre is a must. It is advisable to reserve theater seats as far in advance as possible. Telephone (0789) 269191 for twenty-four-hour information on program and seat availability. (The fax number is [0789] 294810.) To book seats, telephone the theater box office direct at (0789) 295623. The theater has several restaurant/bar facilities. Telephone (0789) 414999 for more information and reservations for special restaurant/theater packages. The Box Tree is a luxuriously appointed restaurant overlooking the Avon River and serving classical cuisine (closed Sundays), and the River Terrace is a modern restaurant/coffee shop/wine bar serving light international dishes. You can even "Pick-up-a-Picnic" by placing your order with the cashier at the River Terrace Restaurant two hours in advance.

Royal Guard stands at castle-hill entrance to Windsor Castle grounds. Changing of the guard ceremony takes place mid-morning daily.

Royal Oak Restaurant, on Datchet Road immediately opposite the Windsor Riverside train station, is a delightful rally point following a castle tour.

From London . . .

A DAY EXCURSION TO WINDSOR
DISTANCE BY TRAIN: 25 miles (41 km)
AVERAGE TRAIN TIME: 50 minutes

Historic Windsor Castle is the official home of English royalty. William the Conqueror built the first structure on this site, a wooden fort that doubled as a royal hunting lodge. Other English kings added to the castle during their reigns, but despite the multiplicity of royalty and architects, the castle has managed to retain a unity of style all its own. It's the largest inhabited castle in the world.

The present queen, Elizabeth II, uses the castle far more than any of her predecessors. For this reason, it is wise to inquire if the queen is in official residence before going to Windsor. When she is, which is usually during the month of April and for periods during March, May, June, and December, the state apartments will be closed to the public. There will still be many areas of Windsor Castle open to the public; however, you will miss seeing the splendor of the various rooms contained within the state apartments. Chances of seeing Her Majesty, should she be in residence, will be rather slim. Nevertheless, during that time you may find Prince Philip watching his son Charles, the Prince of Wales, and his polo team bashing about in the Great Windsor Park. Again, it may be difficult to find the princes, for although the castle itself occupies a mere thirteen acres, the park stretches over 4,000 acres below the battlements of the castle.

For full appreciation of Windsor, we definitely recommend a guided tour. It takes two hours and it is well worth every penny. The tour cost includes the admission charge to St. George's Chapel and the castle precincts. The tours start daily at 1015, 1130, and 1330 from the Windsor tourist information center in Windsor's central rail station. The guides are required to pass a demanding examination set by the Regional Tourist Board.

You have a choice of two rail routes from London to Windsor. For the schedule given here, we have selected the route from Waterloo Station in London to Windsor Riverside Station. This line does not require changing trains en route. The alternate route, which departs Paddington Station in London, requires a change at Slough to a shuttle train before arriving at Windsor Central Station. If you take the Paddington-Slough route, the shuttle train arrives and departs in Slough from track 1. Either route gives you a magnificent view approaching Windsor Castle. On either train, sit on the left-hand side (outbound) to take full advantage of the scenery.

The tourist information center is in the Windsor Central Station. Signs with the traditional "i" will lead the way from either arrival point. The grounds of

WINDSOR—*THE ROYAL CASTLE*

A Day Excursion from London

DEPART FROM WATERLOO STATION	ARRIVE IN WINDSOR RIVERSIDE STATION	NOTES
0812	0903	(1)
0812	0903	(3)
0842	0932	(1)
0850	0945	(4)
0912	1003	(1)(3)
0943	1032	(1)
0950	1045	(4)

(Plus other frequent service)

DEPART FROM WINDSOR RIVERSIDE STATION	ARRIVE IN WATERLOO STATION	NOTES
1440	1532	(2)
1540	1632	(2)
1602	1657	(4)
1640	1732	(2)
1740	1834	(2)
1802	1857	(4)
1902	1957	(4)
1940	2032	(2)
2002	2057	(4)

(Plus other frequent service)

Distance: 25 miles/41 km
References: British Rail Tables 119 and 150

(1) MON–FRI	(3) SAT
(2) MON–SAT	(4) SUN

Train Information: 071–928–5100

Windsor Tourist Information Centre
0753–852010

Windsor Castle are immediately across the street from the tourist information center. The center operates 0930–1800 in summer and 0930–1730 in winter. Be sure to purchase an illustrated guidebook on Windsor Castle even though you plan to take the guided tour. It will become a fond reminder of your visit.

Rare state occasions such as the investiture of the Garter, when the queen proceeds down the walks of Windsor Castle accompanied by a full entourage of castle guards and Knights of the Garter, are difficult for the general public to view. The changing of the castle guard, however, is a daily event conducted in a manner in which the general public can participate. The new guard leaves the Victoria Barracks precisely at 1015, then marches along High Street to the castle. The guard changing takes place at 1025 and the old guard returns by the same route at 1100. By positioning yourself along High Street or Castle Hill, you will have a good view of the pageantry as it unfolds.

From the battlements of Windsor Castle, you may look down and across the stately River Thames onto the playing fields of Eton College, where "how the game is played" has always been more important than the final score. The importance of Eton lies less in what it is than in what it stands for. The school yard and cloisters are open 1400–1700 throughout the year except during school holidays, when they are open 1030–1700.

Your initial entry into the town of Eton may be a bit frightening at first, for you will probably find yourself surrounded by a group of young gentlemen uniformed in pin-striped trousers, white bow ties, and formal black coats with tails. You have not been thrust among a flock of penguins. What you are surrounded by are the students of Eton College, one of Britain's most exclusive educational institutions and a strong reminder that the British on occasion can cling fiercely to their traditions.

A respite from pageantry and tradition during your visit to Windsor may be taken by cruising on the River Thames. At the bottom of High Street, at its intersection with Barry Avenue, the Windsor Boat Pier offers two cruises. The first is a thirty-five-minute trip upstream and the other is a full two-hour trip with light refreshments and a licensed bar aboard.

If you have not yet been introduced to the British public house, there is no better time than now. The Royal Oak, directly across the street from Windsor Riverside Station, is highly recommended. No more prim a pub can you find in all of England. Its impeccable oaken interior matches the high quality of its food and service. The inn was constructed as an ale house in 1736 and restored in 1937. Should we meet you there, we'll buy the first round!

York Minster, largest Gothic church in Britain, stands on a site previously occupied by a Roman military headquarters and a former Norman cathedral. The earlier remains are still visible. Construction of the Minster, begun in 1220, required approximately 250 years.

A DAY EXCURSION TO YORK
DISTANCE BY TRAIN: 188 miles (302 km)
AVERAGE TRAIN TIME: 2 hours, 10 minutes

"The history of York," according to King George VI, "is the history of England." The Romans took it from a Celtic tribe, the Brigantes, in A.D. 71. According to legend, King Arthur captured the city sometime after the Roman legions retreated in A.D. 406. The Saxons took charge of York in the seventh century. The Danes ran the Saxons off the property in 867, only to get their comeuppance from the Anglo-Saxons when Edmund tamed them in 944. In 1066, York saw the fastest turnaround ever when King Harold of England defeated the King of Norway at Stamford Bridge, six miles from York. Nineteen days later, York's management (and all of England, as a matter of fact) passed to the Normans when Harold was killed in the Battle of Hastings.

William the Conqueror, following his victory at Hastings, came north to quell a rebellion, which he did by his version of urban renewal, known in those days as the "scorched-earth" policy. The ruins and rubble of the Romans, the Saxons, the Vikings, and the Anglo-Saxons, however, never was cleaned out thoroughly. Much of it is still there, layer upon layer, and is now being unearthed in York for you to view upon arrival.

Charles I, fleeing the fermenting civil war, left London in 1639 to take residence in York. Cromwell's troops finally took York in July 1644. A condition of surrender was that there would be no pillaging; thus, the fine medieval stained glass of York Minster was saved. It is estimated that the Minster contains more than one-half of all the medieval stained glass in England.

York, similar to Chester, has retained most of its fourteenth-century city walls. You will see a part of them as you exit from York's railway station. The city of York is best explored on foot. You can do it on your own or take a conducted tour. A two-mile walk around the walls provides a panorama of the city.

Following a relaxing ride aboard an InterCity 125 train from King's Cross Station in London, we suggest that you check in with the York tourist information center in the rail station. Once you are armed with a map, we suggest that you proceed on foot into the city. Although it's a ten-to-fifteen-minute walk, you will see a lot of history en route. Turn left leaving the station and proceed along the city wall toward the tower of the York Minster. After crossing the River Ouse, at the intersection of Duncome Place and St. Leonard's Place, you will see the Minster straight ahead. York's main tourist office is nearby in Exhibition Square.

YORK—*FINE MEDIEVAL CITY*

A Day Excursion from London

DEPART FROM KING'S CROSS STATION	ARRIVE IN YORK STATION	NOTES
0730	0926	(1)
0800	0951 (1004 SAT)	(2)
0830	1029	(3)
0900	(1104 SAT) (1141 SUN)	(4)
0930	1132 (1134 SAT)	(2)
1000	1151 (1205 SAT) (1241 SUN)	(2)(4)
1030 (1025 SUN)	1225 (1311 SUN)	(2)(4)

DEPART FROM YORK STATION	ARRIVE IN KING'S CROSS STATION	NOTES
1437 (1443 SUN)	1648 (1715 SUN)	(2)(4)
1532	1739	(3)
1532	1741	(1)
1555	1828	(4)
1720	1910	(1) Pullman Service
1751	2023	(4)
1845	2122	(4)
1941	2155	(1)
2003	2226	(1)

Distance: 188 miles/302 km
References: British Rail Table 26
Thomas Cook Table 570

(1) MON–FRI   (3) SAT
(2) MON–SAT   (4) SUN

Train Information: 0904–642155
InterCity Services: 071–278–2477

York Tourist Information Centre
0904–628666

This center is open October through July and September, 0900–1700 Monday through Saturday; August, 0900–1900 Monday through Saturday; and June through August, its open on Sundays, 1000–1300. City tours leave from the fountain opposite the center. Summer tour hours are 1015, 1415, and 1900 daily. The announcement describing the availability of the tours states: "The tour, which is on foot, will help you to discover the wealth of interest the city offers to its visitors and learn something of its history. There is no charge—our reward is your appreciation of this ancient and historic city." A warmer, more sincere welcome would be hard to find.

York is a compact city, easy to stroll around. Among its points of interest, York Minster draws first choice. Built between 1220 and 1472, the Minster is England's largest Gothic cathedral. As the mother church of the Church of England's northern province, it is outranked in religious importance only by Canterbury Cathedral. York uses the archaic term *minster,* meaning a center of Christian teaching or ministering, for its cathedral.

We suggest that you also visit the National Railway Museum on Leeman Road, a ten-minute walk from the York railway station. It will stand comparison with any railway museum in the world. The Great Railway Show at the museum commemorates the Railway Age from the 1820s to the present day. Visitors walk down station platforms and, in imagination, become passengers on an Edwardian Express or on a boat train to Paris. The Museum's National Railway Collection ranges from a lock of Robert Stephenson's hair to the splendor of the Royal Train.

Another important attraction is the Castle Museum, one of the most interesting folk museums in the world. Famous streets of York have been reconstructed in the museum and depict the daily life and occupations of various periods from Tudor to Edwardian times. The museum also contains an eighteenth-century water mill that operates throughout the summer. Other sections of the museum are devoted to Yorkshire crafts, costumes, and military history.

While walking, no doubt, you will find the narrow, winding streets of York the most fascinating of all the city's attractions. The streets developed from the original Roman street plans. In turn, each century has added a bit more color— and perhaps confusion. The Vikings left their mark in the use of street names ending in "gate," such as *Stonegate* and *Petergate.* The medieval citizens following the Vikings gave York its winding streets. One of these streets, The Shambles, is reputed to be one of the best preserved medieval streets in Europe. Originally the street was crammed with butcher shops in half-timbered, overhanging buildings. The east-west line of the street kept the meat in cool shade for most of the day. It now houses an assortment of interesting stores and book shops, where the meat hooks still hang.

City Chambers, headquarters of the Glasgow District Council, occupies the entire east side of George Square, the city's picturesque "breathing place." Designed by William Young, the building is an impressive treatment of Italian Renaissance architecture. The loggia balcony, marble staircase, and banqueting hall of the building are particularly impressive. (Photo courtesy of the Greater Glasgow Tourist Board and Convention Center, copyright © C. William Long Photography)

11 GLASGOW

In succession to Athens, Florence, Amsterdam, Berlin, and Paris, Glasgow was selected as the Cultural Capital of Europe 1990. Over the past decade, the city has undergone a sweeping renaissance, shaking off the grim, depressed industrial image of the Industrial Revolution to emerge as one of Europe's foremost cities of culture and ambiance.

Now, out from under a century or so of accumulated grime, the cleaning-up process has highlighted, in gleaming gold and red sandstone, some of Europe's finest Victorian architecture. Bustling city streets lined with imposing hand-carved facades pay homage to the optimism of the Victorian city fathers, as do the stunning marble staircases of the opulent City Chambers in central George Square. Glaswegians have reason to be proud of their city and cordially invite you to enjoy it with them.

Direct transatlantic flights into the Glasgow Airport, only fifteen minutes from the city center, as well as regular train services from London and the south, make Glasgow an ideal "base city" site for Scotland. It is conveniently located, as is Edinburgh, for access to our Scottish day excursions. For this reason we are introducing the "Glasgow Connection," wherein the choice of base cities—Edinburgh or Glasgow—becomes a matter of individual selection. The excellent train service between the two cities permits visitors to move with ease between them.

Glasgow is Scotland's largest metropolis, with a population approaching one million. It is the gateway to Loch Lomond and the western Highlands. Glasgow's River Clyde flows into the Firth of Clyde, thus opening its western waterways to a myriad of islands and the Irish Sea. At the height of its shipbuilding boom, Glasgow was launching more than one-third of the world's shipping tonnage. The *Queen Mary,* the *Queen Elizabeth I,* and the *Queen Elizabeth II* (*QE2*) were built there. With the industry now only a shadow of its former self, the River Clyde has become a scenic waterway where you can cruise aboard luxury riverboats or the paddle-wheel steamer *Waverley.*

Glasgow abounds with sights to see and things to do, ranging from its great twelfth-century cathedral to a variety of museums and universities. It is said that Glasgow has more parks than any other European city of its size. One in particular, George Square, opposite the Queen Street railway station, projects a panorama of Scottish and British history in its statuary of those individuals who forged the British Commonwealth through their science, leadership, and literature.

Among the many superb galleries and museums throughout Glasgow, you shouldn't miss the renowned Burrell Collection in the Pollok Country Park, a unique collection of more than 8,000 objets d'art donated to the city by one man, Sir William Burrell.

Glasgow's Railway Stations—Central Station & Queen Street Station

Glasgow has two main railway stations. Trains arriving from southwestern Scotland and England terminate in the Glasgow Central Station. For train travel north and east out of Glasgow to Edinburgh, Perth, and Inverness or west to Oban and Fort William, the Glasgow Queen Street Station becomes the departure point. A convenient city bus service links the two rail stations. The ten-minute walk between them, however, runs through some of the city's finer shopping areas, thereby offering the opportunity to walk off a few British "pounds."

If you choose to walk from the Queen Street Station to the Central Station, walk past George Square to St. Vincent Street. At this point, turn right and walk one block farther to Buchanan Street, a pedestrian shopping precinct. Turn left onto Buchanan Street and walk until your path intersects with Gordon Street. The intersection is easy to locate because this section of Gordon Street is reserved for pedestrians (and shops). Turning right at this point and continuing along Gordon Street for two blocks will bring you to the Glasgow Central Station, on your left.

From the Central Station to the Queen Street Station, merely reverse your line of march. Those who wish to avoid running the shopper's gauntlet on Buchanan Street may proceed between the two stations by traversing Queen and Argyle streets. We suggest that you consult a map of central Glasgow, which is available at the tourist information center in St. Vincent Place.

The Interstation Bus Link provides passenger transfer service between the Central and Queen Street Stations with no stops en route. Departures are approximately every fifteen minutes.

Don't look for a kiosk or a newsstand where you can purchase tickets—you pay your fare when you get on the bus. BritRail Passes are *not* accepted for the bus transfer between rail stations. The time en route varies between five and ten minutes, depending upon traffic conditions. For those in a hurry or those who are heavily ladened with luggage, taxis are standing by in queues at both stations.

If you are arriving in one of Glasgow's rail stations to transfer to the Glasgow Airport at Abbotsinch or to Prestwick Airport near Ayr, a frequent bus service is operated for this purpose out of Anderston Cross Bus Station. The bus terminal is three blocks west of the Central Station, just off Argyle Street. It's quite a distance from the Queen Street Station to the terminal—a taxi is recommended.

Glasgow Central Station, transformed radically in the past few years, caters to those needs of the train traveler ranging from rest rooms with bathing facilities to a grand Victorian hostelry—the Central Hotel. What is more, the station's old ticket office has been transformed into a delightful array of quality shops, bars, and restaurants.

The Glasgow Central Station provides InterCity electric services for English destinations, including Liverpool, Manchester, Birmingham, and London (Euston Station). Also provided are connections for Wales, the west of England, and destinations in south and west Scotland, which include Ayr and Stranraer (for connections to Northern Ireland via Larne). Commuter-train service to Gourock and Wemyss Bay for connections with steamer services on the River Clyde also operate from the Central Station.

Money exchange is available only within the station during times when the banks are closed. An office of the Royal Bank of Scotland is directly across from the main entrance of the station. After banking hours, ticket window No. 9 in the Central Station will exchange foreign currency and cash traveler's checks up to a $50 limit. The American Express office is to the left of the station entrance at 115 Hope Street. The Thomas Cook office is just one block to the right of the station entrance at 15-17 Gordon Street.

Hotel reservations may be arranged at the tourist information center located at 35 St. Vincent Place.

Tourist information is available in Glasgow's information center at 35 St. Vincent Place, telephone (041) 204–4400.

Train information is displayed in the Central Station by means of a huge, digital departures-and-arrivals board located between tracks 2 and 5. For expanded train information, visit the Inquiries and Reservations Office (travel center) on the right side of the main hall at the end of platforms 1, 2, and 3.

Train reservations may be arranged in the travel center. For sleeping-car reservations, you will be directed to the InterCity Sleeper Centre at the entrance to platform 1.

Queen Street Station is the terminal for trains operating on the scenic West Highland Line to Oban, Fort William, and Mallaig, where steamer connections can be made to the Scottish islands. From the Queen Street Station, InterCity express trains depart for Edinburgh and connect with destinations in England including York, Doncaster, and London (King's Cross Station).

Services for north and east Scotland, including Stirling, Perth, Dundee, Aberdeen, Inverness, and the Kyle of Lochalsh, depart from the Queen Street Station. Electric trains to Dumbarton and Balloch (for Loch Lomond cruises) also operate from this station.

Money-exchange services are not available within the Queen Street Station. There are several banks in the general area, including an office of the Royal Bank of Scotland adjacent to the main entrance of the Central Station. After banking hours, however, the only money-exchange facility available in the area is ticket window No. 9 in the Central Station.

Hotel reservations for Glasgow and for all of Scotland may be arranged through the "Book-A-Bed-Ahead" service with the Greater Glasgow Tourist

Tolbooth steeple, erected in 1626, is all that remains at the intersection of High Street and Trongate in Glasgow of a once sprawling complex including the town hall and jail. Other interesting landmarks in this vicinity include the Tron Steeple (1637) and the Mercat Cross (replica–1979).

Information Centre located at 35 St. Vincent Place.

Tourist information in Glasgow is available at the Greater Glasgow Tourist Information Centre. Hours of operation June through September are 0900–1900 (2000 in July and August) Monday through Saturday and 1000–1800 Sunday. From October through May, the center is open Monday through Saturday from 0900 to 1800, closed Sunday until Easter, then open on Sunday through May between 1000 and 1800.

The center has a wealth of Glasgow tourist information on hand. Call there to request a copy of the "Greater Glasgow Quick Guide" booklet. In addition to a listing of city attractions, the booklet contains information on restaurants, pubs, events, and shopping that will be very helpful for getting to know Glasgow. There is a Bureau de Change in operation in the center as well as an office for theater and sporting events tickets.

Train information is available in the British Rail Travel Centre located on the left-hand side of the station as you face the train platforms.

Train reservations can be made in the travel center. For sleeper reservations, however, use the "InterCity Sleeper Centre" in the Central Station.

Glasgow Gazette

Glasgow's modern subway system is a circular line with trains running in both directions beneath the center of the city. It provides a three-minute service from each of its fifteen stations, achieving a circular journey in about twenty-two minutes. A separate subway, the Argyle Line, links the British Rail suburban networks. The main link with British Rail services, however, is the subway station at Buchanan Street, connecting with the Queen Street Station by a moving pedestrian platform similar to those found in airports.

For readers going on the day excursion to Loch Lomond, the rail route departing Glasgow is an electric-train service that departs from subterranean platform 8 in the Queen Street Station. To reach it, after entering the main hall of the station, turn left and exit the station by the side entrance, where you turn right to follow the well-marked PLATFORM 8 signs.

In the Queen Street Station's British Rail Travel Centre, you may obtain full information and tickets for cruising on the Clyde River aboard the *Waverley*. Connecting rail services to the ship's pier originate in the Queen Street Station. The vessel offers a number of interesting cruises on the Clyde River and the Firth of Clyde. On Saturdays during the summer, a special upriver cruise is conducted. Advance bookings for the cruise are recommended.

Throughout the summer, a two-hour bus tour of Glasgow aboard specially converted double-deck buses will take you around some of the best known places—and some of the more out-of-the-way places—in the city. For bus tour schedules and rates, check with the Greater Glasgow Tourist Information Centre.

Every visitor to Glasgow, and model railroad buffs in particular, will not want to miss Glasgow's Museum of Transport in Kelvin Hall on Argyle Street. The museum is located in the west end of Glasgow only ten minutes from the city center by bus or subway. It's open Monday through Saturday from 1000 to 1700 and Sunday between 1100 and 1700. Displays include ship models, Glasgow trams and buses, locomotives of Scottish origins, Scottish-built motorcars, fire engines, and a reconstructed subway station. There is also a section in the museum known as "The Clyde Room," where meticulously detailed models illustrate the story of shipbuilding and shipping on the River Clyde. An operating model railroad is one of the museum's highlights.

Glasgow's Art Gallery and Museum is immediately opposite Kelvin Hall. Home of Britain's finest civic collection of British and European paintings, the museum also features displays of natural history, archaeology, and collections of silver, pottery, arms, and armor. In the performing arts sector, Glasgow's Mayfest (which, of course, occurs in the merry month of May) is a key international festival for theater, dance, music, and related performing arts in Europe.

Previously, we identified that area of the city between the two rail stations as an ideal place to "walk off a few British 'pounds.'" It is. Glasgow is a shoppers' paradise, with more than ample opportunity to find that special souvenir or gift for friends back home—and pick up something for yourself, too. Department stores line the great pedestrianized shopping districts of Argyle and Buchanan streets. Adjacent to them, Princes Square provides some of Europe's top specialty shops blended into an exciting array of restaurants and bars. Slightly farther than a stone's throw from the square, St. Enochs indoor shopping mall offers a wide variety of stores beneath the same roof, and Argyll Victorian Arcade is the place to look for jewelry and fine gifts.

Farther out, but well worth it if you are visiting Glasgow over a weekend, is the city's famous "Barras Street Market." It's a bargain collector's delight with goods ranging from Victorian bric-a-brac to high fashion—all flavored by the antics of the stall holders.

The "Glasgow Connection"

All day excursions described in chapter 12 that depart from Edinburgh also may be taken from Glasgow. In fact, three of the day excursions—Ayr, Loch Lomond, and Stranraer—require passing through Glasgow. For these excursions readers residing in Glasgow need only refer to the appropriate day-excursion schedule in chapter 12 for the "Glasgow Connection."

Two of the day excursions—Dunbar and Dunfermline—can be reached conveniently only through Edinburgh. Consequently, readers need only refer to the Glasgow-Edinburgh shuttle-service schedule to determine the "Glasgow Connection" for these day excursions.

Five day excursions—Aberdeen, Dundee, Montrose, St. Andrews, and Stirling—are so situated on Scotland's rail lines that they may be reached either by direct connection from the Queen Street Station in Glasgow or through Edinburgh. A condensation of the "Glasgow Connections" for direct service appears on page 218.

Three other day excursions—Inverness, Kyle of Lochalsh, and Perth —are reached more conveniently from Glasgow by direct train service from the Queen Street Station rather than through Edinburgh. For a condensation of the "Glasgow Connections," you are referred again to page 218 for details.

The "Glasgow Connection" for express trains to London is given on page 219 of this chapter. All services shown are subject to alteration. Readers are advised to consult with the schedules posted in the train stations or with a British Rail Travel Centre for train information before commencing each journey. The publishers cannot be held responsible for changes or inaccuracies in the schedules.

Regardless of which city you select as your "base," don't forget that the frequent train service between Glasgow and Edinburgh enables you to make a "day excursion" to the one you didn't select as your base. For what to see and do in Edinburgh, consult the following chapter on Scotland's capital for details.

There are times throughout the year when one of the two cities, either Glasgow or Edinburgh, may be "fully booked." This can take place in Glasgow during May when the city hosts a Mayfest—a festival focusing attention on Glasgow's many activities within its cultural sphere. On the other hand, Edinburgh can be filled to overflowing when visitors attend its world famous "Edinburgh Tattoo." When this happens, and your reservationist gives up on the city of your choice—try the other. Your chances of finding accommodations there are very good, and the ease of rail travel between Glasgow and Edinburgh will make it an "easy commute," far better than anything that the Long Island Railroad could come up with!

"GLASGOW CONNECTIONS"

Excursion Destination	Depart Glasgow	Destination Arrive	Destination Depart	Return Glasgow	Notes
Aberdeen	0725	1009	1525	1814	Mon–Sat
	0825	1100	1630	1912	Mon–Sat
	0925	1212	1932	2220	Sundays
	0925	1205	1826	2110	Mon–Sat
Dundee	0725	0852	1545	1710	Mon–Sat
	0825	0950	1745	1912	Mon–Sat
	0925	1057	1645	1824	Sundays
	0925	1050	1907	2035	Mon–Sat
Inverness	0710	1032	1645	2012	Mon–Sat
	1155	1515	2000	2325	Mon–Sat
Montrose	0725	0922	1710	1912	Mon–Sat
	0925	1129	2013	2220	Sundays
	0925	1122	1906	2110	Mon–Sat
Perth	0725	0829	1608	1710	Mon–Sat
	0825	0927	1808	1912	Mon–Sat
	0925	1034	1708	1824	Sundays
	0925	1027	1930	2035	Mon–Sat
Stirling	0825	0853	1740	1814	Mon–Sat
	0925	0955	1744	1824	Sundays
	0925	0953	2039	2110	Mon–Sat
	1025	1053			

St. Andrews Train from Glasgow Queen Street Station to Dundee. Transfer to St. Andrews bus, departing every hour on the half-hour.

Reference: Thomas Cook Table 600

Glasgow-Edinburgh Shuttle Service

Weekday Service: Departs Glasgow Queen Street Station for Edinburgh at 0622, 0655, 0730, and every half-hour thereafter until 2300. Departs Edinburgh at 0700 and every half-hour thereafter until 2330. Journey fifty to seventy minutes.

Sunday Service: Departs Glasgow Queen Street Station for Edinburgh at 0800 and on the hour thereafter until 2300; also at 1830, 1930, 2030, and 2130. Departs Edinburgh at 0830 and on the half-hour thereafter until 1730; also at 1800, 1830, and, every half-hour until 2330. Journey takes fifty-five minutes.

218

GLASGOW-LONDON TRAIN SERVICE
(First- and second-class accommodations for all services listed)

| DEPART FROM GLASGOW CENTRAL | ARRIVE IN LONDON | | | STATION |
	MON–FRI	SAT	SUN	
0700	1241	1240	—	KC
0720(R)	1255	1305	—	ES
0800	1339	1347	—	KC
0950(R)	1449	—	—	ES
1000	1543	1543	1541	KC
0900	—	—	1442	KC
1045	—	—	1727	KC
1140	1658	1708	—	ES
1100	—	—	1641	ES
1200	1741	1739	—	KC
1230(R)	—	—	1833	ES
1245	—	—	1928	KC
1330(R)	—	—	1928	ES
1338(R)	1848	1858	—	ES
1400	1910	1939	—	KC
1445	—	—	2122	KC
1455(R)	—	—	2107	ES
1530	2114	2124	—	ES
1600	2155	2155	—	KC
1630(R)	—	—	2228	ES
1650	—	—	2333	KC
1700(R)	2218	2238	—	ES
1800	0008+1	—	—	KC
2315(R)	—	—	0655+1	ES
2337(R)*	0655+1	0732+1	—	ES

Distance: 402 miles/647 km
References: British Rail Table 26, 26A
           Thomas Cook Table 550

High-speed trains, food service available; reservations recommended for all above-listed trains
(R) Reservations required
KC = King's Cross Station
ES = Euston Station
*Sleeping cars only. Passengers may remain aboard until 0730.

Train Information: 041–204–2844
InterCity Services: 071–387–7070

Glasgow Tourist Information Centre
041–204–4400

The one o'clock gun at Edinburgh Castle is fired every day except Sunday to provide an unusual time check for the city. Visiting shoppers on Princes Street (visible at the lower level in the background), unaware of the firing, may be seen doing their own version of the "One O'clock Jump" at precisely the same moment.

12   EDINBURGH

"This profusion of eccentricities, this dream in masonry and living rock," wrote Robert Louis Stevenson of Edinburgh, "is not a drop-scene in a theater, but a city in a world of everyday reality!" There is an understandable feeling of rocklike perpetuity enveloping Edinburgh. Formed by volcanic heat, scoured and shaped by ice-age glaciers in a valley punctuating its skyline with upward-thrusting crags, Scotland's capital city of Edinburgh is nothing short of dramatic in its setting.

Edinburgh's exact origins are lost in antiquity. Although dissenting opinions exist, it appears that the historical jigsaw of Edinburgh was pieced together in the following pattern. A primitive fortress was established around A.D. 452 by the Picts on the sloping ground leading from the great Castle Rock on which Edinburgh Castle stands today. There have been fortresses on Castle Rock since that time, each in turn razed by a challenger, rebuilt by the challenger, only to be razed again by another challenger. By the time of the eleventh century, however, Edinburgh began to calm down and get on with the task of becoming a civilized and prosperous town.

From its earliest days, Edinburgh's stern, almost aloof countenance has retained and fostered those enduring qualities that have inspired great men to great achievements. Edinburgh is actually two cities. The Old Town, built on a rocky ledge running from Edinburgh Castle to the Royal Palace of Holyroodhouse, is steeped in ancient history. It huddled on high ground in typical medieval fear of attack.

The New Town, which took form on the lower side of Nor' Loch, a lake created from a swamp and eventually drained in 1816, spread serenely in a succession of streets and avenues reflecting the optimism of the latter centuries. The New Town was conceived in 1767 when the Scottish Parliament approved an extension of the city and the Town Council lost no time in proceeding with the work. The city planning that followed made possible Edinburgh's present wide streets and spacious squares.

Its contrasts of two cities within a city are further reflected, on the one hand, by Edinburgh's reserved exterior and, on the other, by its ability to express great warmth and, upon occasion, a high degree of gaiety. Edinburgh has been termed one of the most attractive capital cities in the world. As Oliver Wendell Holmes aptly put it, "Edinburgh is a city of incomparable loveliness."

From the beauty of its setting, enhanced by its architecture, to the turbulence of its history and the quality of its citizens, Edinburgh is a city of inexhaustible delight. Edinburgh Castle, the Palace of Holyroodhouse, the Royal Mile, and Princes Street await you. Welcome to Scotland's capital!

Day Excursions

A "baker's dozen," thirteen exciting day excursions, have been selected for our readers. All were chosen so that those who prefer staying in Glasgow rather than in Edinburgh can enjoy them as well. (See "Glasgow Connections" in chapter 11.)

Scotland is known as "the land that likes to be visited." To ensure that your opportunity to visit this marvelous country by rail includes seeing as many of its features as possible, we have divided the selected day excursions into Scotland's four geographic areas: the east coast, central region, west coast, and Highlands.

East Coast. Along the east coast of Scotland, starting at the North Sea fishing port of Dunbar near the English border, we then swing north from Edinburgh through the trio cities of Dundee, Montrose, and Aberdeen—not overlooking a stop en route at the golf capital of the world, St. Andrews.

Central Region. In the central part of the country, we have selected excursions to two of Scotland's most historic cities—Perth and Stirling—plus a visit to Andrew Carnegie's birthplace, Dunfermline, and a visit to Linlithgow to view the castle where Mary Queen of Scots was born.

West Coast. For our forays to the western coast, we delve deep into the heart of Robert Burns's country by a visit to Ayr, the poet's favorite town. Further west on the Firth of Clyde, we call at Stranraer, the gateway to the Irish Sea and the "Emerald Isle" of Ireland.

Highlands. North in the Highlands, Inverness serves as a gateway to explorations of Loch Ness, with its legendary monster, "Nessie," and as a "base city" for a dash to the west to Kyle of Lochalsh and the Isle of Skye.

Scotland has often been compared to an iceberg—in that there is much more than first meets the eye. Come to Scotland with an open mind, a keen eye, and a sense of adventure.

Arriving and Departing

By Air. Glasgow, Scotland's international airport, located ten miles west of the city from which it takes its name, is a convenient port of entry for visitors arriving in Britain from overseas. The airport is situated in an area that is relatively fog free throughout the majority of the year, for the wind moving across the Irish Sea has few natural obstructions to interrupt its flow. Prestwick airport (twenty-nine miles southwest of Glasgow), which for years served as the international airport for the area, is the most fog-free airport on the British Isles.

Along with its excellent weather, the Glasgow airport offers travelers the opportunity of "open jaw" airline ticketing—arriving or departing on one leg of their transatlantic flight in Scotland rather than flying both in and out of the

London complex of Gatwick, Stansted, or Heathrow. Currently, transatlantic service is provided by the following air carriers: Air Canada, American Airlines, British Airways, Icelandair, and Northwest Airlines.

The airport information desk also provides tourist information to incoming passengers. The office is open from 0715 to 2230 daily. Currency exchange services are operated by Thomas Cook. The office is open daily in the summer between 0700 and 2300; in the winter (November to April), it is open from 0800 to 2000 Monday–Saturday, and Sunday, 0800–1800.

Airport coach service is available between the airport and Glasgow every thirty minutes from 0555 to 2325 weekdays; Sunday service is hourly from 0825 to 2325. Journey time is approximately twenty-five minutes and the fare is £2.00. Bus service direct to Edinburgh departs the airport at fifty-five minutes past the hour from 0655 to 2255 weekdays; Sunday, service is every two hours. Journey time is one hour and forty-five minutes; the fare is £6.00.

In Glasgow, buses terminate at the Buchanan bus station. In Edinburgh, buses terminate at the St. Andrew Square bus station.

By Train. There is only one major train station in Edinburgh—Waverley Station. Some InterCity trains from London go on to Aberdeen after a brief station stop in Edinburgh. If you are aboard one of these trains, be prepared to "set down" in the Waverley Station as quickly as possible following your arrival. Edinburgh does have another station, Haymarket, where all trains halt en route to Glasgow or Aberdeen. Trains arriving from England via Newcastle and York, however, bypass Haymarket Station.

Edinburgh's Railway Station—Waverley

The train terminal in Edinburgh appears to be completely immersed in an open ravine. The area was once a swamp that was converted into a lake as a northern defense for Edinburgh Castle during the reign of King James II (1437–1460). The lake was drained in 1816 to become the site of the Princes Street Gardens separating the Old Town and New Town in Edinburgh.

In 1847, rail lines were laid through the middle of the Princes Street Gardens to the east end, where Waverley Station was constructed. The tracks are now all but concealed by landscaping. Today's Waverley Station complex is the second largest in Britain.

Waverley Station is equipped with twenty-one tracks strewn about in a labyrinth of steps and passageways that could easily drive a laboratory white rat berserk. But a plenitude of signs and the helpful presence of Edinburghers (who appear to be specially trained to assist visitors) will help you put it all together.

Basically, there are three accesses to Waverley Station. The first is a set of rather steep steps connecting the north side of the station (the trackage runs

Floral clock attracts Edinburgh's citizens and visitors alike. Built in 1903 in the city's West Princes Gardens, it is the oldest floral clock in the world. A cuckoo pops out to herald every quarter hour, and the flowers are changed frequently for important events.

east and west) with Princes Street, the city's main artery. The second and third approaches are ramps leading from the main floor of the station to the Waverley Bridge, which runs between the Old Town and the New Town. Both ramps have pedestrian walkways. The northern ramp serves incoming vehicles; the one to the south is for outgoing vehicles.

Many of the facilities sought by incoming passengers, such as banking, city information, and hotel accommodations, are located nearby in the combined offices of the Scottish Tourist Board and Edinburgh City Information Centre beyond the north end of Waverley Bridge at the corner of Waverley and Princes streets. To reach the center, use the pedestrian ramp on the north side of the station, turning right as you reach the Waverley Bridge level. There are several TOURIST INFORMATION signs to help guide the way.

Tracks 12 to 18 form the backbone, or center, of the Waverley Station. At the entrance to these tracks is a digital-display bulletin board for train arrivals, departures, and special announcements. If your train is departing from tracks other than 12 to 18, ask the railroad personnel at the ticket barriers for directions; otherwise, you may end up in some dark corner like a berserk white rat.

Pay special attention to multiple train departures from the same track. In other words, a line of coaches on a single train track can actually be two trains departing for two separate destinations. They are announced with red-bannered FRONT TRAIN or REAR TRAIN signs. It pays to ask questions however—one advantage you have over the rat!

The British Rail Travel Centre (train information center) is located in the waiting-room area of the station. Covered by a huge glass dome, the waiting area also contains digital arrival/departure information and a series of facilities, including rest rooms, a magazine kiosk, and the Talisman Bar and the Talisman Buffet. The principal entrance to this area is located across the main-station concourse from the stub ends of tracks 16 and 17.

Since 1902, a landmark for Edinburgh as well as the Waverley Station is the Balmoral Hotel (formerly known as the North British Hotel), situated between the station and Princes Street. Topped by a mammoth 200-foot Gothic clock tower, the hotel served as a transition between the hustle of commerce on Princes Street and the bustle of the passengers arriving and departing the station. Erected during the Age of Steam, the hotel's spacious foyer and well-appointed lounges provided a brief but necessary respite for weary travelers.

Victorian throughout, the hotel underwent a £23 million restoration. It has emerged new in face but old in grace as the Balmoral Hotel. Undoubtedly, the hotel is still one of Edinburgh's most familiar and most elegant landmarks, commanding an important position at the east end of Princes Street.

Two bus departure points serve the area surrounding the Waverley Street rail station. The first, at Waverley Bridge, is located immediately up the ramps leading out of the rail station. This departure point serves the city bus system as well as the sightseeing buses. Coach service for the Glasgow Airport utilizes the bus terminal on St. Andrew Square. To reach it, cross Princes Street where it intersects with Waverley Bridge at the city's tourist information center. Then, walk north one block to St. Andrew Square.

Money exchange (Bureau de Change) is available from the Edinburgh & Scotland Information Centre. Hours of operation are 0900–2000 Monday through Saturday and 1000–2000 on Sunday (July and August). During May, June, and September, the hours are 0900–1900 Monday through Saturday and 1100–1900 on Sunday. April and October, it is open 0900–1800 Monday through Saturday and 1100–1800 Sunday; November through March, the hours are 0900–1800 Monday through Saturday.

 Hotel accommodations are provided by the Edinburgh tourist information center. Hours are: (July and August) Monday through Saturday, 0900–2000, and Sunday, 1000–2000; (May, June and September) Monday through Saturday, 0900–1900, and Sunday, 1100–1900; (April and October) Monday through Saturday, 0900–1800, and Sunday, 1100–1800; (November–March) Monday–Saturday, 0900–1800. The hotel-accommodations reservation fee is £3.00 per booking.

Tourist information is available at two locations within Edinburgh's information center, both operating at the same hours as the "Hotel Accommodations" section mentioned above. The first section has information on Edinburgh and all of Scotland; go straight ahead as you enter for self service. Go to the right for counter service. For entertainment information, proceed through the shopping section, where Scottish books, maps, and posters are available and turn to the left.

For bus tours of Edinburgh, we refer you to the tourist information office and its selection of bus tour brochures. Among those available, we have found that the Guide Friday bus tour of the city is complete and the commentary of their guides accurate and amusing. Guided walking tours (Robin's Walking Tours) depart daily from outside the tourist information center. There are several to choose from: The "Grand Tour of the City" departs at 1000, the "Royal Mile" tour at 1100, and 1900 for "Ghosts and Witches." Telephone (031) 661–0125.

Train information is available at the British Rail Travel Centre in the waiting-room area of Waverley Station. City information is *not* available in this office. Operating hours are 0700–2300 daily.

Train reservations may be made in the travel center at any one of the counters in operation during the time of your visit.

Shopping in Edinburgh

The city of Edinburgh is well known for its fine boutiques, shops, and department stores. You can still find bargains in the famous Harris tweeds, Fair Isle sweaters, and Tartan plaids. Princes Street is lined with shops displaying a variety of Scottish wares from argyles and bagpipes to whiskey. And when you run out of stores and shops to visit on Princes Street, turn north two blocks to George Street and continue your shopping there. (You may need to stop by the bank on the way.)

Shoppers' havens on Princes Street include large department stores such as Jenners and C. & A., opposite the Scott Monument in the Waverley Street Station area. If you've not been in a store 180 years old, try Romanes & Paterson, Ltd. at 62 Princes Street. You will find traditional Scottish tweed, exquisite Edinburgh crystal, Caithness glass, knitwear from the borders, and, of course, tartans.

Still not tired of shopping? The Scotch House next door contains more than 300 tartans available by the meter, along with Shetland knitwear and original gifts. If you know a wee person, check out Hop Scotch, The Scotch House's special department for children.

With all that shopping, you may be ready for a libation and a snack. You don't have far to go—between, and parallel to, Princes Street and George Street is Rose Street—which probably has more convivial pubs to the meter than any other street in the world.

Greyfriars Bobby

On Candlemaker Row, a short distance from Edinburgh's Royal Mile, stands a statue in tribute to a small dog's affection and fidelity to his master. In 1858, a wee Skye terrier followed the remains of his master, Auld Jock, to Greyfriars churchyard, where the dog lingered and slept on his master's grave for fourteen years until his death in 1872.

People tried to take Bobby away. They even found a home for him in the country. Still, Bobby returned to the churchyard, where friends began bringing food to sustain him during his vigil. The story of Greyfriars Bobby spread throughout Edinburgh, and soon Bobby's tale of devotion reached Queen Victoria in London. She sent a special envoy, Lady Burdett-Coutts, to investigate this unusual story.

Bobby, in the meantime, had made friends with a number of children in a nearby orphanage. The terrier brought joy and love to the children, particularly to Tammy, a crippled boy with whom Bobby would play by the hour. Bobby lived his own life, however, and returned nightly to his master's grave—at first secretly, for the presence of a dog in a churchyard was unthinkable in those times. But as Bobby won hearts, he gained privileges, too. He even won

Greyfriars Bobby, a small Skye terrier whose devotion to his master in both life and death captured hearts throughout Edinburgh, is commemorated there by a fountain with his statue on it. A film by Walt Disney has made Bobby world-famous. The Greyfriars Bobby Bar may be seen in the background.

the heart of the Lord Provost of Edinburgh, who had a collar made for the dog in 1867 and paid Bobby's licensing fee. (The collar can be seen today in the Huntly House Museum on Canongate Street.)

Bobby never went to London to see the Queen, but royal annals reflect that the Queen actually was planning to pay *him* a visit at Greyfriars. Bobby died, however, before that honor became a reality.

The dog's body was buried alongside that of his master. Although Bobby is no longer visible, his presence is felt so strongly by the residents of the area that they frankly admit to opening their doors briefly before retiring at night—just in case. Perhaps, when the door to heaven is opened for them, they will see Bobby again, running on the green pastures at the heels of his master, beside the still waters. Bobby is there. If there wasn't room enough in God's heaven for the love of this dog for his master, Bobby would not have kept the vigil at his master's grave—he would just have gone away.

Bobby's statue stands close to the iron gates of Greyfriars churchyard, where Auld Jock and his faithful dog are interred. The story of Greyfriars Bobby was filmed by Walt Disney. We think it's worth your while to visit Greyfriars, just as we do each time we return to Edinburgh.

Enticing Edinburgh

Amid the contrasting charms of its Old Town and New Town, Edinburgh takes its place among an elite group of European cities conspicuous for their romance and physical attributes. As more and more enclosures were built during the post-medieval period, the term *close* came into existence in old Edinburgh to describe the narrow passageways giving access or right of way to the buildings in the rear of others. There are well over one hundred closes in Old Town, many of which have brass tablets at their entrances to explain their historical significance.

There are many aspects of Edinburgh to see on conducted tours, but the city's real beauty is best seen by exploring it on foot at your own pace. Walk the Royal Mile in Old Town from Edinburgh Castle to the Palace of Holyroodhouse. En route, you'll pass a fantastic assembly of picturesque old buildings, such as Brodie's Close, the John Knox House, the Cannonball House, Anchor Close, and the Canongate Tolbooth.

Brodie's Close housed Deacon Brodie, a respectable town councilor by day and a burglar by night. Brodie's life-style supposedly provided the basis for Robert Louis Stevenson's *Dr. Jekyll and Mr. Hyde.* The John Knox House dates from the sixteenth century. It's traditionally connected with both John Mossman, Keeper of the Royal Mint to Mary Queen of Scots, and John Knox, Scotland's religious reformer. A brief video presentation amid original timber-framed galleries and oak paneling will take you back to the sixteenth century.

The John Knox House is located at the halfway mark of The Royal Mile in The Netherbow. Admission is £1.20.

The Cannonball House, dating from 1630, got its name from a cannonball lodged in its gable, ostensibly fired from the castle by an errant cannoneer during the blockade of 1745. Anchor Close is the site where the first edition of the *Encyclopedia Britannica* was printed. The Edinburgh edition of Robert Burns's poems was also printed there. Reportedly, Burns himself read the proofs on the premises. Last renovated in 1591, the Canongate Tolbooth has been used as the Town Council House and a prison for the ancient village of Canongate, now incorporated into the city of Edinburgh. The Canongate Tolbooth now houses the People's Story Museum, which relates the life and work of ordinary people in Edinburgh from the late eighteenth century to the present.

Although the Palace of Holyroodhouse originated as a guest house for the Abbey of Holyrood, most of the palace we see today was built for Charles II in 1671. The most famous figure associated with the palace, however, was Mary Queen of Scots, who spent six years of her tragic reign there. On the palace grounds, you can view Queen Mary's Bath House where, according to today's Scottish tour guides, Mary Queen of Scots bathed daily. The guides also explain that her cousin, Queen Elizabeth I, bathed once a month—whether she needed it or not.

The Royal Mile was for many centuries the center of Edinburgh life. Its citizens lived and conducted their affairs on this busy, crowded street. At the point where High Street changes into Canongate, you will find a line of the letter "S" embedded in the pavement. Until 1880, it marked the limits of sanctuary extended by Holyrood Abbey. It is said that debtors were often seen running toward the line with creditors in hot pursuit and bystanders wagering on the outcome.

EDINBURGH-LONDON TRAIN SERVICE
(First- and second-class accommodations for all services listed)

DEPART WAVERLEY STATION	ARRIVE LONDON KING'S CROSS STATION		
	MON–FRI	SAT	SUN
0600	1055	—	—
0630*	1039	—	—
0700	1139	1146	—
0800	1239	1240	—
0830	—	1310	—
0900	1339	1347	1442
0930	—	1408	—
0945	—	1412	—
1000	1440	1450	1541
1030	1457	1457	—
1100	1543	1543	1641
1130	1600	1600	—
1200	1649	1648	1727
1230	1657	1654	1750
1300	1741	1739	1828
1330	—	1801	1928
1400	1835	1840	—
1500	—	1939	2023
1500*	1910	—	—
1530	—	—	—
1600	2038	2038	2122
1630	—	—	2143
1700	2155	2155	2208
1730	2229	2217	—
1800	0010	—	2333
1900	0010+1	—	—
2200	0500+1	—	—
2310(R)**	—	0751+1	—
2335	—	—	0635+1
2355(R)**	0620+1	—	—

Distance: 393 miles/632 km
References: British Rail Table 26A
Thomas Cook Table 570
High-speed trains, food service available; reservations recommended
(R) Reservations required
*Pullman service, supplement payable
** Sleeping cars only, arrives in Euston Station

Tourist Information
British Tourist Authority: 071–499–9325
Edinburgh: 031–557–1700

Train Information
Edinburgh: 031–556–2451
InterCity Services: 071–278–2477

Aberdeen's many faces (above) are depicted in its harbor and academic countenances. Its harbor bustles with commercial fishing craft, outlying-island ferries, and vessels resupplying offshore oil rigs. Kings College (below) provides tranquillity with its seventeenth-century crown tower.

From Edinburgh ...

A DAY EXCURSION TO ABERDEEN
DISTANCE BY TRAIN: 131 miles (211 km)
AVERAGE TRAIN TIME: 2 hours, 30 minutes

Since the discovery of oil in the North Sea, Aberdeen has earned the title of "Europe's offshore oil capital." The city, however, has not been spoiled by this new industry. Oil does not come ashore in Aberdeen; moreover, only occasionally can an oil rig be seen on the horizon—under tow to a new location or at anchor awaiting a new contract.

The development of North Sea oil plus the gathering strength of northeast Scotland's agriculture, fishing, and manufacturing industries have combined to give Aberdeen the highest growth rate of any city in Great Britain. Therefore, you will find Aberdeen a city of many moods. It is steeped in history. It is an ancient university town and a thriving seaport as well. It has grown very cosmopolitan, yet it remains old in grace. Above all else, the Aberdonians always have time—time to help, time to be interested, and time to talk.

Aberdeen lies between the rivers Dee and Don with two miles of golden sand connecting them. But don't think of Aberdeen merely as a large city with a beach. Union Street bisects the city and provides a mile-long shopping center lined with excellent shops. If you can make it out of bed and down to the docks no later than 0730, you'll see one of the city's biggest attractions, the fish market, in full operation.

Aberdeen University comprises Kings College and Marischal College. Both are architecturally attractive yet totally different. Marischal College is one of the largest granite buildings in the world. It was founded in 1593 and united with Kings College in 1860 to form the University of Aberdeen. King's College, in Old Aberdeen, was founded in 1495. The ivy-covered building with its distinctive crown tower has stood for centuries as a symbol of Aberdeen.

Standing like a sentinel, the gleaming white Girdleness Lighthouse guarding Aberdeen's harbor will be the first welcoming sign you'll see in Scotland's third largest city. It becomes visible on the right as the train curves away to the left from Nigg Bay to cross the River Dee, then glides to a halt in Aberdeen's rail station.

The port of Aberdeen is the jumping-off place for adventurers bound for the Orkney Islands and Shetland Islands to the north. Don't be surprised if you see a cruise ship or two in Aberdeen's harbor. Aberdeen has attracted the cruise ships by constructing a passenger landing stage in its Victoria Dock area. It appears that everyone wants to visit Europe's offshore capital, Aberdeen. Enjoy your visit.

ABERDEEN—*THE GRANITE CITY*

A Day Excursion from Edinburgh

DEPART FROM WAVERLY STATION	ARRIVE IN ABERDEEN STATION	NOTES
0705	0942	(2)
0810	1045	(2)
0855	1124	(3)
0910	1138	(2)
1020	1250	(2)
1055	1325	(3)

DEPART FROM ABERDEEN STATION	ARRIVE IN WAVERLY STATION	NOTES
1455 (1510 SUN)	1720 (1741 SUN)	(1)(3)
1615	1848	(2)
1712	1950	(2)
1815	2042	(2)
1900	2127	(3)
2000	2223	(2)
2050	2320	(3)

Distance: 131 miles/211 km
References: British Rail Table 229
            Thomas Cook Table 600

(1) MON–FRI   (3) SUN
(2) MON–SAT

Train Information: 0224–594222
InterCity Services: 071–278–2477

Aberdeen Tourist Information Centre: 0224–632727
Aberdeen Whats on Line—24-Hour Service
0224–636363

Aberdeen maintains tourist information in the form of a well-stocked literature stand alongside the Travel Centre information counter in the rail station. There's also a twenty-four-hour "View Data" service—a very user-friendly computerized inquiry unit.

The main tourist information center is in St. Nicholas House on Broad Street. When leaving the station, turn right onto Guild Street and walk until you arrive at Market Street, where the docks come into view. A left turn onto Market Street followed by a right turn onto Union Street will keep you on course (mind the shops!) until you spy Aberdeen's Town House at the head of Broad Street leading to your left. The center is a short distance up Broad Street on the left-hand side, opposite Marischal College and its award-winning Museum of Human History.

This information center is open daily throughout the year except on Sundays from October through May. During summer (June through September), the center is open Monday through Saturday, 0900–1800, and Sunday, 1000–1600 (closes two hours later July and August). From October to May, it is open Monday through Friday, 0900–1700, and Saturday, 1000–1400. On public and local holidays, with the exception of Christmas and New Year's Day, the center is normally open 0900–1700.

The Aberdeen information center has a wide variety of booklets, leaflets, and posters of Aberdeen and the surrounding area. Also available are the publications of the Scottish Tourist Board covering the entire country. The center is divided into three operating sections: inquiries, accommodations, and tickets. Walking-tour and bus-tour information is also available here.

Clustered around the tourist information center on Broad Street, many of Aberdeen's places of interest are only a short walk away. In the restored Provost Skene's House on Broad Street, the oldest domestic dwelling in Aberdeen, dating from 1545, you will find rooms furnished in styles covering different periods in Aberdeen's history.

The Aberdeen Maritime Museum is housed in Provost Ross's House overlooking the city's harbor. Here, attractive displays not only depict Aberdeen's maritime heritage of fishing, shipbuilding, and trade, but also its offshore oil industry (with scale-model oil rigs). Provost Ross's House, a restored sixteenth-century dwelling, also houses a visitor's center featuring audiovisual displays of National Trust for Scotland properties, a fascinating collection of more than 100 properties representing a rich variety of castles, gardens, scenic areas, islands, and historic sights.

Tam o'Shanter Inn on High Street is a part of the lore of Scotland's bard, Robert Burns. The city of Ayr is a principal point for starting out on the Burns Heritage Trail, developed by the Scottish Tourist Board. The trail tours places linked to the history of Scotland's greatest poet.

A DAY EXCURSION TO AYR
DISTANCE BY TRAIN: 88 miles (142 km)
AVERAGE TRAIN TIME: 1 hour, 30 minutes

What William Shakespeare is to England, Robert Burns is to Scotland. Ayr is the acknowledged center of the celebrated "Burns Country." The town is rich in the history of Scotland's bard. Many famous landmarks remain in Ayr today to tell the Burnsian stories.

The Tam o'Shanter Inn on High Street is where Tam began his celebrated ride. The Auld Brig (old bridge) that for 500 years was the only bridge in town still offers a delightful passage across the River Ayr. In a conspicuous location outside the Ayr train station, a statue of Robert Burns waits to greet travelers.

In Alloway, a pleasant southern suburb of Ayr, you will find the Land O'Burns Interpretation Centre, where visual displays introduce you to the life of Robert Burns and acquaint you with locations in and around Ayr that you may later want to visit. A brief walk from the Interpretation Centre will bring you to Burns's Cottage, where the poet was born on 25 January 1759. More than 100,000 visitors pass through the center and the cottage annually. The ruins of the Alloway Auld Kirk (old church), also close to the center, were the inspiration for Burns's narrative poem "Tam o'Shanter."

It was from the ruins of the Auld Kirk that witches pursued Tam, but he escaped over the Auld Brig O'Doon—the bridge over the River Doon—and eluded his pursuers, because according to legend witches were unable to cross running water. Maggie, the mare that Tam rode, was less fortunate: "Ae spring brought off her master hale,/But left behind her ain gray tail:/The carlin claught her by the rump,/And left poor Maggie scarce a stump."

Ayr was a seaside resort long before the term was invented. Well-heeled Glasgow merchants came to Ayr for short vacations, liked what they saw, and built houses there. In addition to providing Scottish gentry with suburban abodes, Ayr is also an industrial town, a market center, and a fishing port—for good measure. With all these assets, Ayr is assured of retaining its prosperous, bustling atmosphere even after the summer visitors have gone.

Throughout the year on Tuesdays and Thursdays, the farmers bring their cattle to market in Ayr. Year-round, the town's harbor provides the locale for those who enjoy watching the fishermen bringing in their catch. As the shopping center for the district, Ayr surprises visitors with the range and size of its stores and shops.

After arriving in Ayr, head for the town's tourist information center which is a very short walk from the rail station. Depart the train station through the main exit and walk directly across the street for Burns Statue Square. The

237

AYR—*BURNS'S TAM O'SHANTER INN*

A Day Excursion from Edinburgh

DEPART FROM EDINBURGH WAVERLEY STATION	ARRIVE IN GLASGOW QUEEN STREET STATION	NOTES
0700 or 0900	0750 or 0950	(1)
0830	0940	(2)

Transfer to Glasgow Central Station (See chapter 11)

DEPART FROM GLASGOW CENTRAL STATION	ARRIVE IN AYR STATION	NOTES
0800 or 1000	0852 or 1052	(1)(2)

(Plus other frequent service)

DEPART FROM AYR STATION	ARRIVE IN GLASGOW CENTRAL STATION	NOTES
1543	1634	(1)(2)
1613 or 1813	1709 or 1909	(1)

Transfer to Glasgow Queen Street Station (See chapter 11)
(Plus other frequent service)

DEPART FROM GLASGOW QUEEN STREET STATION	ARRIVE IN EDINBURGH WAVERLEY STATION	NOTES
1700 or 1930	1750 or 2020	(1)
1700	1759	(2)

Distance: 88 miles/142 km
References: British Rail Table 221
Thomas Cook Tables 590, 591

(1) MON–SAT   (2) SUN

Train Information: 345–212282
InterCity Services: 071–387–7070

Ayr Tourist Information Centre: 0292–284196

tourist information office is in Burns House. From Easter to the end of May, the office is open Monday through Friday, 0915–1700, and Saturday and Sunday, 1000–1700. June–September, hours are Monday through Friday, 0915–1800, and Saturday and Sunday, 1000–1800. October to Easter, it is open Monday through Friday, 0915–1700.

Literature on Ayr, the district surrounding it, and Scotland's famous poet, Robert Burns, abounds by the pound in the information center. You will want to collect such informative booklets as the one published by the district that's crammed with facts and photos. In addition, ask for a copy of the city map. It is the best authority for a tour of Ayr on foot that we have found.

You will hear mention of the Burns Heritage Trail during your visit in Ayr. If you are interested in taking it or a bus to "Burns Country," you should gather all the details from the information center. The Burns Heritage Trail has been developed by the Scottish Tourist Board. It is a tour of the places linked with Scotland's poet. On the trail, you can see many places that have been developed to tell the story of Burns and his lifetime. The trail tour includes a visit to Tarbolton and the Lochlea Farm, where the Burns family lived from 1777 to 1784, and a stop at Mauchline, where it is said that Robert Burns met his wife to be, Jean Armour.

With more than two miles of golden, sandy beach, Ayr gets more than its fair share of the summer Scottish sun. Golf, bowling, and tennis are among the many sports activities that can be enjoyed there. The town has three golf courses, forming part of the famous fifteen-mile stretch of "golfing coast" you'll see from the train approaching Ayr. All the traditional seaside amusements can be enjoyed in Ayr, as well as horse racing, held at the Ayr Racecourse throughout the year.

Away from the beaches, there are many beautiful parks and gardens, noteably Belleisle, Craigie, and Rozelle. Rozelle is also the home of Ayr's Art Gallery and displays one of the very few Henry Moore sculptures to be seen in Scotland. Ayr's beauty has frequently brought it the coveted titles, "Britain's Floral Town" and "Scotland's Floral Town." If you delight in old houses, Ayr has many, including one that was built in 1470—twenty-two years before Columbus discovered America!

Following your visit to Ayr, you probably will be in accord with "Robbie" Burns when he wrote, "Auld Ayr, wham ne'er a town surpasses/For honest men and bonnie lasses."

RNLB *Margaret*, a Royal National Life Boat, stands ready for rescue duty in Dunbar's Victoria Harbor. The ruins of Dunbar Castle mark the narrow passageway leading from the harbor into the North Sea. The old lifeboat house on the harbor's quay is now a museum.

A DAY EXCURSION TO DUNBAR
DISTANCE BY TRAIN: 29 miles (46 km)
AVERAGE TRAIN TIME: 30 minutes

Put on your walking shoes—we're going to Dunbar. The town offers two wonderful walking opportunities: one through the historic center of old Dunbar to appreciate the great and varied wealth of its traditional Scottish buildings, the other along the cliffs brooding over the North Sea in the John Muir Country Park. Those unaccustomed to walking or slower of pace can take solace in Dunbar's harbor area by watching fishermen and their customers on the quay buying and selling freshly caught fish as their colorful fishing boats bob about on the tide. Further assurance of a pleasant outing for all is the presence of several public houses in the harbor area. Among them is the Volunteer Arms, which houses the Volunteer Bar and the Haven Lounge, where one can either seek haven or volunteer.

Dunbar is situated amid some of the most beautiful countryside and coastline in Scotland. There are few other places where it is possible to witness the full range of history of a Scottish east-coast fishing port and market center. Dunbar has always played an important part in Scotland's history. Due to its strategic location, the town has been a stronghold down through the centuries. Dunbar, Gaelic for "the fort on the point," had a castle fortress at least as early as 856. The remains of the castle stand on the promontory overlooking Dunbar's Victoria Harbor.

The Dunbar Castle was the place where Bothwell brought Mary Queen of Scots when he abducted her in 1567. That same year, the Scottish Parliament ordered that Dunbar Castle should be demolished. When the Victoria Harbor was constructed in the nineteenth century, the channel leading into the harbor was cut through the rocky palisade where the ruins of the castle lay. The remains that you may inspect during your visit to Dunbar are only a fragment of the original great castle.

There are two harbors: the old harbor, extended by Oliver Cromwell, and Victoria Harbor. Construction on the old harbor began in 1655, and it was improved and extended in the eighteenth century. This harbor, now nearly deserted, still retains the old paving stones as well as a fishermen's barometer that was erected in 1856. As part of the redevelopment, the harbor areas have had cottage-type houses built since 1951 to the special design of Sir Basil Spence, the architect of the new Coventry Cathedral. Perhaps the best evidence of Dunbar's beauty is the large number of visitors walking about simply admiring the scenery.

An interesting part of Victoria harbor is Dunbar's RNLB (Royal National

DUNBAR—*"FORT ON THE POINT"*

A Day Excursion from Edinburgh

DEPART FROM EDINBURGH WAVERLEY STATION	ARRIVE IN DUNBAR STATION	NOTES
0600	0621	(1)
0700	0720	(3)
0930	0951	(1)
1000	1023	(3)
1200	1220	(4)
1400	1421	(1)

DEPART FROM DUNBAR STATION	ARRIVE IN EDINBURGH WAVERLEY STATION	NOTES
1600	1639	(4)
1657	1725	(1)
1713	1738	(3)
1826	1856	(4)
2108	2134	(3)
2148	2218	(1)
2242	2312	(4)

Distance: 29 miles/46 km
References: British Rail Table 26
                    Thomas Cook Table 570

(1) MON–FRI   (3) SAT
(2) MON–SAT   (4) SUN

Train Information: 031–556–2451
InterCity Services: 071–278–2477

Dunbar Tourist Information Centre
0368–63353

Life Boat) *Margaret.* Opposite its mooring is the Lifeboat Museum, which is well worth a visit. Lifeboats out of Dunbar have saved more than 200 lives since beginning operation in 1808.

The Dunbar tourist information center is at 143 High Street, near the Town House. Part of the Town House, incidentally, is a tolbooth (toll gate) dating back to the seventeenth century, when a toll road between Edinburgh and Newcastle ran through Dunbar. The center is a short walk from the railway station. Station Road runs from the front of the station to where it crosses Countess Road and becomes Abbey Road. When you reach the general post office on your left, the thoroughfare has another name change to High Street and remains so until you reach the information center.

The information center is open during summer 0900–2000 Monday through Saturday and 1100–1800 on Sunday. During the balance of the year, it is open Monday through Friday, 0900–1700, and closed Saturday and Sunday. Note the sundial on the tolbooth tower as you enter the information center. You can still set your watch by it—provided, of course, that the sun is shining during your visit.

For the town tour we mentioned, ask for a copy of *A Walk Around Historic Dunbar* (£2.50). A guidebook for the self-guided trail laid out along the cliffs running out of Dunbar is also available. This cliff-top trail is prominently marked on the previously mentioned street plan, as are other features of the town, including the two harbors.

If you brought your walking shoes with you, the place to try them out is the John Muir Country Park, which begins at Dunbar harbor and extends to the Ravensheugh sands to the west, on the south approaches to the Firth of Forth. The cliff-top trail has controlled public accesses to the beaches below. Throughout the summer, a ranger is normally on duty in the park and is available to answer your questions and provide directions. You may join the ranger on a ramble along the cliff-top trail, but times and routes may vary. Check with the tourist office. There are several horse riding routes within the park. If interested in equestrian pursuits, ask the tourist information center for a copy of *Horse Riding Guide.*

If you are a golf nut and have not been able to obtain a tee time for the Old Course at St. Andrews, try the par-64 Winterfield Golf Course maintained by the city of Dunbar. Call Dunbar 62280 to get a tee time.

There is a bowling green on the right-hand side of the Station Road as you proceed toward town. We asked an old Scot, "How can such a green be so smooth and flat?" "It's easy," he explained, "you just plant the best of grass seed and then roll it for a few hundred years."

Unicorn figurehead of the frigate *Unicorn* glistens at the bow of Britain's oldest warship still afloat. Moored at the Victoria Dock in Dundee, the vessel is open to visitors year-round and features an exhibition of Royal Navy development.

From Edinburgh . . .

A DAY EXCURSION TO DUNDEE
DISTANCE BY TRAIN: 60 miles (96 km)
AVERAGE TRAIN TIME: 1 hour, 30 minutes

As your train approaches the city of Dundee, you will be able to witness a scene of railroading history—one of disaster and yet one of triumph. Following the station stop at Leuchars, where you detrain for St. Andrews, watch as the train passes through the local station of Wormit and on to the railway bridge crossing the Firth of Tay inbound to Dundee. The bridge, a double-track structure 11,653 feet long, was opened in 1887 and was considered at that time (as it is even now) to be a triumph of railroad engineering. Look alongside the present bridge and you will see a series of old bridge piers. These once supported a single-track bridge that was swept away during a violent storm in 1879, along with a train and seventy-five of its passengers.

Turn your gaze to the east during the crossing of the great Firth (estuary) where the Tay River empties into the North Sea and you will see a two-lane vehicular bridge 7,365 feet in length that was opened by Queen Elizabeth II in 1966. The River Tay and its rail and vehicular bridges are a vital part of Dundee's existence.

Dundee, the capital of Tayside and Scotland's fourth largest city, lies in a magnificent setting between the Sidlaw Hills and the banks of Britain's finest salmon river, the Tay.

Dundee was famous for generations as the city of "jute, jam, and journalism." Its prolific writers still abound and Dundee marmelade is still made locally, but jute is slowly sinking into the shadows of time as synthetic fibers take over in the cordage industry.

Dundee lies in the heart of Scotland, where the game of golf originated. The latest count reveals forty golf courses within one hour's drive of the city. Five actually lie within the city's district. In Dundee, the name of the game is golf, and its citizens have proven to the world that they can construct courses that can confound, confuse—but always entertain. In Dundee and throughout the area, you also will note that the hospitality in the nineteenth holes throughout the region is second to none.

By the way, if your original day-excursion plans were for St. Andrews but you failed to leave the train at Leuchars Station, you can still make it back to the golf capital by bus out of Dundee in less than one hour. You also can capitalize on your error, however, and enjoy Dundee.

Dundee's tourist information center is easy to find. From within the rail station proceed across the pedestrian bridge, then exit and follow Whitehall Street to the right until you come to Crichton Street. Turn left up this street until you

DUNDEE—*CITY OF DISCOVERY*

A Day Excursion from Edinburgh

DEPART FROM EDINBURGH WAVERLEY STATION	ARRIVE IN DUNDEE STATION	NOTES
0705	0827	(2)
0810	0926	(2)
0855	1010	(3)
0910	1024	(2)
1020	1135	(2)
1055	1208	(3)

DEPART FROM DUNDEE STATION	ARRIVE IN EDINBURGH WAVERLEY STATION	NOTES
1427	1548	(2)
1501	1618	(3)
1606	1720	(1)
1627	1741	(3)
1727	1858	(2)(3)
1827	1950	(2)
1927	2042	(2)(3)*
2109	2223	(2)

* Arrives 2058, Sunday

Distance: 60 miles/96 km
References: British Rail Table 229
                  Thomas Cook Table 600

(1) MON–FRI   (3) SUN
(2) MON–SAT

Train Information: 0382–28046
InterCity Services: 071–278–2477

Dundee Tourist Information Centre
0382–434664

reach the top. Turn right again and you have reached the City Square. The tourist information center is at No. 4. You can phone the center from the railway station on (0382) 434664. The center is open Monday through Saturday, 0830–2000; Sunday, 1100–2000 during May, June, and September. It closes one hour later during July and August. From October through April, it is open Monday through Friday, 0900–1800, and Saturday, 1000–1600.

The cultural aspects of Dundee are enhanced by its McManus Galleries as well as the University Botanical Gardens. Camperdown Park and the Wildlife Centre are also stellar attractions for those who prefer outside activities. Among Dundee's many other attractions, one that we think will prove to be of interest to all is the frigate *Unicorn*, Britain's oldest warship still afloat. The *Unicorn* is one of the world's four remaining frigates, those fast, lightly armed sailing ships of yesteryear now replaced by the destroyer class of naval vessel. Launched in 1824, the *Unicorn* remained in naval service until 1968. Ask the information center for the *Unicorn* and RRS *Discovery* brochures and instructions to reach Victoria Dock and Discovery Quay.

Dundee's newest attraction is *Discovery* Point, a state of the art visitor's center portraying the history of Captain Scott's Royal Research Ship *Discovery* and her Antarctic voyages. Built in Dundee, Britain's first scientific research vessel set sail on her voyage to the Antarctic in 1901. You can visit *Discovery* berthed adjacent to the visitor's center.

Dundee's other points of interest include its old steeple, its four castles—Dudhope, Mains, Claypotts, and Broughty—and the Mercat Cross, which is moved about as the population center changes. The old steeple, standing at a height of 156 feet above the ground, dates from the fourteenth century. The steeple has withstood many storms, both natural and manmade. It was the site of the siege of 1651, when the town was invaded by Cromwell's army. The old steeple and all of the castle sites can be reached by public transport buses from the city bus station close to the British Rail terminal.

The Mercat Cross, a replica of the old structure that was demolished in 1877, is currently located at the end of High Street. The original cross was erected in the Seagate area. About the beginning of the fifteenth century, however, the city's population began to increase, and the town began to spread westward. The Seagate was abandoned as the principal center of the city in favor of a more open space to the west, which is now High Street.

Dundee has a passion for plaques and has erected a number of them on buildings having historical associations. At latest count, twelve such monuments are located throughout the city. Of particular interest to visitors is the plaque marking the Greyfriars monastery, which was granted to the city as a burial site by Mary Queen of Scots in 1564 and is now known as the Howff.

Humble weaver's cottage in Dunfermline (above), birthplace of steel millionaire Andrew Carnegie, is open to the public. Carnegie's benevolence brought amenities such as a concert hall, library, and sports center to the city. Old Pug Engine No. 11 (below) stands in Pittencrieff Park close by the Carnegie memorial statue.

From Edinburgh . . .

A DAY EXCURSION TO DUNFERMLINE
DISTANCE BY TRAIN: 17 miles (27 km)
AVERAGE TRAIN TIME: 32 minutes

Dunfermline was once the capital of Scotland and holds an important position in Scottish history. The majestic spires of the Dunfermline Abbey dominate the town's skyline. Within the abbey are the graves of seven Scottish kings, including the tomb of Robert the Bruce. The abbey was founded by Scotland's King David in the twelfth century as a Benedictine monastery. In the course of time, through royal gifts and other extensive endowments, it became one of the most magnificent establishments in Scotland. In its time, the monastery has played host to a wide range of people, from Edward I of England to Oliver Cromwell.

A second attraction in Dunfermline is Pittencrieff Park, a lovely area with its flower gardens, music pavilion, aviary, and museum. It was given to the town by Andrew Carnegie, the Scottish-American philanthopist who was born in a humble weaver's cottage in Dunfermline in 1835. His birthplace is open to the public, and it attracts thousands of visitors every year. A statue of the steel millionaire stands in the center of Pittencrieff. It was erected by the citizens of Dunfermline in grateful appreciation of his many gifts to his native city.

Arriving in Dunfermline by train, you can go to the center of the city either by bus or by taxi. The walk is not too distant to the abbey and the other attractions in town. It is a bit longer, however, than the stationmaster's advice, "Not more than a four-minute walk from here." Allow fifteen minutes to cover the ground between the train station and the center of the city. The tourist information center, the abbey, Pittencrieff, and Carnegie's birthplace lie between these two points. Taxis queue at the front of the station. About £2.00 will see you to the city center. The bus stop is close to the station at an underpass on the left.

The tourist information center is located near the historic sixteenth-century Abbot House, right next to the abbey in the Maygate. It is open from Easter to October, 1000–1800 Monday through Saturday (closed 1400–1430); Sunday, 1100–1500. October through March the center is open 1100–1600 daily, closed Wednesday and Sunday. To contact the center by telephone, call 0383–720999.

Of course, Dunfermline's tourist information center specializes in the features of the abbey and Carnegie's cottage, but you'll find that the staff is very helpful in suggesting other things to do, too.

249

DUNFERMLINE—*ANDREW CARNEGIE BIRTHPLACE*

A Day Excursion from Edinburgh

DEPART FROM EDINBURGH WAVERLEY STATION	ARRIVE IN DUNFERMLINE STATION	NOTES
0815	0845	(1)
0955	0945	(1)
0955	1027	(2)
1015	1045	(1)
1115	1145	(1)
1155	1227	(2)

DEPART FROM DUNFERMLINE STATION	ARRIVE IN EDINBURGH WAVERLEY STATION	NOTES
1504	1538	(1)
1604	1636	(1)
1704	1736	(1)
1740	1812	(2)
1809	1845	(1)
1904	1936	(1)
1940	2012	(2)
2021	2053	(1)
2121	2153	(1)
2140	2212	(2)
2221	2253	(1)

Distance: 17 miles/27 km
Reference: British Rail Table 242

(1) MON–SAT   (2) SUN

Train Information: 031–556–2451
InterCity Services: 01–278–2477

Dunfermline Tourist Information Centre
0383–720999

To reach the tourist information center on foot from the railway station, cross St. Margaret's Drive in front of the station and walk down Comley Park. After crossing New Row, Priory Lane joins St. Margaret's Street. Bear right and continue on St. Margaret's to the intersection of Abbot Street, where you'll find the center to your near left round the corner.

The triangle of interest is the Dunfermline Abbey, Pittencrieff Park, and the Andrew Carnegie birthplace. We suggest visiting the park first, due to its close proximity to the information center. Stop at the abbey, next, then the Carnegie cottage as you proceed back to the rail station.

The site of the Dunfermline Abbey has had continual Christian worship for about 1,500 years. In the fifth or sixth century, the first building on the site was the Culdee Church. Later, it was rebuilt on a larger scale by Malcolm III, father of King David I, and was dedicated in 1072. Traces of both buildings are visible beneath gratings in the floor of the abbey's Old Nave.

April through October, the abbey church is open 0930–1700 daily and 1400–1700 on Sunday. Between November and March, the abbey is closed, except for services. The abbey shop is open during the same hours as the church between April and October.

It was Andrew Carnegie who generously donated Pittencrieff Park to Dunfermline and gave funds for its upkeep. It has become a popular place for visitors to pause and reflect on his donations of a library, public baths, and a theater in addition to the park. During your stroll through the park, swing aboard Old Pug and marvel at the advances that have been made in railroading since its engine's fires were banked for the last time.

Andrew Carnegie's birthplace is open to the public daily from April through October from 1100 to 1700 (Sunday opening, 1400). From November through March, it's open 1400–1600 daily. From his humble beginnings, Andrew Carnegie found his fortunes in the new world. Nevertheless, with his philanthropist attitude, he never forgot his home town of Dunfermline. At age thirty-three, with an annual income of $50,000, Carnegie said, "Beyond this never earn, make no effort to increase fortune, but spend the surplus each year for benevolent purposes." This, he certainly did. His generosity in Dunfermline is administered today by a trust fund.

When you visit Dunfermline, you will be following in the footsteps of British royalty. Both Queen Victoria and Queen Mary visited there, and in 1972, Queen Elizabeth and Prince Philip were present to dedicate a Royal Pew in celebration of the abbey's 900th anniversary. You'll find, however, that Dunfermline extends a royal welcome to all of its visitors.

River Ness, as viewed from Inverness Castle, leads southwest to Loch Ness, mythical lair of "Nessie," the Loch Ness monster. Known as the "Capital of the Highlands," Inverness, because of its increasing popularity, has expanded its hotels and recreational facilities to meet its visitors' needs.

From Edinburgh . . .

AN "OUT-AND-BACK" EXCURSION TO INVERNESS
DISTANCE BY TRAIN: 176 miles (283 km)
AVERAGE TRAIN TIME: 4 hours, 20 minutes

The position of Inverness at the eastern head of Loch Ness, Scotland's famous inland sea, earns the city its title, "Capital of the Highlands." From Inverness, you can get to more places in the Highlands than you can from any other location in Scotland. For this reason, we have termed the excursion to Inverness an "out-and-back" excursion, for you may want to use Inverness as your "base city" for exploring the Highlands.

Should your schedule for visiting Inverness be limited, you may want to utilize the excellent British Rail sleeper services. For example, you could board a sleeper one night in London and awaken the following morning in Inverness. You could spend an entire day sightseeing, followed by boarding another sleeper back to London.

It is an ambitious program, but going in and out of Inverness by sleeper could permit you to board the 1040 train from there to the Kyle of Lochalsh (see page 257), where you arrive at 1305, then ferry to the Isle of Skye, soak in the sights, and leave Lochalsh on the 1705 to be back in Inverness by 1948 with some time to spare before boarding the sleeper again.

But why hurry? The scenery is superb and the climate is invigorating. Take our advice and plan to spend at least several days in hospitable Inverness, exploring the Highlands at a leisurely pace.

The tourist information center in Inverness is at Castle Wynd. To reach it by the shortest route turn left when leaving the train station and continue until you see Marks & Spencer. Cross the street and continue up Inglis Street, then turn right onto Hight Street walking until you come to McDonald's. Cross the pedestrian walk, past the Town House and across Castle Wynd where the tourist information center is located at the top of a short flight of stairs.

The tourist information center is open Monday through Saturday, 0900–2030; and Sunday, 0930–1800. During the off-season, we suggest that you call the center at (0463) 234353 for information.

There is so much to do in and around the "Capital of the Highlands" that not even a series of action-packed days could absorb all the possible activities.

Here are but a few of the sightseeing possibilities in and around Inverness. Visit the castle grounds and walk along the garden paths at the River Ness. Cruise on Loch Ness, as far away as Urquhart Castle if you like, where most of the sightings of the Loch Ness "monster" (or "beastie," as the locals call it) have occurred. Journey on the renowned railway line between Inverness and

INVERNESS—*HIGHLAND GATEWAY*

An "Out-and-Back" Excursion from Edinburgh, Change in Perth

DEPART FROM EDINBURGH WAVERLEY STATION	ARRIVE IN INVERNESS STATION	NOTES
0648	1032	(2)(4)
0925	1310	(2)(5)
1125	1514	(2)(4)
1540	1940	(2)
1640	2010	(2)
1808	2140	(3)
1940	2310	(2)

DEPART FROM INVERNESS STATION	ARRIVE IN EDINBURGH WAVERLEY STATION	NOTES
0638	1013	(2)
0750	1120	(2)
0940	1318	(3)
1015	1412	(2)
1430	1825	(2)
1830	2106	(3)
1830	2210	(2)
2005	2356	(1)(6)

Distance: 176 miles/283 km
References: British Rail Table 231
                    Thomas Cook Table 605

(1) MON–FRI	(4) Change in Perth
(2) MON–SAT	(5) Sunday: depart 0935, arrive 1310
(3) SUN	(6) Change in Stirling

NOTE: London-Inverness sleeper service: Depart London Euston Station 2130 Monday–Friday; arrive Inverness 0840+1. Saturdays, depart 2000; arrive Inverness 0940+1. Sundays, depart 2055; arrive 0840+1. Returning sleeper service: Depart Inverness 2020 daily; arrive London Euston Station 0753+1 (1027 Saturday).

Train Information: 0463–238924
InterCity Services: 071–278–2477

Inverness Tourist Information Centre
0463–234353

Kyle of Lochalsh along eighty-two miles of railroad right of way that involved beauty, romance, history, and endurance in its building. Forge northward to Thurso, Scotland's most northerly town, on a dramatic rail route holding 162 miles of Scotland's better scenery captive for your viewing. If you prefer the solitude that surf breaking on a shore can bring, take a train east to Nairn, fifteen miles from Inverness. Or train south a mere thirty-five miles to Scotland's St. Moritz—where the ski boom has transformed the town of Aviemore into a continental sports village.

Eons ago, Loch Ness was carved out along a geological fault between two land masses in northern Scotland. The earth's forces formed a long narrow lake of approximately twenty-four miles with depths of up to 750 feet, possibly 1,000 feet in some parts. To go to Inverness and not have a look at Loch Ness would be like eating one potato chip and throwing the rest of the bag away. We urge you to dip into the mystery, the history, and the beauty of Loch Ness.

Loch Ness is reportedly the home of "Nessie," the Loch Ness monster, which has often been described as one of the world's greatest mysteries. The first recorded sighting of Nessie was made by an unimpeachable witness (Saint Columba, no less) in A.D. 565. According to the report, the monster attacked one of the members of his group. Since then, there have been too many visual and photographic sightings of the monster for it to be easily explained.

Fact or fiction, there is a continuing similarity in the descriptions of Nessie given by most of those who claim to have seen the monster over the years. Photographs also support a common description, that of a small head at the end of a long thin neck with an overall body length between twenty to thirty feet. Underwater evidence gathered by every means from space-age technology to yellow submarines suggests that it may have four flippers. Zoologists recognize this description as a plesiosaur, a type of marine dinosaur that existed more than seventy million years ago and should have become extinct.

Scientific data notwithstanding, the fact that malt whiskeys have been produced in large volumes throughout the area since the beginning of recorded time may account for many or all of the sightings!

Kyle of Lochalsh, a narrow channel (Kyle) connecting Loch (Lake) Alsh with the open sea through the Sound of Raasay, offers superb views to its visitors. The Lochalsh Hotel is located conveniently beside the ferry dock for transport to the Isle of Skye, seen in the background.

A DAY EXCURSION TO KYLE OF LOCHALSH
DISTANCE BY TRAIN: 258 miles (415 km)
AVERAGE TRAIN TIME: 7 hours, 35 minutes

The railway between Inverness and Kyle of Lochalsh has been accorded the distinction of being the premier scenic rail line in Britain. It offers a lovely journey through the Highland towns of Dingwall, Garve, Achnasheen, and Stromeferry before terminating on the western shores of Scotland overlooking the Isle of Skye. The rail line passes through a region of superlative natural beauty loaded with Scottish folklore. This eighty-two-mile journey, which appears rather uninspiring in the cold prosaic type of the timetable, is in reality a rare mixture of beauty, romance, history, and endurance.

When the railroad opened in 1870, the western terminal was the town of Stromeferry on the saltwater Loch Carron. Although the original intention was to build right through to Kyle of Lochalsh, construction money ran out and Stromeferry remained the terminus for twenty-seven years. Completing the remaining twenty-six miles of right of way proved to be a formidable task of engineering. Most miles were forged through solid rock, requiring cuts up to eighty-eight feet deep. Even the area of the train terminal at Kyle required blasting and removing rock. When you reach Kyle of Lochalsh, pause to appreciate the backbreaking toil that created the train station and the right of way leading to it.

A ferry plies between Kyle of Lochalsh and Kyleakin on the Isle of Skye. The ruins of Castle Moil stand on a promontory close to the Kyleakin ferry dock. During the time of the Vikings, the castle was the home of a Norwegian princess. History relates that the princess made quite a bundle during her stay in the castle by exacting a toll from ships passing through the narrow straits. To ensure prompt payment, she had a heavy chain attached between the castle and the Kyle of Lochalsh, which was drawn taut when a ship approached. The chain was probably depreciated and charged off as a business expense, for there's no evidence of its existence today.

During the summer, the 1040 train from Inverness includes a special observation car, for which a supplement is payable. The special car returns to Inverness in the late afternoon, departing from Kyle of Lochalsh at 1705. A guide aboard the observation car offers interesting commentary en route. If you're unable to obtain a seat in that car, ask at the railway-station magazine stand for the British Rail illustrated booklet *Inverness to Kyle of Lochalsh.* It describes much of the scenery en route, along with a sprinkling of Scottish folktales.

257

KYLE OF LOCHALSH AND THE ISLE OF SKYE

A Day Excursion from Edinburgh through Inverness

DEPART FROM INVERNESS STATION	ARRIVE IN KYLE OF LOCHALSH STATION	NOTES
0800	1030	(1)
1025*	1315	(1)
1040	1320	(1)(2)
1240	1508	(1)
1838	2115	(1)(2)

DEPART FROM KYLE OF LOCHALSH STATION	ARRIVE IN INVERNESS STATION	NOTES
0710	0939	(1)
1000	1230	(2)
1148	1420	(1)
1510*	1752	(1)(2)
1705	1948	(1)

Distance: 82 miles/132 km
References: British Rail Table 239
                  Thomas Cook Table 597

* Conveys observation car

(1) MON–SAT   (2) SUN

Train Information: 0463–238924
InterCity Services: 071–278–2477

Kyle of Lochalsh Tourist Information Centre
0599–4276

In Kyle of Lochalsh, you'll find the tourist information center conveniently located midway between the train station and the ferry dock. It is open Monday through Saturday, 0930–2130, and Sunday, 1230–1630. To reach it, use the stairs to the overpass and then walk downhill.

Don't pass up the opportunity of visiting the Isle of Skye. You'll be treated to one of the finest land-and-seascapes in the world during the seven-minute crossing. The ferry service operates year-round and departs every fifteen minutes during peak season and every half-hour after 2100. Rest assured that you will not be left on the Isle when your train departs the Kyle. For a quick review of the village of Kyleakin and its points of interest, check the tourist-information three-sided sign just outside the Castle Moil Restaurant, a short distance from the ferry dock. It is a relatively short walk from Kyleakin to Castle Moil.

Scottish legends leap out at you as the train plies between Inverness and Kyle. The castle at Dingwall was said to have been ruled by Finlaec, the father of MacBeth. In a graveyard opposite the castle ruins, the ghost of a young girl wanders nightly in search of her faithless lover. Approaching Garve, you'll pass Loch Garve, where even in the dead of winter there is a small part that never freezes—attributed to the water-horse monsters who carry off local girls. The inn at Garve purveys Athole Brose, a libation of whiskey, oats, and honey, several drafts of which could produce a whole herd of water horses.

The right of way passes areas that stir the imagination. Departing Achnasheen en route to Stromeferry, passengers may get a fleeting glance at the Torridon range of mountains—the oldest mountains on earth. They are so old that geologists have been unable to find any trace of fossils, indicating the mountains were formed long before life of any description began. The range, consisting of peaks such as Liathach (3,456 feet), Beinn Eighe (3,300 feet), and Beinn Alligin (3,021 feet), has sparkling quartzite peaks, often mistaken for snow.

In the seventeenth century, Brahan Seer, the Highland's prophet extraordinaire, said, "The day will come when every stream will have its bridge, balls of fire will pass rapidly up and down the Strath of Peffery and carriages without horses will cross the country from sea to sea." And so it came to pass when, on 10 August 1870, the railroad steam engines began operating from sea to sea.

Linlithgow Palace (top), birthplace of Mary Queen of Scots, broods over Linlithgow Loch. The waters of the loch provide recreational opportunities for townspeople and tourists alike. **Union Canal** (below), once the main water artery for coal from nearby Falkirk, runs through the center of the town as an additional asset to the attractions offered by Linlithgow and the Forth Valley. (©Terence Hughes Photography)

From Edinburgh . . .

A DAY EXCURSION TO LINLITHGOW
DISTANCE BY TRAIN: 18 miles (29 km)
AVERAGE TRAIN TIME: 20 minutes

Linlithgow lies between Edinburgh and Glasgow and stands in the midst of Scotland's history. To its visitors, the town offers a bevy of attractions, so many in fact that our advice on going there is to go early and plan to stay late, *very late.*

Linlithgow Palace, the birthplace of Mary Queen of Scots, is the town's main attraction; however, a variety of others will vie for your attention. A mere 100 yards from the Linlithgow Station, there's a canal where you may board a replica of a Victorian steam packet boat. A scant distance from the town you can visit The Binns—one of the most "lived in" mansions in Scotland, and a short bus ride will take you to the town of Bo'ness with its unique set of attractions ranging in historical significance from Roman ruins to the Industrial Revolution.

Bo'ness also has a reconstructed Victorian railway station where you may board a steam train for a delightfully romantic 7-mile round-trip—including a stop in Birkhill where you can go down in a mine. Also nearby is Blackness Castle, at one time one of Scotland's most important strongholds, with a prison cell that's under water at high tide! Meanwhile, back at the palace . . .

Linlithgow Palace lies in what historians would describe as a splendid ruin. Nevertheless, it tells a poignant tale of Scotland's royal history in an intriguing manner. The palace was the successor to a wooden fortress that burned down in 1424. King James V, father of Mary Queen of Scots, was born in Linlithgow Palace on 10 April, 1512. Mary's mother, Mary of Guise-Lorraine, described the palace as equal to the noblest chateaux in France. Defeated by the English at the battle of Solway Moss in November 1542, the king died on 14 December of that year, only six days after the birth of his daughter. The infant child became Mary Queen of Scots at the age of six days.

In the years to follow, Bonnie Prince Charlie and Oliver Cromwell took brief residence in the palace. At the beginning of 1746, troops belonging to the Duke of Cumberland's army were billeted in the palace. As they marched out of the palace on 1 February, fires were left burning that soon spread throughout the building. Since that time, the palace has remained unroofed and uninhabited. Through the years, there has always been talk about restoring Linlithgow Palace. In 1906 the fireplace in the great hall was restored; King George V held court there in 1914; and now you can let your imagination "restore" it.

The Union Canal runs through the center of Linlithgow. Some 31 miles in length, the canal was once a major thoroughfare for taking coal from the mines

LINLITHGOW—BIRTHPLACE OF MARY QUEEN OF SCOTS

A Day Excursion from Edinburgh or Glasgow

DEPART EDINBURGH WAVERLEY STATION	ARRIVE LINLITHGOW STATION	NOTES
0818	0837	(1)(2)
0848	0907	(1)
0918	0937	(1)
0930	0948	(2)
0948	1007	(1)
1018	1037	(1)(2)
1048	1107	(1)
1118	1037	(1)(2)

DEPART GLASGOW QUEEN STREET STATION	ARRIVE LINLITHGOW STATION	NOTES
0800	0828	(1)
0800	0836	(2)
0900	0928	(1)
0900	0936	(2)
1000	1028	(1)
1000	1036	(2)
1100	1128	(1)

(Plus other frequent service)

DEPART LINLITHGOW STATION	ARRIVE EDINBURGH WAVERLEY STATION	NOTES
1628	1650	(1)
1633	1656	(2)
1733	1756	(2)
1750	1811	(1)
1758	1820	(1)
1800	1823	(1)
1833	1850	(2)
1928	1950	(1)(2)
2028	2050	(1)(2)
2128	2150	(1)(2)
2332	2353	(1)(2)

DEPART LINLITHGOW STATION	ARRIVE GLASGOW QUEEN STREET STATION	NOTES
1648	1720	(1)(2)
1748	1820	(1)(2)
1848	1920	(1)(2)
1948	2020	(1)(2)
2048	2120	(1)(2)
2148	2220	(1)(2)
2248	2325	(1)(2)

Distance: 18 miles/29 km
References: British Rail Passenger Timetable, Tables 228 and 230
(1) MON–SAT   (2) SUN

in Falkirk to Edinburgh. You can cruise the Union Canal on board the *Victoria* or *Janet Telford,* two diesel-powered replicas of Victorian steam packet boats, every half hour on Saturday and Sunday afternoons from Easter until the end of September. Short trips of about twenty minutes' duration depart from the Canal Basin at Manse Road, located about 100 yards from the rail station. The Canal Museum at the basin has a small restaurant and is open when the *Victoria* operates from 1400 until 1700. The last boat trip departs at 1630. Admission to the museum is free; boat trips are £1.00 for adults; children, 50 pence.

The Binns has been occupied by the Dalyell family for three and a half centuries. The house dates from the sixteenth century. General Tam Dalyell (1599–1685) had some hair-raising adventures in his lifetime, including an escape from the Tower of London and military service in Russia. The house reflects the early seventeenth-century transition from the fortified castle to a more comfortable and gracious house. You'll enjoy a visit there.

Bo'ness is a seaport on the Firth of Forth. It has been the site of many activities including coal mining, iron founding, and maritime trading. You can get the full details from the tourist center in Linlithgow or from the center in Bo'ness. The Bo'ness center is housed in Hamilton's Cottage, a re-creation of a working man's home from the 1920s.

The Bo'ness & Kinneil Railway runs to the Birkhill clay mine where fireclay was mined. Without fireclay, many say there could never have been an Industrial Revolution. While in Kinneil, you can visit the Kinneil Estate, where there is an interesting museum, an ancient mansion, and the remains of the Roman Antonine Wall.

The running dates for the Bo'ness & Kinneil Railway are on Saturdays and Sundays from April 2 through October 16; daily from July 9 through August 21. The standard fare, including the stop at Kinneil, is £3.20 for adults, £1.60 per child. If you have the whole gang with you, you can take advantage of the £8.00 family rate.

Despite the possible objection by the tourist boards of both Edinburgh and Glasgow, the Forth Valley Tourist Board (headquartered in Linlithgow) suggests that our readers consider booking accommodations in Linlithgow when either of the larger cities is fully booked. The train trip from Edinburgh takes twenty minutes; thirty minutes from Glasgow. If there are no objections, the motion is passed. The Forth Valley Tourist Board can be contacted by phone at (0506) 843306, by fax at (0506) 670427, or by writing to them at Annet House, High Street, Linlithgow, West Lothian EH49 7EJ.

We're certain that no one will object to our suggestion to call at the Four Marys' Public House on High Street in Linlithgow. A great atmosphere, excellent libations, and superb food will reward you. Don't miss it!

Eighteenth-century Town Hall dominates the broad main street of Montrose, a city that has served as a fashionable Scottish spa for almost three centuries. Montrose profited from trade with the Low Countries, consequently bringing Flemish-style architecture into its own decor.

A DAY EXCURSION TO MONTROSE
DISTANCE BY TRAIN: 90 miles (145 km)
AVERAGE TRAIN TIME: 2 hours, 10 minutes

Travelers who have visited many villages, towns, and cities throughout Continental Europe and the British Isles can "read" the history of a place in its architecture and street names. Montrose is an outstanding example of this point.

Even at first glance, Montrose does not look like a typical Scottish town. Its broad main street, High Street, has many elegant houses with the gabled ends on the street side. There was a time in the city's history when only Edinburgh surpassed it in prosperity and elegance. The Town House of Montrose—Americans would more properly term it the city hall—is fronted by a broad piazza. From its facade, Montrose looks more like a page out of a Flemish picture book rather than a Scottish one. Its great houses are surrounded by garden walls—not ordinary ones, but remarkably high garden walls. There are oddly named streets, such as "America" and "California"—another hint that the history of Montrose is different in many ways.

When Glasgow was still a village, Montrose was one of Scotland's principal ports. For centuries, the merchants of Montrose traded with the Low Countries. It was only natural that they would bring back to Montrose some of the things they admired on the Continent: for example, houses with gabled ends to the street side as they are constructed in Holland. The wide streets? From the promenades of Europe, no doubt. And what about the street names? Almost within living memory, ships sailed from Montrose to America carrying emigrants and returned ladened with lumber.

For many years, Montrose was Scotland's primary port for tobacco with its fleet sailing regularly to and from Virginia. Today, North Sea oil is virtually pumping life back into the city's harbor, where, until the recent past, an air of sleepiness prevailed as the trade with America began to subside. The first part of the civic motto of Montrose—*Mare ditat* (the sea enriches)—is again coming true.

Baffled by the high garden walls? History relates that more than 300 years ago, the streets of Montrose ran red with blood when a band of Highlanders raided the town. Its inhabitants were defenseless as they slept without the protection of a city wall and with only low garden walls about their residences. The carnage was swift and horrible. Within months, the majority of the walls within the town were built up to their present height to prevent attacks from intruders.

When you arrive in Montrose from Edinburgh, take a moment at the train station to direct your gaze to the west, away from the town. You will see a

MONTROSE—*SEASIDE RESORT*

A Day Excursion from Edinburgh

DEPART FROM EDINBURGH WAVERLEY STATION	ARRIVE IN MONTROSE STATION	NOTES
0705	0859	(2)
0810	1002	(2)
0855	1042	(3)
0910	1057	(2)
1020	1207	(2)
1055	1240	(3)

DEPART FROM MONTROSE STATION	ARRIVE IN EDINBURGH WAVERLEY STATION	NOTES
1534	1720	(1)
1552	1741	(3)
1605	1809	(2)
1652	1848	(2)
1754	1950	(2)
1940	2158	(3)
2037	2223	(2)

Distance: 90 miles/145 km
References: British Rail Table 229
            Thomas Cook Table 600

(1) MON–FRI   (3) SUN
(2) MON–SAT

Train Information: 0224–594222
InterCity Services: 071–278–2477

Montrose Tourist Information Centre
0674–72000

tidal basin where thousands of wild fowl forage for food, including the pink-footed Arctic goose during the winter. Seasonally, there is a great gathering of swans in the basin dotting the water with their white tufts of plumage like so many bread crumbs scattered on a watery lawn.

From the station, turn right on Western Road until it reaches Hume Street, where a quick left followed by a right turn one block away onto High Streets puts you in view of the town hall and its grand piazza. Stay on the right-hand side of High Street and walk a short distance south. Just before reaching the town's public library, you will come to the tourist information center at 212 High Street.

The office has a wealth of information available regarding both Montrose and the area surrounding it. A Heritage Trail leaflet provides information on walks through Montrose. It is available at the information office for a nominal fee. The information office also has a street map for sale that lists many points of interest.

Montrose is one of Scotland's leading seaside resorts, and it can become crowded during the peak summer season. Four miles of magnificent sandy beaches attract many an inlander to seek the sea. Beaches have a way of indicating their latitudes, however, just as places reflect their history in their names and facades. Beaches in Britain, for example, attract huge crowds in summertime, but note the distribution of the people on the beach. With exception of a hardy few, the majority of holiday makers are on the sands and not in the water.

The city's large indoor swimming pool and two eighteen-hole golf courses, plus numerous other sports facilities, make up for the other-than-tepid temperature of the North Sea waters off Montrose. The seaside also offers something rather unusual—something you'd never find at Atlantic City. On the beaches beside Elephant Rock, you can search for semiprecious stone such as agates, amethysts, cornelian, and onyx.

Cultural life is not lacking in Montrose. The name of William Lamb immediately relates to the world of art in fine sculptures and etchings. This well-known artist maintains a studio at 24 Market Street. On Panmure Place, the Montrose Museum houses an excellent collection of art relating to the natural and maritime history of the area.

If you've been waiting for us to drop the other shoe, the second part of the Montrose civic motto is *rosa decorat* (the rose adorns). If you walk in the Mid Links Park on a summer day, the air is scented with the perfume of roses. Although the city's name has nothing to do with roses—it was originally called "Monros" (the mossy promontory)—there are few towns in Scotland where roses grow more abundantly.

Pretty pedestrian passes Perth's tourist information center, situated in the pedestrian section of the city's old town. To reach it from the railway station, follow King's Place just outside the station to where it intersects with Scott Street. Four blocks up Scott Street lies High Street and the information center—or go for the taxi queue at the station.

A DAY EXCURSION TO PERTH
DISTANCE BY TRAIN: 58 miles (93 km)
AVERAGE TRAIN TIME: 1 hour, 30 minutes

"Behold a river more mighty than the Tiber!" History relates that these words were uttered by a Roman commander as, approaching what is now the city of Perth, he caught his first glimpse of the River Tay. Beginning as a mountain stream at Ben Laoigh, the Tay trickles down the hillsides, gaining tributaries as it flows on its 120-mile journey to the sea. Perth stands astride the Tay, her history inexorably linked with the "river more mighty than the Tiber."

Two vehicular bridges, plus a rail bridge (all with pedestrian footpaths), cross the River Tay today, but "Old Man River" Tay kept the locals quite busy in earlier years, when floods swept away the first bridge in 1210 and its successor in 1621, leaving travelers no alternative but ferries for the 150 years to follow.

Perth is often referred to as "the gateway to the Highlands," but this is far from being its only attraction. Its prominent position in the history of Scotland has left a legacy of distinctive buildings in an area that is compact enough so that they can easily be examined on foot. Perth's architecture mixes the modern with the ancient. City fathers are justly proud of Perth's sports centers with an ice rink, swimming pools, tennis courts, and indoor bowling stadium.

Tay Street fronts the river on the city side. Without straying too far from the river, it is possible to enjoy the riverside and visit places of interest such as St. John's Kirk, the Perth Art Gallery and Museum, the Fergusson Gallery, the Lower City Mills, and the Fair Maid's House, as described in Sir Walter Scott's novel *The Fair Maid of Perth.* Turn left off Tay Street at Queen's Bridge and proceed two blocks to sight St. John's to your right. One of Perth's most famous landmarks, St. John's Kirk is where the Protestant reformer John Knox, following his return from exile in Geneva, preached his famous sermon against idolatry in 1559. The congregation was so taken with his sermon that as a result, they wrecked the church and then went on to create similar outrages on the monastic houses of the friars. Originally founded in 1126, St. John's is a fine example of Gothic-style architecture from the mid-sixteenth century.

Returning to Tay Street, continue to walk to the Perth Bridge, where you will find the art gallery and museum on George Street close to the bridge approach. In quest of the Fair Maid's House, ask directions when leaving the museum. It is at North Port, a short distance away, but there are several ways to reach it.

Close by the Fair Maid's House is the North Inch, a beautifully situated park bordered by Georgian terraces and the River Tay and overlooked by

PERTH—*FIRST CAPITAL OF SCOTLAND*

A Day Excursion from Edinburgh

DEPART FROM EDINBURGH WAVERLEY STATION	ARRIVE IN PERTH STATION	NOTES
0935	1048	(2)
0925	1046	(1)

DEPART FROM PERTH STATION	ARRIVE IN EDINBURGH WAVERLEY STATION	NOTES
1500	1615	(1)
1655	1812	(1)
2050	2206 (SUN)	(1)(2)
	2210 (MON–SAT)	

Distance: 58 miles/93 km
References: British Rail Table 230
             Thomas Cook Table 600

(1) MON–SAT   (2) SUN

Train Information: 0738–37117
InterCity Services: 071–278–2477

Perth Tourist Information Centre
0738–38353

Balhousie Castle, the historic home of the Black Watch Regimental Museum. Across the river lies the colorful Branklyn Garden, owned by the National Trust for Scotland and said to be "the finest two acres of private garden in the country." It sits on the wooded slopes of Kinnoull Hill and offers an excellent view over the town.

For centuries, Perth has been a prosperous market town, serving a rich agricultural hinterland and profiting from its geographical position in the heart of Scotland. The town's livestock markets flourish, with the famous Perth Bull Sales in February and October attracting buyers from all over the world. Perth's reputation as a trading center, however, rests principally with its excellent shops. Much of Perth's center is traffic-free and bedecked with floral displays thanks to the city-wide "Perth in Bloom" campaign.

In the pedestrianized High Street, call at the modern Perth Tourist Information Centre, located at the intersection of Kirkgate and Skinnergate. Operated by the Perthshire Tourist Board, the center is open from March 29 to June 27 and September 5 to October 31 from 0900 to 1800 on weekdays and 1200–1800 Sundays. From June 28 to September 4, the hours are daily, 0900–2000. From November 1 to March 21, the office is open only from Monday through Saturday, 0900–1700.

An excellent addition to Perth's city center attractions is the Fergusson Gallery in the Round House (Perth's old waterworks) at Marshall Place. Here you can view the largest and most important collection of the works of the famous Scottish colorist John Duncan Fergusson. Three specially designed galleries display rotating exhibits taken from a total collection of 6,000 items.

Scone Palace, a mile north of Perth, stands close to the historic spot where Scottish kings were crowned through 1651. The Moot Hill, which stands in front of the palace, is an artificial mound that was constructed in the Dark Ages. Traditionally, Scottish chiefs and lairds came to Scone to pledge their allegiance to the king. This they did, filling their boots before they left home with the earth of their own districts. Thus, with the earth still in their boots, they were standing on their own land when they swore allegiance to their king. Afterwards they ceremoniously emptied their boots on the Moot Hill (or Boot Hill, as it is more appropriately known today).

The palace is open to the public, and there is an admission charge. It is included in the two-hour city bus tour on Wednesdays during July and August, or you can reach it by bus No. 58 from the Leonard Street bus station or No. 8 from South Street Post Office. Check with the information center for details if you plan to go. By the way, don't plan to heist the stone of Scone—it's safely back in Westminster Abbey.

Home of golf, St. Andrews *lives* golf. The clubhouse of the Old Course (above) lies almost within the city itself. Founded in 1160 and consecrated in 1318, St. Andrews Cathedral (below) was destroyed by fire in 1380, then rebuilt, only to be destroyed again during the Reformation.

A DAY EXCURSION TO ST. ANDREWS
DISTANCE BY TRAIN: 57 miles (92 km)
AVERAGE TRAIN TIME: 1 hour

No town in the world is so completely identified with one game as St. Andrews is with golf. No matter where in the world they have played the game, there is nothing as exhilarating to devoted golfers as a round on the Old Course at St. Andrews. Anyone may play the Old Course, provided they can produce a current, official handicap certificate or a letter of introduction from a bona fide golf club, together with proof of identity. This rule applies only to play on the Old Course. Play on the other five courses at St. Andrews is not affected. The links belong to the townspeople and, as such, are open to all.

In summer and autumn, most available tee times on the Old Course are reserved—in many instances, a year in advance. To be certain of obtaining a starting time for the Old Course, it is essential to make application well in advance of the date of play. Latecomers still have a chance because some starting times are retained each day for issue by a random ballot procedure. To enter your ballot, it is necessary to apply to the starter by 1400 on the previous day. (The Old Course is closed on Sunday.)

To obtain full details and reservations for golf in St. Andrews, we suggest you telephone the St. Andrews links secretary at (0334) 475757 at least one day in advance of your intended visit. In total, St. Andrews and its surrounding area list sixteen courses from which to choose.

How old is the game of golf? Apparently, no one knows. Seemingly it originated on the stretches of grassland along Scotland's east coast next to the sandy beaches—the ground known in Scotland for centuries as "links." The sand dunes interspersed throughout the grasslands became the original traps or bunkers. A round of golf consisted of whatever number of holes were possible in the terrain of a particular link. For more on the history of golf, ask the tourist information center about the British Golf Museum.

At first, the pastime of golf was indulged in predominantly by the Scottish aristocracy. With the advent of the inexpensive golf ball, however, golfing in Scotland soon became a mass sport. Aristocracy again moved to the fore by establishing clubhouses for the leisured gentlemen, where they could attend dinners to observe the end of matches between players.

Such was the case at St. Andrews in 1754 when twenty-two "noblemen and gentlemen being admirers of the ancient and healthful exercise of the golf," founded the Society of St. Andrews Golfers, which is now known throughout the world as the Royal and Ancient Golf Club.

St. Andrews and history go together hand in hand. Such stellar sights as the

ST. ANDREWS—*WORLD'S GOLF CAPITAL*

A Day Excursion from Edinburgh

DEPART FROM EDINBURGH WAVERLEY STATION	ARRIVE IN LEUCHARS STATION	NOTES
0705	0811	(1)
0810	0911	(1)
0855	0955	(2)
0910	1009	(1)
1020	1121	(1)
1048	1136	(2)

DEPART FROM LEUCHARS STATION	ARRIVE IN EDINBURGH WAVERLEY STATION	NOTES
1639	1741	(2)
1656	1809	(1)
1739	1858	(2)
1839	1950	(1)
1939	2042 (2058 SUN)	(1)(2)
2006	2123	(1)
2025	2127	(2)

Distance: Train, 51 miles/82 km; then bus, 6 miles/10 km
References: British Rail Table 229
Thomas Cook Table 600

(1) MON–SAT   (2) SUN

Train Information: 0382–28046
InterCity Services: 071–278–2477

St. Andrews Tourist Information Centre
0334–472021

St. Andrews Castle, with its bottle dungeon and secret passage, vie for your attention along with the ruins of St. Andrews Cathedral, once the largest in Scotland. Mary Queen of Scots had a house in St. Andrews that you can still see. The town is the home of Scotland's oldest university (1412). Long before Columbus discovered America or Cooke discovered Australia, students were attending classes at St. Andrews University. Another attraction is St. Mary's College and its unique quadrangle. Founded in 1537, St. Mary's is a part of the university complex. To visit St. Andrews and to roam its streets and scenes is to establish a tangible link with the past.

Leuchars is the rail station serving St. Andrews. This becomes rather obvious when you arrive, for there are signs at both ends of the station announcing LEUCHARS ALIGHT FOR ST. ANDREWS. The bus fare to St. Andrews is inexpensive, and taxis are readily available for about £5.00–£6.00.

From the bus station in St. Andrews, cross City Road, and continue along Market Street. The tourist information center is at No. 70 Market Street, on the right-hand side after Church Street. The center is open 0930–1900 Monday–Saturday and 1100–1700 Sunday during July and August. In June and September, hours are 0930–1800 Monday–Saturday and 1100–1700 Sunday. October through April, it's open 0930–1700 Monday–Friday; Saturday, 1400–1700. The hours in May are 0930–1700 Monday–Saturday; 1400–1700 on Sunday.

St. Andrews Castle may be reached by proceeding along North Street until reaching Castle Street, where you turn left and then proceed one block to the castle. Continuing one block farther on North Street will put you in front of the cathedral ruins.

Golfer or not, you must see the Royal and Ancient Clubhouse of St. Andrews during your stay. Though founded in 1754, the present clubhouse was built in 1854. The Royal and Ancient Golf Club is now the ruling authority of the game, and its clubhouse is recognized as the world headquarters for the game of golf. From the castle ruins, walk along The Scores until you come to Gillespie Terrace. From this point, the clubhouse and the eighteenth hole of the Old Course come into view.

Of all the places and views in St. Andrews, we give our nod to St. Andrews Castle overlooking St. Andrews Bay. Initially constructed in 1200, the castle was destroyed and rebuilt during a war between Scotland and England, only to be demolished again during the Reformation. The savagery of those times may be noted on a stone outside the castle gate where George Wishart was burned at the stake. The castle has lain in ruins since the seventeenth century, when much of its stone was removed for repairing the harbor.

Stirling Castle, astride its great 250-foot rock promontory, has dominated much of Scotland's history. Showplace of Stirling, the castle and its surrounding buildings house a variety of exhibitions, including the Regimental Museum of the Argyll & Sutherland Highlanders.

A DAY EXCURSION TO STIRLING
DISTANCE BY TRAIN: 37 miles (59 km)
AVERAGE TRAIN TIME: 50 minutes

Stirling Castle cannot be ignored. Standing on a 250-foot rock overlooking the River Forth valley, it offers one of the finest panoramic views in Scotland. The area surrounding the crag on which the castle sits has given up relics of early man's presence from the Stone Age down through the Bronze Age. There is no evidence that the Romans occupied the area, but it seems implausible that they didn't "take the high ground."

Stirling Castle has witnessed endless struggles for power. Kings and Queens have been crowned in its halls and great battles fought on the plain below it. Originally named Striveling—which may be translated as "a place of strife"—Stirling has been the scene of strife within the Scottish nation since before the time of recorded history. The town of Stirling and its castle truly stand at the crossroads of Scotland. Its position overlooking the Forth Valley and the crossing of the River Forth at its tidal limits has contributed to its past and present importance.

The castle, as seen today, began to develop around 1370 with the accession of the Stewart kings. It served as a royal residence from then until Mary Queen of Scots' son, James VI of Scotland, departed for London in 1603 to become James I of England. Scotland's tragic queen spent the first five years of her life in and around Stirling Castle. The castle is perhaps the finest example of renaissance architecture in Scotland, most of its buildings dating to the fifteenth and sixteenth centuries. It having been the royal Stewart residence, Scotland's kings and queens held court there, and parliaments met on its premises.

Between the castle and the old town of Stirling is a tourist information center. The operating hours are daily, 0930–1830. At press time the building is being refurbished. The center will combine a multilanguage audiovisual presentation and photographic exhibition with a bookstore and a crafts shop. According to its innovators, it is the first building in Europe to be designed specifically to bring alive the history of a town. The theme is Stirling Castle through seven centuries. All is bustle and noise as ships from France and Holland unload their cargoes and farmers drive their cattle to market. Stirling's market, now the city's Broad Street, is lined with shops selling everything from swords to spices. Meanwhile, back at the castle, a roistering banquet is being held in the great hall, packed with honored guests.

All of the information you might need for an enjoyable day excursion in Stirling also is available in Stirling's tourist information center on Dumbarton

STIRLING—*AND STIRLING CASTLE*

A Day Excursion from Edinburgh

DEPART FROM EDINBURGH WAVERLEY STATION	ARRIVE IN STIRLING STATION	NOTES
0748	0836	(1)
0848	0936	(1)
0918	1005	(1)
0948	1036	(1)
1048	1136	(1)(2)

DEPART FROM STIRLING STATION	ARRIVE IN EDINBURGH WAVERLEY STATION	NOTES
1602	1655	(1)
1713	1755	(1)
1802	1856	(1)
1902	1955	(1)
2006	2056	(1)

Distance: 37 miles/59 km
References: British Rail Table 230
                   Thomas Cook Table 598

(1) MON–SAT   (2) SUN

Train Information: 0786–64754
InterCity Services: 071–387–7070

Stirling Tourist Information Centre
0786–475019

Road. To get there from the train station, make a left turn onto Murray Place, a short distance in front of the station. Walk to the first traffic light and turn right onto Dumbarton Road, immediately opposite the city wall. The center's hours of operation during July and August are Monday through Saturday, 0900–1930, and Sunday, 0930–1830. The center operates on more restricted hours during winter.

Several publications describing walks around Stirling are available in the center. One of particular interest is *Stirling Heritage Trail,* published by the Stirling District Council. It covers a course starting and ending at Stirling Castle and includes photographs and drawings as well as colorful text on the history of Stirling Old Town.

Throughout Stirling during the summer months, the presence of flowers is always evident. You will notice this first in the railway station, and it continues all around town. Possibly Stirling developed its love for flowers from the King's Knot, an octagonal, stepped mound that was laid out as the royal gardens in 1627–28 beneath the walls of Stirling Castle by an Englishman, William Watts, who was brought from London to supervise the project. The raised central portion of the Knot is thought to have originated as a Bronze Age burial mound. It was probably used as an outdoor royal court for tournaments before being incorporated into the formal gardens by Mr. Watts.

There are many historic buildings in Stirling. Below the castle stands the imposing Church of the Holy Rude. It has seen great moments in history. Here, at its altar, the infant son of Mary Queen of Scots, James VI of Scotland and subsequently James I of England, was crowned at the tender age of eighteen months to succeed his exiled mother. The tower of the church still bears the marks of the 1745 rebellion, during which Bonnie Prince Charles's troops attempted to capture Stirling Castle. In the overture to the Reformation, the strident voice of John Knox boomed from the church pulpit.

Stirling is indeed a historic center that has played a vital role in the making of Scotland. It purveys an atmosphere that is hard to match in any other part of Scotland. Over the centuries of its involvement in historical events, it has preserved its heritage.

Gateway to Ireland, Stranraer's importance stems primarily from its being the terminal for ferry service to Larne in Northern Ireland.

From Edinburgh . . .

A DAY EXCURSION TO STRANRAER
DISTANCE BY TRAIN: 147 miles (237 km)
AVERAGE TRAIN TIME: 4 hours, 45 minutes

Stranraer is primarily the terminal for passenger and car ferry service to Larne or Belfast Harbor in Northern Ireland. Rail connections from Larne to Belfast take about forty-five minutes, so it's possible for rail travelers to go to Northern Ireland via this route. We emphasize, however, that the BritRail Pass *is not accepted* for travel on trains operated by the Northern Ireland Railways. Travelers wanting to cross from Stranraer to Larne and then on to Belfast are advised to purchase regular rail tickets or a BritIreland Pass, which would include the sea crossing plus rail travel in England, Scotland, Wales, Northern Ireland, and the Republic of Ireland.

All arrangements for visiting Northern Ireland should be completed prior to departing on the journey rather than en route. One important requirement is a control ticket each passenger *must* have prior to boarding the Larne-Stranraer ferry. These tickets are issued free of charge. Ticketing and reservations are available in the ferry terminal, along with a comfortable passenger lounge with rest rooms and refreshments.

The crossing between Stranraer and Larne usually takes two and one half hours, and trains are waiting at the terminals to take travelers to their final destinations. In both ports, the train terminal is directly alongside the ferry dock. Porter service is available. The crossing from Stranraer to Belfast Harbor is by SeaCat (catamaran) and takes only one and one half hours.

Stranraer has direct, daytime express-train connections to London. For sleeper services to London, proceed from Stranraer to Glasgow for departures out of Glasgow Central. The last train leaves Stranraer for Glasgow at 2105. Frequent train service connecting with the ferries to and from Larne is also available out of Glasgow. Edinburgh passengers should use the Edinburgh-Glasgow train service for the fastest connections to Stranraer.

The Stranraer tourist information center operates from 1, Bridge Street, close to Hanover Square car park. During July and August it is open daily, including Sunday, 0930–1800. Hours vary during the remainder of the year.

The old section of Stranraer clusters around its port area. There are interesting streets and small alleyways with a variety of sights. The Stranraer Castle, which houses a Visitor's Centre with audiovisual displays, is a relic of the sixteenth century and adds a certain attraction to the area. The information center can provide you with a map of Stranraer and suggest various sights to see on a walking tour. The area is renowned for its golf and fishing, and there are a number of beautiful gardens, which flourish in the mild climate.

281

STRANRAER—*GATEWAY TO NORTHERN IRELAND*

A Day Excursion from Edinburgh or Glasgow

DEPART FROM EDINBURGH WAVERLEY STATION	ARRIVE IN GLASGOW QUEEN STREET STATION	NOTES
0700	0750	(1)(2)
1030	1120	(1)(2)

Transfer to Glasgow Central Station (See chapter 11)

DEPART FROM GLASGOW CENTRAL STATION	ARRIVE IN STRANRAER STATION†	NOTES
0823	1034*	(1)
0848	1100	(2)
1123	1340	(1)

DEPART FROM STRANRAER STATION	ARRIVE IN GLASGOW CENTRAL STATION	NOTES
1430	1645	(1)(2)
1840**	2055	(1)(2)

Transfer to Glasgow Queen Street Station (See chapter 11)

DEPART FROM GLASGOW QUEEN STREET STATION	ARRIVE IN EDINBURGH WAVERLEY STATION	NOTES
1730	1820	(1)(2)
2130	2220	(1)(2)

Distance: 147 miles/237 km

References: Thomas Cook Tables 590, 591; British Timetable 218

* Connects with ferry service to Belfast, via Larne

** Connects with ferry service from Belfast, via Larne. Consult train information offices for train/ferry schedules for Sundays and holidays.

† Food service is available at entrance to Stranraer Pier

(1) MON–SAT   (2) SUN

Train Information: 041–204–2844
InterCity Services: 071–387–7070

Stranraer Tourist Information Centre: 0776–702595

The Stranraer Castle, with the formal title of Castle of St. John, is known locally as the "Old Castle." Built in what is now the heart of Stranraer around 1510, it was erected on a site that gave the settlement its original name, Chapel. The name was later changed to Chapel of Stranrawer and finally shortened to Stranraer. *Stranrawer* was believed to have referred to a row of original houses on the strand, or beach, now buried beneath the town's streets.

There is an interesting hotel in Stranraer, one which you might mistake as the town's castle when you first see it. Its name is the North West Castle Hotel, and it's complete with a castle tower that cleverly conceals two well-stocked bars. Again, if you are anticipating a long train trip, you may want to bolster your spirits here in the quaint tower. In the lower bar, there are some fossiliferous wooden beams (no, they are not former patrons), while topside in the Explorers Lounge you are treated to a fine view of the harbor.

The hotel was originally the home of Sir John Ross, the famous Arctic explorer. He gave it the name North West Castle as a reminder of his journeys to the northern and western reaches of the Arctic. Although the "castle" has been transformed into the largest hotel in southwest Scotland, its origins with Sir John have been carefully preserved. Here you will find an indoor ice rink to cater to curling fans, and the hotel proprietor has also added a swimming pool, sauna baths, and several restaurants. A brochure at the hotel desk gives the full history of this most interesting hostelry.

Stranraer lies at the southern end of Loch Ryan, known since Roman times as a safe harbor. At the point where Loch Ryan meets the Irish Sea, the granite bulk of Ailsa Craig stands as a sentinel guarding the enclosed waters of the loch from the ravages of the storms that sweep into the area from the Atlantic across Ireland.

At one time Stranraer was a small fishing community, but it became the main port serving Northern Ireland and a busy shipping center by the middle of the nineteenth century. Involved in the shipment of ammunition from the United States at the end of World War II, the shipping firm of Townsend-Thoresen (now P&O European Ferries) turned the port into a ferry terminal for what is now the shortest sea route to Ireland.

Train departure and arrival notices are posted throughout Glasgow's Central Station on digital boards. Always check at the station for departure time, destination, and loading platform prior to boarding your train.

RECOMMENDED INFORMATION SOURCES

British Tourist Authority Offices in North America

New York: 551 Fifth Avenue, Suite 701, New York, NY 10176. Telephone:
(212) 986–2200. Fax: (212) 986–1188
Atlanta: 2580 Cumberland Parkway, Suite 470, Atlanta, GA 30339–3909.
Telephone: (404) 432–9635. Fax: (404) 432–9641
Chicago: 625 North Michigan Avenue, Suite 1510, Chicago, IL 60611–1977.
Telephone: (312) 787–0490. Fax: (312) 787–7746
Los Angeles: World Trade Center, 350 South Figueroa Street, Suite 450, Los
Angeles, CA 90071. Telephone: (213) 628–3525. Fax: (213) 687–6621
Toronto: 111 Avenue Road, Suite 450, Toronto, Ontario M5R 3JB Canada.
Telephone: (416) 961–8124. Fax: (416) 961–2175

BritRail Travel International Offices in North America

New York: 1500 Broadway, New York, NY 10036–4015.
Los Angeles: 800 South Hope Street, Suite 603, Los Angeles, CA 90017.
Toronto: 94 Cumberland Street, Toronto, Ontario M5R 1A3 Canada.
Vancouver: 409 Granville Street, Vancouver, British Columbia V6C 1T2
Canada.

Rail Pass Express, Inc.
2737 Sawbury Boulevard
Columbus, Ohio 43235–4583
Telephone: **(800) 722–7151**
Fax: (614) 764–0711

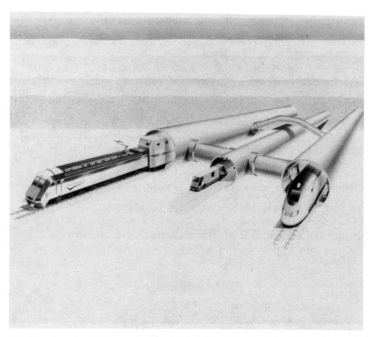

The Eurotunnel, or "Chunnel," opened officially on May 6, 1994. There are actually three tunnels: one servicing the Le Shuttle rail cars, which carry automobiles and trucks; one used as a service tunnel; and one for the Eurostar service for individual passengers. (Photo courtesy of Eurostar Passenger Services)

BRITISH TOURIST INFORMATION CENTERS

Below is a listing of British tourist information centers applicable to cities appearing in this edition of *Britain by BritRail*. When telephoning or faxing from the United States, dial 011–44 (the country code for the United Kingdom) and omit the "0" prior to the city code. For example, to telephone the tourist information office in Brighton from the United States, dial 011–44–273–23755.

Key to Listing:
* Provides summer service only
† Accommodation services available to personal callers (for same or next night)
(B) "Book-a-Bed-Ahead" accommodations service for personal callers (for same or next night) in any town with a Tourist Information Centre also offering this service

ENGLAND/WALES

Bath (B)†
The Colonnades
11–13 Bath Street
General: (0225) 462831
Fax: 481062

Birmingham (B)†
2 City Arcade
(021) 643–2514
Fax: 616–1038

Brighton (B)†
10 Bartholomew Square
(0273) 323755
Accommodations:
(0273) 327560
Fax: 377–7409

Bury St. Edmunds (B)†
6 Angel Hill
(0284) 764667
Accommodations:
757082
Fax: 757124

Cambridge (B)†
Wheeler Street
(0223) 322640
Fax: 463385

Canterbury (B)†
34 St. Margaret's Street
(0227) 766567
Accommodations:
455567
Fax: 459840

Cardiff (B)†
8–14 Bridge Street, South
(0222) 227281

Chester (B)†
Vicars Lane
(0244) 318356
Fax: 324338

Coventry †
Central Library,
Smithford Way
(0203) 832304
Fax: 832370

Dover (B)†
Townwall Street
(0304) 205108
Fax: 225498

Folkestone (B)†
Harbour Street
(0303) 850388
Fax: 221720

Gloucester (B)†
St. Michael's Tower,
The Cross
(0452) 421188
Accommodations:
504273
Fax: 396599

Greenwich (B)†
46 Greenwich Church
Street
(081) 858 6376

Hastings (B)†
4 Robertson Terrace
(0424) 718888
Fax: 716411

Ipswich (B)†
St. Stephen's Church,
St. Stephen's Lane
(0473) 693396

Isle of Wight, Shanklin †
67 High Street
(0983) 862942
Fax: 863047

King's Lynn †
The Old Gaol House
Saturday Market Place
(0553) 763044

287

Lincoln (B)†
9 Castle Hill
(0522) 529828
and 21 The Cornhill
(0522) 512971
Fax: 510822

**London British
Travel Centre**
12 Regent Street,
Piccadilly Circus
(071) 730–3400

London Tourist Board
(B)†
(071) 730–3488
26 Grosvenor Gardens
Accommodations:
(071) 824–8844
Fax: 730–9367

Also at Harrods (Basement Banking Hall);
Tower of London*;
Selfridges (Basement
Services);
and at Victoria Railway
Station

Clerkenwell Heritage
Centre
(071) 250–1039

Margate †
22 High Street
Thanet (0843) 225511
Fax: 226289

Nottingham (B)†
1–4 Smithy Row
(0602) 470661
Fax: 350883

Oxford (B)†
St. Aldate's Chambers,
St. Aldate's
(0865) 726871
Fax: 240261

Penzance (B)†
Station Approach
(0736) 62207

Plymouth
Civic Center
(0752) 264849/51
Fax: 674303

Portsmouth (B)†
City of Portsmouth
Civil Offices
(0705) 834116
Fax: 834975

Ramsgate †
Argyle Centre,
Queen Street
(0843) 591086

St. Albans (B)†
Town Hall,
The Market Place
(0727) 864511
Fax: 863533

Salisbury (B)†
Fish Row
(0722) 334956

Sheffield (B)†
Town Hall Extension,
Union Street
(0742) 734671/2

Southampton (B)†
Above Bar Precinct
(0703) 832695
Accommodations:
832712
Fax: 631437

Stratford-upon-Avon (B)†
Bridgefoot
(0789) 293127
Fax: 295262

Windsor *(B)†
Central Station
(0753) 852010

York (B)†
De Grey Rooms,
Exhibition Square
(0904) 621756
Fax: 650998

SCOTLAND

Aberdeen (B)†
St. Nicholas House,
Broad Street
(0224) 632727 or
Railway Station
Fax: 644822

Ayr (B)†
Burns House
(0292) 262555

Dunbar (B)†
Town House,
143 High Street
(0368) 63353
Fax: 64999

Dundee(B)†
4 City Square
(0382) 434282
Fax: 434655

Dunfermline *(B)†
Abbot House
(0383) 720999

Edinburgh (B)†
Waverly Market, Princes
Street
(031) 557–1700
Fax: 557–5118

Glasgow (B)†
39 St. Vincent Place
(041) 204–4480
Fax: 204–4472

Inverness (B)†
Castle Wynd
(0463) 223512
Fax: 710609

288

Kyle of Lochalsh *(B)†
(0599) 4276

Linlithgow (B)†
Annet House
High Street
(0506) 843306
Fax: 670427

Loch Lomond *(B)†
Balloch
(0389) 53533

Montrose *(B)†
212 High Street
(0674) 72000

Perth (B)†
45 High Street
(0738) 627958
Fax: 630416

St. Andrews (B)†
70 Market Street
(0334) 472021
Fax: 478422

Stirling (B)†
Dumbarton Road
(0786) 475014
Fax: 71301

Stranraer *(B)†
1 Bridge Street
(0776) 2595

USEFUL PHONE NUMBERS—LONDON

Calling the U.K.

To telephone or send a fax to the United Kingdom from the United States, you must first use the international dialing code 011. Then dial the United Kingdom country code 44. All of the area codes within Britain start with a "0," but you do not use it when you are dialing from the United States. For example, to call the British Hotel Reservation Centre in London from the United States, dial 011–44–71–828–1849.

Accommodations	Telephone No.
(credit card holders only)	(071) 824–8844
British Hotel Reservation Centre	(071) 828–1849
Victoria Station, outside Platform 8	
Expotel Hotel Reservations	(071) 328–1790
Kingsgate House, Kingsgate Place	Fax (071) 328–8021
British Travel Centre	(071) 930–0572
Hotel Finders	(081) 202–7000
20 Bell Lane	Fax (081) 202–3871

Airlines	
Aer Lingus (Irish)	(081) 569–5555/745–7017
Air Canada	(081) 759–2331/(0800) 181313
Alitalia	(071) 602–7111
American Airlines	(081) 572–5555
British Airways	(081) 897–4000/897–4567
Delta Air Lines	(0800) 414767
Icelandair	(071) 388–5599
Trans World Airlines	(071) 439–0707

Airport Information	
Heathrow, general inquiries	(081) 759–4321
Heathrow, Terminal 1	(081) 745–7702/4
Terminal 2	(081) 745–7115/6/7
Terminal 3 check-in	(081) 745–7067
Arrivals Concourse	(081) 745–7412/3/4
Terminal 4	(081) 745–4540
London City Airport	(071) 474–5555
Gatwick	(0293) 535353
Stansted	(0279) 680500

American Express
6 Haymarket, Piccadilly   (071) 930–4411

Bike Rentals
On Your Bike, 52 Tooley Street   (071) 407–1309
22 Duke St. Hill   (071) 357–6958

British Tourist Authority, British Travel Centre,
12 Regent Street, Piccadilly Circus SW1   (071) 730–3404

Canadian Embassy
Canada House, Trafalgar Square   (071) 629–9492

Emergency
Police or Ambulance   999

Express Bus Information
National Express   (071) 730–0202

London Tourist Board (main office)
26 Grosvenor Gardens, SW1W 0DU   (071) 730–3488
Medical Help
Middlesex Hospital, Mortimer Street   (071) 636–8333
Medical Express, 117a Harley Street   (071) 499–1991

Post Office
Paddington Main Post Office   (071) 723–0279

Rail Information
InterCity Services to:
East Anglia, Essex, Southern England, Northeast,
South, and East London   (071) 928–5100
South Midlands, West of England, South Wales
and West London   (071) 262–6767
East and West Midlands, North Wales, Northwest
England and Scotland via the West Coast and
Northwest London   (071) 387–7070
East and Northeast England, Scotland via East Coast
and North London   (071) 278–2477
Continental Europe, general inquiries   (071) 834–2345
Continental Europe, to make credit card bookings   (071) 828–0892

Recorded Timetable Announcements for Services to:
    Amsterdam   (071) 828–4264
    Brussels/Köln   (071) 828–0167
    Paris   (071) 828–8747
Special Rail Offers   (071) 828–6708
Sleeper Reservations:
    Euston Station   (071) 388–6061
    Paddington Station   (071) 922–4372
London Regional Transport (bus/underground)   (071) 222–1234
Hoverspeed Reservations   (0304) 240241

River Trips and Canal Cruises
    River Boat Information Service   (071) 730–4812
    London Waterbus Co., Camden Lock Place   (071) 482–2660
    RiverBus   (071) 512–0555
    Catamaran Cruisers   (071) 839–3572
    Jenny Wren Canal Cruises   (071) 485–6210

U.S. Embassy
    24 Grosvenor Square   (071) 499–9000

Victoria Student Travel Service
    Need student I.D. to book accommodations   (071) 730–8111

USEFUL PHONE NUMBERS — EDINBURGH

Tourist Information
City of Edinburgh Tourist Information and
    Accommodations, Waverley Market, Princes Street.   (031) 557–1700

The Tattoo Office   (031) 225–1188
British Rail
    Waverley Station   (031) 556–2451
    Sleeper reservations   556–5633
Edinburgh Airport, information   (031) 333–2167
Scheduled Airlines
    Aer Lingus (Irish)   (031) 225–7392
    British Airways   (031) 225–2525
    British Caledonian Airways   (031) 225–5162

City Transport Information	(031) 556–5656
Student Travel Centre	(031) 668–2221
American Express	
139 Princes Street	(031) 225–7881
Emergency	
Fire, Police, Ambulance	999
Guide Friday—city tours by open-top	
double-decker bus	(031) 556–2244

USEFUL PHONE NUMBERS — GLASGOW

Tourist Information

Tourist Information, 35 St. Vincent Place	(041) 204–4400
Glasgow Travel Centre	(041) 226–4826
British Rail	
Passengers inquiries	(041) 204–2844
Sleeper reservations	(041) 221–2305
Airport Information	(041) 887–1111, Ext. 4552
	or (041) 848–4440

Scheduled Airlines

Aer Lingus (Irish)	(071) 734–1212
Air Canada	(0800) 181313
Air France	(0345) 581393
British Airways	(041) 332–9666
British Midland	(0332) 810552
Northwest Airlines	(041) 226–4175
American Express	
115 Hope Street	(041) 221–4366
Emergency	
Fire, Police, Ambulance	999

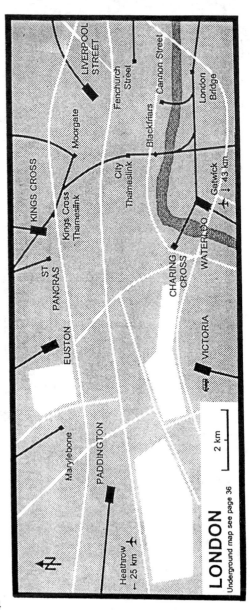

LONDON

Underground map see page 36

LIVERPOOL STREET

Fenchurch Street

Cannon Street

London Bridge

Moorgate

Blackfriars

KINGS CROSS

Kings Cross Thameslink

City Thameslink

Gatwick ✈ 43 km

ST PANCRAS

WATERLOO

CHARING CROSS

EUSTON

VICTORIA

Marylebone

PADDINGTON

2 km

Heathrow ✈ 25 km

N

Inter-terminal links
by London Underground

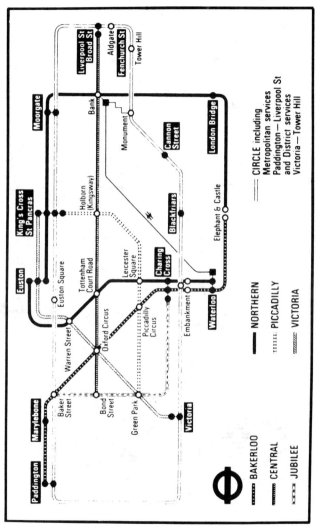

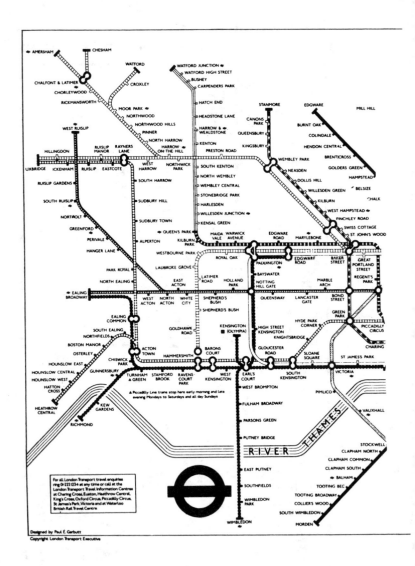

For all London Transport travel enquiries
ring 01-222 1234 at any time or call at the
London Transport Travel Information Centres
at Charing Cross, Euston, Heathrow Central,
King's Cross, Oxford Circus, Piccadilly Circus,
St James's Park, Victoria and at Waterloo
British Rail Travel Centre

A Piccadilly Line trains stop here early morning and late
evening Mondays to Saturdays and all day Sundays

Designed by Paul E. Garbutt
Copyright London Transport Executive

296

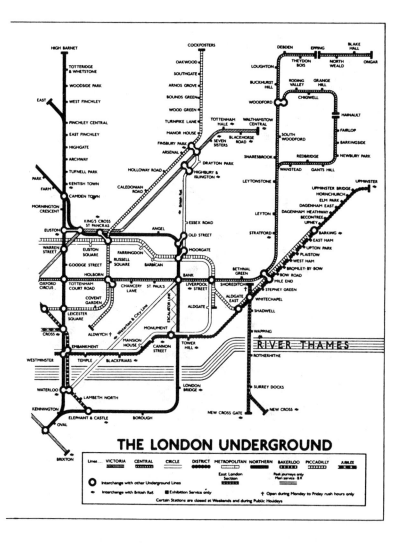

THE LONDON UNDERGROUND

Lines.... VICTORIA CENTRAL CIRCLE DISTRICT METROPOLITAN NORTHERN BAKERLOO PICCADILLY JUBILEE

East London Section

Peak journeys only Mon service B.R.

⬭ Interchange with other Underground Lines

⊷ Interchange with British Rail

■ Exhibition Service only

† Open during Monday to Friday rush hours only

Certain Stations are closed at Weekends and during Public Holidays

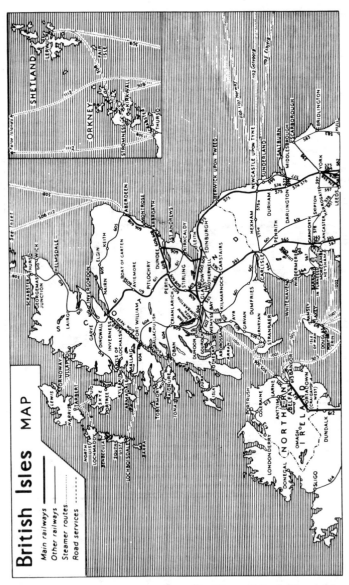

British Isles MAP

Main railways
Other railways
Steamer routes
Road services

Courtesy Thomas Cook Timetable

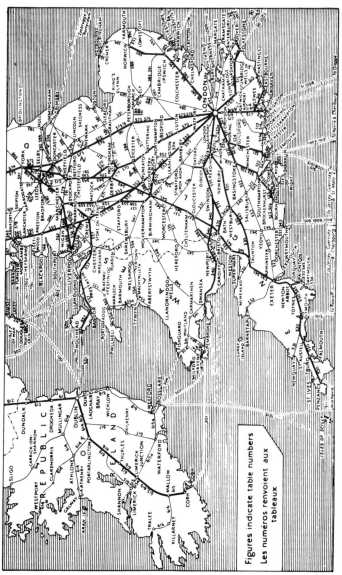

Figures indicate table numbers
Les numéros renvoient aux tableaux

299

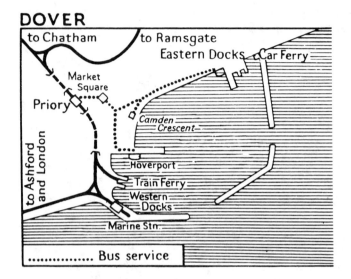

The plans shown here are provided for orientation of readers for those day excursions to points on the English Channel with cross-channel port facilities. (Ref: Dover p-119; Folkestone p-123; Ramsgate p-175)

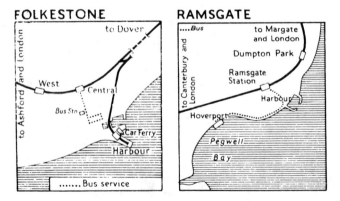

Courtesy Thomas Cook Timetable

British & European Rail Passes
BRITRAIL PASS
(Prices applicable as of January 1, 1995, in U.S. Dollars)

BRITRAIL PASS* gives you unlimited rail travel in England, Scotland, and Wales for periods ranging from 8 days to one month.

| | First Class | | | Standard Class | |
| | Adult | Senior | | Adult | Senior |
		(60 & over)			(60 & over)
8 days	$299	$279		$219	$199
15 days	$489	$455		$339	$305
22 days	$615	$555		$425	$379
1 month	$715	$645		$495	$445

BRITRAIL YOUTH PASS (ages 16–25, Standard Class only)

8 days	$179	22 days	$339
15 days	$269	1 month	$395

BRITRAIL FLEXIPASS* Travel by rail for any 4, 8, or 15 days within one month (within two months for Youth 15-day). Days of travel need not be consecutive.

		Adult	Senior	Youth
4 days/1 month	First Class	$249	$229	—
	Standard	$189	$169	$155
8 days/1 month	First Class	$389	$350	—
	Standard	$269	$245	$219
15 days/1 month	First Class	$575	$520	—
	Standard	$395	$355	—
15 days/2 months	Standard	—	—	$309

* Children under 5 travel free. Children 5 through 15 years pay half adult fare for Britrail Pass and Flexipass. Youth is 16 through 25 years, and Senior Citizen is 60 years and over.

LONDON VISITOR TRAVELCARD Hop on and off of the subway and red double-decker buses in Central London. (Days of travel are consecutive.)

	Adult	Child (5–15 years)
3 days	$25	$11
4 days	$32	$13
7 days	$49	$21

Call 1–800–722–7151 to order!
With your order, you receive a FREE timetable and fold-out rail map.

BRITFRANCE RAILPASS Unlimited rail travel in Britain and France plus round-trip channel crossing by catamaran.

	Adult First Class	**Adult Standard**	**Youth (12–25) Standard**
15 days/15	$359	$259	$220
10 days/1 month	$539	$399	$340

Call about BritFrance Rail & Drive Passes. Children 4–11 pay half fare; under 4 travel free.

BRITIRELAND PASS Unlimited rail travel in England, Scotland, Wales, Northern Ireland, and the Republic of Ireland, and round-trip Sealink ferry service between Holyhead and Dun Laoghaire, Fishguard and Rosslare, or Stranraer and Larne.

	First Class	**Second Class**
5 days/15	$389	$269
10 days/1 month	$599	$419

Children 5–15 pay half fare; under 5 travel free.

EURAIL PASS

(Prices applicable as of January 1, 1995, in U.S. Dollars)

EURAIL PASS* is a convenient card for *unlimited first class rail travel* throughout 17 countries of Europe.

15 days	$498	2 months	$1,098
21 days	$648	3 months	$1,398
1 month	$798		

EURAIL SAVERPASS* For three or more people traveling together. *Unlimited first class rail travel.* Same privileges as the regular Eurailpass but requires that the group always travel together. (Saverpass for two people traveling together is valid between October 1 and March 31 only.)

15 day Eurail Saverpass (price per person)	$430
21 day Eurail Saverpass (price per person)	$550
1 month Eurail Saverpass (price per person)	$678

EURAIL FLEXIPASS* Unlimited first class rail travel for any 5, 10, or 15 days within a 2-month period with the same privileges as the regular Eurailpass.

Any 5 days within 2 months Flexipass	$348
Any 10 days within 2 months Flexipass	$560
Any 15 days within 2 months Flexipass	$740

Call **1–800–722–7151** to order!
With your order, you receive a FREE timetable and fold-out rail map.

EURAIL YOUTHPASS is designed only for people under 26 years of age, It entitles you to 15 days, 1 or 2 full months of *unlimited second class rail travel* through 17 countries of Europe.

15 day Youthpass	$398
1 month Youthpass	$578
2 month Youthpass	$768

EURAIL YOUTH FLEXIPASS Designed only for people under 26 years of age, entitles you to *unlimited second class rail travel* for any 5, 10, or 15 days within a 2-month period.

Any 5 days within 2 months	$255
Any 10 days within 2 months	$398
Any 15 days within 2 months	$540

EUROPASS Designed for travel in the five most frequently visited countries of Europe: France, Germany, Italy, Spain, and Switzerland. You determine the number of countries visited based on the number of travel days purchased. Optional add-on countries: Austria, Belgium and Luxembourg (considered one country), and Portugal.

	Adult First Class	Youth* Second Class
3 COUNTRIES		
Any 5 days within 2 months	$280	$198
Any 6 days within 2 months	$318	$226
Any 7 days within 2 months	$356	$254
4 COUNTRIES		
Any 8 days within 2 months	$394	$282
Any 9 days within 2 months	$432	$310
Any 10 days within 2 months	$470	$338
5 COUNTRIES		
Any 11 days within 2 months	$580	$366
Any 12 days within 2 months	$546	$394
Any 13 days within 2 months	$584	$422
Any 14 days within 2 months	$622	$450
Any 15 days within 2 months	$660	$478
ASSOCIATE COUNTRIES		
Austria	$35	$25
Belgium and Luxembourg	$22	$16
Portugal	$22	$16

Associate countries extend the geographic area of the pass, they do not extend the pass' length in days.

*Youth pass for persons under 26 years.

Passes not refundable in case of loss or theft or once validated. An insurance option is available for $10 per pass, which refunds 100% of the unused portion of the pass in the event of loss or theft. Unused, unvalidated passes must be submitted to the issuing office within one year of issue date. Any refund is subject to a 15% cancellation charge. Please read the "Conditions of Use" on your pass. Prices applicable as of January 1, 1995. Children under 12 pay half price; under 4 travel free.

COUNTRY & REGIONAL PASSES

AUSTRIAN RABBIT CARD Unlimited travel, for the 4 days you choose, on the entire Austrian rail network.

	First Class	**Second Class**
Any 4 days within 10	$153	$103
Junior* 4 days within 10	$95	$64

*Junior: Available only for passengers under 26 on their first date of travel. Children under 7 free.

BENELUX Unlimited travel, for the days you choose, on the entire national rail networks of Belgium, the Netherlands and Luxembourg.

	First Class	**Second Class**
Any 5 days in 17	$185	$124
Junior* Any 5 days within 17	—	$92

*Junior: Available only for passengers under 26 on their first date of travel. Children under 4 free.

CENTRAL EUROPE Unlimited travel, for the days you choose, on the entire national rail networks of Czech Republic, Germany, Poland, and Slovakia.

	First Class
Any 10 days/1 month	$398

Children under 14 half adult fare; under 4 free.

GERMANY Unlimited rail travel for any 5, 10, or 15 days within a one-month period for the entire German Rail system.

	First Class		**Second Class**		
	1st Person	**2nd Person Twinpass***	**1st Person**	**2nd Person Twinpass***	**Junior**
5 days/1 month	$250	$200	$170	$130	$130
10 days/1 month	$390	$308	$268	$200	$178
15 days/1 month	$498	$400	$348	$250	$218

*Twinpass: Two people traveling together; first person pays normal German Railpass price (first or second class). Second person pays Twinpass price in applicable class. Junior: Under 26 years of age.

ITALY Unlimited travel, for the days you choose, on the national rail networks of Italy, including Intercity, Eurocity, and Rapido trains, with no surcharge. A supplement is required for TR450 trains.

ITALIAN RAIL PASS	**First Class**	**Second Class**
8 days	$226	$152
15 days	$284	$190
21 days	$330	$220
30 days	$396	$264

ITALIAN FLEXI RAILCARD		
4 days within 9 days	$170	$116
8 days within 21 days	$250	$164
12 days within 30 days	$314	$210

Children from 4–11 half adult fare; under 4 free.

304

PRAGUE EXCURSION Enjoy a side trip to the historic Czech capital. First class rail travel from any Czech border crossing to Prague and return.

	Adult	**Youth (12–25)**	**Child (4–11)**
7 days	$49	$39	$25

Children under 4 free.

SCANDINAVIA Unlimited travel, for the days you choose, one the national rail networks of Denmark, Finland, Norway, and Sweden.

	First Class	**Second Class**
Any 4 days in 15	$189	$155
Any 9 days in 21	$325	$265
Any 14 days in 1 month	$475	$369

Children from 4–11 half adult fare; under 4 free.

Call about BritRail/Drive, Eurail/Drive, Europass/Drive, and German Rail/Drive Passes.

To order call:
RAIL PASS EXPRESS, INC.
2737 Sawbury Blvd., Columbus, OH 43235
Payment by Visa or MasterCard

1–800–722–7151

FAX: 1–614–764–0711
With your order, you receive a FREE rail timetable and a fold-out rail map.

Pass availability and prices are subject to change.

24-HOUR TIME CONVERTER

AN EASY GRAPHIC MEANS OF CONVERTING STANDARD 12-HOUR TIME TO 24-HOUR TIME AND VICE VERSA

Courtesy of Thomas Cook Ltd.
Thomas Cook International Timetable
Peterborough, England

A SELECTION OF BRITISH RAIL ONE-WAY FARES

Deciding whether or not you should purchase a BritRail Pass becomes a matter of simple arithmetic. Plan your trip to Great Britain, decide what places you want to visit, and use the fares listed below to determine if the cost of the individual rail segments has exceeded the cost of a BritRail Pass. Round-trip fares are slightly less than double the one-way charge. Children five to fifteen years of age, inclusive, pay half fare. All fares are applicable as of press time and subject to change without prior notice. Fares are given in U.S. dollars. To convert to pounds sterling, apply current rate of exchange. For example, at press time, the rate was approximately $1.00 = £.65.

	One-Way Fares			**One-Way Fares**	
	First Class ($)	Standard Class ($)		First Class ($)	Standard Class ($)
From London to:			**From London to:**		
Aberdeen	167.00	115.00	Oxford	24.00	16.00
Aviemore	167.00	115.00	Penzance	117.00	87.00
Ayr	136.00	91.00	Perth	147.00	103.00
Bath Spa	49.00	33.00	Plymouth	88.00	59.00
Birmingham	61.00	44.00	Portsmouth	28.00	19.00
Brighton	17.00	13.00	Salisbury	28.00	14.00
Cambridge	29.00	16.00	Sheffield	74.00	50.00
Canterbury	17.00	13.00	Southampton	28.00	19.00
Cardiff	74.00	50.00	Stratford-upon-Avon	49.00	36.00
Chester	91.00	65.00	Windermere	100.00	66.00
Coventry	49.00	36.00	Windsor	12.00	8.00
Dover	17.00	13.00	York	101.00	67.00
Dundee	147.00	103.00			
Edinburgh	136.00	91.00	**From Glasgow to:**		
Folkestone	17.00	13.00	Aberdeen	46.00	36.00
Glasgow	136.00	91.00	Birmingham	117.00	84.00
Gloucester	49.00	36.00	Dundee (Tay Bridge)	26.00	19.00
Hastings	17.00	13.00	Inverness	46.00	36.00
Inverness	167.00	115.00	Manchester	100.00	72.00
King's Lynn	34.00	22.00	Oxford	127.00	87.00
Leamington Spa	49.00	36.00	Perth	26.00	19.00
Lincoln	66.00	47.00	Sheffield	74.00	50.00
Manchester	91.00	65.00	Stirling	9.00	5.00
Nottingham	74.00	50.00	York	91.00	65.00

To order rail tickets prior to your departure for Britain call the information department at Rail Pass Express at (800) 722–7151.

TIPS AND TRIVIA

Do not be surprised to see a 17.5 percent value–added tax (VAT) added to your bill for items purchased or services rendered. The VAT appears on just about everything, excluding bus/rail transportation.

Tipping: For luggage, generally tip 75 pence per bag; taxis, 15 percent, with a 50-pence minimum; for service staff in hotels, 10–15 percent if service charge not included in bill.

Imports: You can import into Britain 200 cigarettes, two liters of table wine along with either two liters of sparkling wine or one liter of liquor, two ounces of perfume and nine ounces of cologne, and photographic film for your own use.

Shops: Most shops are open from 0900 to 1730. Shops in smaller towns may close for one hour at lunchtime. In London, shops in the Knightsbridge area (Harrods, for example) remain open until 1900 on Wednesday, while those in the West End (Oxford Street, Regent Street, and Piccadilly areas) stay open until 1900 on Thursday.

Banks: Banks are usually open Monday through Friday from 0930 to 1530. Some are open on Saturday mornings. Most banks in Scotland are closed for one hour at lunchtime. The banks at London's Heathrow and Gatwick airports are open twenty-four hours a day.

Holidays: Most banks, shops, and some museums, historic houses, and other places of interest are closed on Sundays and public holidays. Public transport services generally are reduced, especially during Christmas time.

1995 Holidays

January 1	New Year's Day	May 8	May Day
January 2	Bank Holiday	May 29	Spring Bank Holiday
January 3	Bank Holiday (Scotland only)	July 12	Orangeman's Day (Northern Ireland only)
March 17	St. Patrick's Day (Northern Ireland only)	August 7	Bank Holiday (Scotland only)
April 14	Good Friday	August 28	Summer Bank Holiday (England and Wales only)
April 17	Easter Bank Holiday (not Scotland)	December 25	Christmas Day
		December 26	Boxing Day

CLIMATE

	Jan	Feb	Mar	Apr	May	June	July	Aug	Sept	Oct	Nov	Dec
Average Low (F)	35°	35°	37°	40°	45°	51°	55°	54°	51°	44°	39°	36°
Average High (F)	44°	45°	51°	56°	63°	69°	73°	72°	67°	58°	49°	45°
Average Rainfall (in inches)	2	2	1	2	2	2	2	2	2	2	3	2

PASSPORT OFFICES THROUGHOUT AMERICA

You may apply for a passport at any passport agency and at many Clerks of Court Offices or Post Offices designated to accept passport applications. The regional offices are as follows:

Boston: Thomas P. O'Niell Federal Building, 10 Causeway Street, Suite 247, Boston, Massachusetts 02202-1094; (617) 565–6990.

Chicago: Kluczynski Office Building, 230 South Dearborn Street, Room 380, Chicago, Illinois 60604; (312) 353–7155.

Honolulu: New Federal Building, 300 Ala Moana Boulevard, Room C-106, P.O. Box 50815, Honolulu, Hawaii 96850-0001; (808) 541–1918.

Houston: Mickey Leland Federal Building, 1919 Smith Street, Suite 1100, Houston, Texas 77002-8049; (713) 653–3153.

Los Angeles: Federal Building, 11000 Boulevard, Los Angeles, California 92061; (310) 575–7070.

Miami: Claude Pepper Federal Office Building, 51 Southwest First Avenue, Room 1616, Miami, Florida 33130-1680; (305) 536–4681.

New Orleans: 701 Loyal Avenue, Postal Services Building, T-12005, New Orleans, Louisiana 70113; (504) 589–6166.

New York: Rockefeller Center, International Building, 630 Fifth Avenue, Room 270, New York, New York 10020; (212) 541–7710 or (212) 399–5290.

Philadelphia: Federal Building, 600 Arch Street, Room 4426, Philadelphia, Pennsylvania 19106; (215) 597–7480.

San Francisco: Tishman Speyer Building, 525 Market Street, Room 200, San Francisco, California 94105; (415) 744–4010.

Seattle: Federal Building, 915 Second Avenue, Room 992, Seattle, Washington 98174; (206) 553–7745 or (206) 553–7747.

Stamford: One Landmark Square, Broad and Atlantic streets, Stamford, Connecticut 06901; (203) 325–3538.

Washington, D.C.: Room G62, 1425 K Street NW, Washington, D.C. 20522-1705; (202) 326–6060.

PASSPORT INFORMATION

Passport Services, located at the Bureau of Consular Affairs, Department of State, 2201 C Street NW, Room 5813, Washington, D.C. 20520, provides a recorded message at (202) 647–0518 that describes the documents you need and the application process for obtaining a passport as well as reporting the loss or theft of your passport. It also explains how you can obtain a copy of the report of a birth or death or a U.S. citizen abroad. The message will direct you to the proper agencies for information regarding naturalization, travel advisories, customs regulations, and shots required by various countries.

TOLL-FREE AIRLINE NUMBERS
(Dialing from U.S.)

Air Canada (AC) 800–776–3000
Air France (AF) 800–237–2747
American Airlines, Inc. (AA) ... 800–433–7300
Austrian Airlines (OS) 800–843–0002
British Airways (BA) 800–AIRWAYS
Continental Airlines (CO) 800–525–0280
Delta Air Lines, Inc. (DL) 800–221–1212
Finnair (AY) 800–950–5000
Icelandair 800–223–5500
KLM Royal Dutch
   Airlines (KL) 800–374–7747
Lufthansa German
   Airlines (LH) 800–645–3880
Northwest Airlines,
   Inc. (NW) 800–225–2525

Sabena Belgian World
   Airlines (SN) 800–955–2000
Scandinavian Airlines
   System (SK) 800–221–2350
Swissair (SR) 800–221–4750
TAP Air Portugal (TO) 800–221–7370
Trans World
   Airlines, Inc. (TWA) 800–221–2000
United Air Lines, Inc. (UA) 800–241–6522
USAir (US) 800–428–4322
Virgin Atlantic
   Airways Ltd. (US) 800–862–8621

TOLL-FREE HOTEL RESERVATIONS NUMBERS
(Dialing from U.S.)

Choice Hotels
   International, Inc. 800–4–CHOICE
Consort Hotels Ltd. 800–55–CONSORT
Forte Hotels, Inc. 800–225–5843
Golden Tulip International 800–344–1212
Hilton Reservations
   Worldwide 800–HILTONS
Holiday Inn Worldwide 800–HOLIDAY
Hyatt Worldwide Reservation
   Centres 800–233–1234
Inter-Continental Hotels Corp .. 800–327–0200
Inter-Europe Hotels 800–221–6509
ITT Sheraton Corporation 800–325–3535
Kempinski International 800–426–3135
Leading Hotels of the World 800–223–6800
Loews Representation
   International 800–223–0888

Marriott Corportation 800–228–9290
MinOtels Intl. 800–336–4668
Mount Charlotte Thistle Hotels 800–847–4358
Movenpick Hotels
   International 800–34–HOTEL
Nikko Hotels International 800–645–5687
Preferred Hotels & Resorts
   Worldwide 800–323–7500
Radisson Hotels
   International, Inc. 800–333–3333
Ramada International
   Hotels & Resorts 800–854–7854
Romantik Hotels &
   Restaurants Intl. 800–826–0015
SRS Steigenberger Reservation
   Service 800–223–5652
Swissotel 800–63–SWISS

GEOGRAPHIC INDEX

All places that have a main entry appear in bold–face type.

AUTHOR'S NOTE

We take this opportunity to thank the British Tourist Authority, British Rail, BritRail Travel International, and the British tourist information offices for their cooperation. Thanks also to our British and European research teammates who are invaluable aids to us in our annual revisions: Elissa Austria, Major Robert S. Bean, Benoit and Simone Drillon, Margaret Keith, Matthew Palma, Shellie and Daniel Rubin, Andrea Simkins, and Dorothy and Emil Turansky.

Our well-trained rail-specialist colleagues at Rail Pass Express, Inc., deserve profuse praise as well. Mary Kish, general manager at Rail Pass Express, runs a tight ship—must be her Navy background. Mary's leadership and organizational skills coupled with her business and computer experience are incomparable. Like a talented orchestra leader, Mary keeps the music playing.

Our assistant editor, Christian Martin, helps keep us on the right track and up to date. Christian actually wears several hats. In addition to his research and editorial duties, he's also director of marketing for Rail Pass Express, Inc. Busy guy!

Ben Sehgal, Mary DiThomas, and Tonya Young specialize in rail schedules and rail reservations. Novices may become confused and frustrated when trying to decipher rail schedules or make seat reservations, but for Ben, Mary, and Tonya, it's elementary.

Holly Bovie, Emma-Jane Clowes, and Jill Schmid are very knowledgeable about all the different European rail passes available—and there are many of them! Gone are the days of the simple choice between one or two types of rail passes. Holly, Emma, and Jill's expertise can take the confusion out of deciding which rail pass best meets the needs of the traveler.While handing out laudatory comments, we cannot forget our most capable editor at The Globe Pequot Press, Mace Lewis. Thanks!

Most of all, we thank *you,* our readers. We enjoy hearing from you and receiving your helpful comments and suggestions. Things do change rapidly— if you find that something is not the way we say it is, please let us know. We want to keep both *Europe by Eurail* and *Britain by BritRail* as current and as accurate as possible. We do acknowledge your letters personally, but because of our research trip schedule and publishing deadlines, we are sometimes unable to answer as soon as we (or you) would like. We appreciate your help.

George & LaVerne Ferguson
Rail Pass Express
2737 Sawbury Boulevard
Columbus, OH 43235–4583
(800) 722–7151
(614) 889–9100

INTERNATIONAL TRAVEL

Here are some other guides on various international destinations. All Globe Pequot travel titles are published with the highest standards of accuracy and timeliness. Please check your local bookstore for other fine Globe Pequot titles, which include:

Europe by Eurail, $14.95
Exploring Europe by Car, $12.95
Exploring Europe by Boat, $12.95
Exploring Europe by RV, $14.95
Guide to Eastern Canada, $15.95
Guide to Western Canada, $16.95
The Best Bed & Breakfast in England, Scotland, and Wales, $18.95
The Best Hotels of Great Britain, $21.95
The Best Restaurants of Great Britain, $21.95
Hotels and Restaurants of Britain, $18.95
Ireland: The Complete Guide and Road Atlas, $19.95
The Vineyards of France, $14.95
The Traveler's Handbook, $19.95

Berlitz Travel Guides
Bradt Travel Guides
Cadogan Travel Guides
Karen Brown's Travel Guides
Off the Beaten Track Travel Guides

To order any of these titles with MASTERCARD or VISA call toll-free, 24 hours a day, (800) 243–0495. Free shipping for orders of three or more books. Shipping charge of $3.00 per book for one or two books ordered. Connecticut residents add sales tax. Ask for your free catalogue of Globe Pequot's quality books on recreation, travel, nature, personal finance, gardening, cooking, crafts, and more. Prices and availability subject to change.

NOTES

NOTES

NOTES

NOTES

I purchased a copy of the Ferguson's ☐ *Europe by Eurail*
☐ *Britain by BritRail*

Please send me **FREE** rail pass information.

Name _____

Address ____ _____

City _____ State _____ Zip _____

We'd like to know more about our readers. Information is for internal use only.

1. Expected departure date for Europe _____

2. Expected length of trip _____

3. What is the expected cost of your trip to Europe_____

4. Number of people in your party_____

5. Is this your first trip to Europe: 01 ☐ Yes   02 ☐ No

      03 If no, how many times _____

6. This trip is for: 01☐ Pleasure   02☐ Business   03☐ Both

7. Countries you expect to visit:

01 ☐ Austria	08 ☐ Germany	15 ☐ Norway
02 ☐ Belgium	09 ☐ Greece	16 ☐ Poland
03 ☐ Britain	10 ☐ Hungary	17 ☐ Portugal
04 ☐ Czechoslovakia	11 ☐ Ireland	18 ☐ Spain
05 ☐ Denmark	12 ☐ Italy	19 ☐ Sweden
06 ☐ Finland	13 ☐ Luxembourg	20 ☐ Switzerland
07 ☐ France	14 ☐ Netherlands	

8. What other types of European travel services are you interested in:

01 ☐ Car Rental	04 ☐ Cruises	07 ☐ Package Tours
02 ☐ Group Tours	05 ☐ Hostels	08 ☐ Other _____
03 ☐ Hotels	06 ☐ Discounted Airfare	_____

9. What is your age:

01 ☐ Under 18	03 ☐ 26-35	05 ☐ 46-54
02 ☐ 18-25	04 ☐ 36-45	06 ☐ 55+

10. Highest level of education:

01 ☐ Attended High School	05 ☐ Postgraduate Study - No Degree
02 ☐ Graduated High School	06 ☐ Masters Degree or MBA
03 ☐ Attended College	07 ☐ Ph.D., MD, JD or other
04 ☐ Graduated College	08 ☐ Other Professional Degree

11. Please list up to three Travel Related magazines and/or newspapers you read on

a regular basis: _____

_____

Rail Pass Express, Inc.
2737 Sawbury Blvd.
Columbus, OH 43235-4583